'We're trying to do things differently'

The challenges of relationships and recognition in Higher Education

'We're trying to do things differently': the challenges of relationships and recognition in Higher Education

A reflexive review of King's College London's Social Sciences BA programme

---

Freya Aquarone, Laura Nehéz-Posony, Propa Rezwana Anwar, Samira Salam, Eleni Koutsouri, Minkyung Kim, SooYeon Suh, Tope Mayomi, Julia Pilarska, Emily Houghton, and Yara Boodai

Centre for Public Policy Research

Published in 2020 by the Centre for Public Policy Research (CPPR)
King's College London
The School of Education, Communication & Society
Waterloo Bridge Wing
Franklin-Wilkins Building
Waterloo Road
London, SE1 9NH

ISBN 978-1-8382998-0-4 (paperback)
ISBN 978-1-8382998-1-1 (e-book)

A catalogue record for this book is available from the British Library

Cover design by Neil Brogan

This book's publication and the research on which it is based were funded by the London Interdisciplinary Social Science Doctoral Training Partnership (LISS-DTP)

Printed on recycled paper by Premier Print Group, London

To find out more about CPPR visit
https://www.kcl.ac.uk/research/centre-for-public-policy-research-cppr

This book is dedicated to Laura's father, Dr Márton Nehéz-Posony, who passed away in April 2020. Márton devoted his career to striving for social justice in Hungary; his life stands as testimony to the value of fighting for change.

Márton was a big supporter of this project from the start and was so looking forward to seeing it completed. So Márton, if you're listening, here goes…

Contents

Acronyms

BAME – Black, Asian and Minority Ethnic
BASS – BA Social Sciences
CCM – Course Community Meeting
CPPR – Centre for Public Policy Research
ECS – (School of) Education, Communication and Society
GTA – Graduate Teaching Assistant
HE – Higher Education
KCL – King's College London
LGBTQ+ – Lesbian, Gay, Bisexual, Transgender, Queer/Questioning 'plus' other sexual orientations/gender identities that fall within the umbrella term
LISS-DTP – London Interdisciplinary Social Science Doctoral Training Partnership
UCU – University and College Union

Foreword

Sometime in the late autumn of 2019, just a couple of months into working on the BA Social Sciences programme at KCL, it began to dawn on me that you only get to do something for the first time *once*. An obvious realisation perhaps, but one which had – in the pace and the intensity of the day to day – escaped me. The first year of the programme was slipping through our fingers, and Higher Education is hectic at the best of times – not least when you're starting a whole new course from scratch. For the staff team, having spent hours over coffees and email, at Away Days and in corridors, debating and discussing the principles of education which we were hoping to realise, 'normality' suddenly kicked in. And come September, there just wasn't enough time in the week for in-depth reflection and discussion. Snatched conversations in stairwells came to feel like luxuries; moments of pausing in a storm to take stock of where we'd washed up.

Some of those conversations became about how to capture this journey – for posterity and for our own community's learning and maybe for a few outside people with an interest. A group of us put our heads together and the idea of a reflective research project – carried out for and by members of the programme community – emerged. The idea became a possibility primarily because of a generous grant from the London Interdisciplinary Social Science Doctoral Training Partnership, which enabled me to take a funded break in my PhD. But the project's viability was also grounded in the support of Dr John Owens and Professor Alan Cribb who, despite the aforementioned workloads faced by HE practitioners, gave hours and hours of their time and emotional energy to making this project happen, from co-writing the grant application right through to proof-reading the drafts. More than anything though, this project is the result of the enormous work, dedication, and creativity of the rest of the research team – all of whom are first-year undergraduates.

This project was meant to last three months. In the end, it took us seven. Of course, research projects famously overrun, but we weren't really anticipating doing ours in the context of a pandemic. For the vast majority of the project, our research team of thirteen has been scattered across six countries – the UK, Greece, Poland, Hungary, South Korea, and Thailand – and has been communicating largely through an unhealthy reliance on video conferencing and a bit of dabbling in interactive post-it-note software. It has not always been an easy journey, and many team members have had to deal with complex personal challenges resulting from the fallout of COVID-19. I'm still blinking in pleasant surprise that we've reached this point without becoming thoroughly sick of one another, and without burning out completely.

This book is trying to capture a moment in a journey. That journey is still very much in its infancy. But we hope what we've written provides a useful snapshot of a work in progress for those of us – students and practitioners alike – who have an interest and belief in the possibility that Higher Education can look a little more like our ideals, and a little less like tick-boxes and marketing.

- Freya

Background and project approach

A brief introduction to the BA Social Sciences programme

The BA Social Sciences (BASS) programme is a relatively new undergraduate programme at King's College London (KCL), hosted by the School of Education, Communication and Society (ECS). The programme was developed over several years by staff at ECS and launched with its first cohort of forty-three students in September 2019. The ideas and aims which motivated the programme's creators, and which were developed further by staff to form the programme's official 'philosophy and ethos statement', are oriented around four core commitments, to: social justice and human wellbeing, rigour and criticality, social action and social change, and collaborative and inclusive learning. There is also a strong emphasis on the idea that meaningful human relationships are fundamental to education.

Many aspects of the programme's philosophy will feel familiar to students and practitioners, perhaps especially those working in the social sciences. However, partly because the course was built from scratch, it has been able to embed some practices which are arguably relatively unusual. For instance, while lectures do form part of the timetable, a large proportion of contact time consists of workshops and small-group seminars, with a strong emphasis on student participation and discussion. There is a whole-community forum for deliberation and decision-making based on democratic principles. There are no exams, and the programme combines conventional academic essays with more diverse forms of assessment such as presentations, media articles and reflective diary-writing.

The research team and how it worked

This project drew on the principles of Participatory Action Research (PAR). PAR has many definitions, but at its core, it is about people becoming *researchers of their own social context* in order to better understand and/or change it (Galletta and Torre, 2019). In education research, this tends to mean "center[ing] the wisdom and experience of students [...] and educators, positioning them as architects of research rather than objects of study" (Galletta and Torre, 2019:1). Accordingly, our research team was made up of ten students and three staff members from the BASS programme; the majority of the research team (nine out of thirteen) were also research participants.

PAR is an explicit attempt to "redistribute power and legitimacy" (Galletta and Tore, 2019:1) when it comes to *who generates claims about education spaces*. HE is a sector increasingly characterised by competitive data comparison and top-down performativity metrics. Among these is the Teaching Excellence Framework (TEF), which implies good learning and teaching can be captured through a range of standardised data, such as 'student satisfaction', 'lifelong skill acquisition', and 'employment outcomes' (Neary, 2016; Gunn, 2018). The TEF has its uses, but an enduring reliance on such metrics – at the expense of other forms of 'knowing' – risks normalising the idea that what matters is what can be quantified through big data. As Berliner argues, this does "great harm" to our understanding of education (2002:18) – it misses, by technical necessity, large chunks of what truly matters. In such a policy context, it feels important to contribute to accounts of HE which foreground narratives over numbers and which – crucially – are generated by people actually learning and teaching within the sector.

As a team, we worked collaboratively to discuss the project scope and design, to build our research questions and methodology, to collect and analyse data and, finally, to write up our findings. The writing team consisted of Freya, Laura, Propa, Samira, Eleni, SooYeon, Minkyung and Tope – their names are listed in order of their work's appearance. However, the other student team members (Julia, Emily and Yara) also contributed analysis, feedback and proof-reading which has been integral to the process of write-up. Therefore, even though most sections have a designated author, in much of the writing we use the plural pronoun 'we' in recognition of the collaborative nature of the project. Sometimes, individual authors have drawn explicitly on their lived experience as participant researchers. At these times, they have spoken in their own voice, with the singular pronoun 'I'. And in chapter 5, various student authors take different normative stances on the 'politics of difference';

because these are to some extent personal responses, they have not been written in a collective voice.

Scope of the project

In this book, we haven't focused on every aspect of the programme's official philosophy and ethos identified earlier. Rather, we have been led by the core themes which emerged from our data; these centred around the role and nature of educational relationships. As explained in chapter 1, we analyse this focus on relationships through a common social justice concept known as *'recognition'*. We explore the various ways in which the programme can be seen to embed – or at least seek to embed – recognition in its practice, as well as how this can be problematised.

Many of the themes we explore crossover with the official philosophical aspirations and practices of the programme. But there are also gaps in the scope of our research: for instance, there is limited discussion of the programme curriculum[1], or its academic disciplines/themes. This is as much of a surprise to us as authors as it may be to readers: surely a review of an education programme would have analysis of curriculum at its centre? And yet, reflections on the programme's curriculum and academic disciplines were simply quite marginal in our dataset. In a way, it's reassuring that curriculum was hardly mentioned by participants – except through some passing references to 'interdisciplinarity' and favourable comparisons to the dominance of 'white men' too often associated with HE reading lists[2]. It may suggest that the programme is doing something right. Alternatively, the relative silence around curriculum may be an artefact of our methodology: although our interview question guide contained a specific question around curriculum/thematic content, this wasn't raised by researchers in every interview.

---

[1] For more information about the programme's curriculum, see the KCL website: https://www.kcl.ac.uk/study/undergraduate/courses/social-sciences-ba

[2] Such concerns are precisely why campaigns around curricula are at the heart of many campaigns for change within HE – e.g. the 'Why Is My Curriculum White?' (see Peters, 2018) and 'Rhodes Must Fall' (see Gebrial, 2018) campaigns.

Nonetheless, the breadth of participants' focal points in their narratives – covering issues of emotional care and concern, hierarchy and partnership, HE access, class/'race'[3] consciousness, and trust and freedom of speech in the classroom – clearly demonstrates that there is much *more* to a programme than its curriculum. This is not to deny that reading lists / thematic and disciplinary structures are important, or that ours are imperfect or need work, but it does indicate that – even when there are no starkly obvious concerns around these aspects of a programme – there are many more things to consider when it comes to promoting social justice in education.

In spite of its lack of total comprehensiveness, then, we hope that this text provides important insights into our programme and its practice. One aspect of the programme which was highlighted with particular consistency by our research participants (and which is also emphasised in official programme documents) is the importance of 'co-creation' or 'co-production' – that is, on partnership between students and staff in the common task of building meaningful educational experiences. We would invite readers to consider this a core aspect of the text. We hope it achieves this in two ways: a) by offering an in-depth review of the aspirations, successes and challenges entailed by the relatively distinctive co-productive ethos of the programme, and b) as itself an exercise in reflexivity and co-production – both literally in the creation of the text and in (we hope) usefully contributing to the *future* of the programme.

---

[3] The term race is in single quotation marks here to highlight the fact that race is a social construct which has arisen from practices of racism and racialisation, rather than objectively, biologically or genetically fixed or 'real'. For ease of reading, we will not be using quotation marks going forwards, but wanted to flag the problematic nature of the term and confirm that its use should not be read as upholding essentialist ideas around identity.

Methodology

Sampling and recruitment

This book is based primarily on data from qualitative interviews and focus groups with members of the programme. Nineteen students (out of forty-three in the cohort) were interviewed, and eight staff (all but one of the core teaching staff from year one, plus a member of the wider staff team).

All members of the programme community were invited to participate. Some people were individually approached because it was felt they would have particularly valuable insights to share. Thus, sampling was partly purposive. The sample was also to some extent (and perhaps unavoidably) self-selecting. That is, it is likely that our participants constitute the group of students with the most time to take part in a voluntary activity like a research project. This may have an impact on their level of positivity about the programme. For instance, the team noted that the vast majority of those who took part are also those who are most engaged and involved with the programme in ways which go beyond formal learning and teaching time – e.g. its democratic meetings and its social and community aspects. This is perhaps especially true of the students who constitute the research team, and thus the authorial perspective of the piece. There is thus a risk that the book underrepresents the views of those who are – whether for practical reasons or otherwise – more disengaged with or ambivalent about the programme.

This is a common challenge of qualitative sampling, but we have tried in several ways to militate against it. Firstly, there are a number of participants in the sample who described themselves explicitly as less engaged in the programme community, or who had quite critical things to say. We encouraged all participants to speak openly and honestly about their experiences of the programme and were reassured by the fact that data was by no means all positive. Secondly, we interviewed both elected student representatives (reps) who – due to their role – have regular contact with most members of the programme community, and often field student concerns. The reps referred to such concerns in their interviews, and at various points we have used these reflections as indicative of broader issues on the programme. Thirdly, nineteen out of forty-three students constitutes 45% of the programme cohort overall; even if not all voices are present, we nonetheless feel that the sample represents the experiences and perspectives of a significant proportion of the programme community, and thus has relevance for thinking about the programme as a whole.

We did not specifically collect demographic information from our participants. However, there are times when participants make reference to their positionality – including along lines of race/ethnicity, gender, class, and nationality – in ways which have deep relevance to the analysis. Sometimes, with participants' permission, we have identified aspects of their identity/positionality (even when not mentioned in the data). Partly on this basis, we feel we can describe the sample in broad terms as follows: there are very few men, and very few who explicitly identify as working-class. Although the majority of participants are white, there are a number of participants who identify, varyingly, as 'Brown', 'Asian', 'South Asian', 'Black' or as 'a person of colour'. There is a very large range of nationalities, with the majority of students being from outside the UK (mostly from Europe and Asia).

These factors broadly mirror the demographics of the programme community (at the time of writing). They also mirror the demographics of the research team. We are mostly women, mostly middle-class, and from a range of national contexts. However, we are a slightly more racially/ethnically diverse group than the programme as a whole: two of us identify as British Bangladeshi, two as Korean, one as Black, one as Middle Eastern/Arab, one as non-religious part-Jewish Hungarian, and four as white European, from Poland, the UK and Greece. Identifying the position from which people are speaking is important, not least in the context of a book about recognition. Accordingly, at certain points throughout the text (especially in chapter 5) we offer more explicit, detailed explanations of our author positionality, as a way of increasing the reader's understanding of the perspectives informing our analysis. We feel that the diversity of the research team's lived experience on various counts – including but not limited to race/ethnicity – enriches the range of perspectives that we are able to bring to the table as authors, particularly on issues around structural marginalisation.

Data collection

All interviews and focus groups were semi-structured, based on flexible guideline questions. All staff interviews were conducted by Freya. The majority of student interviews (which took place both one-to-one and in pairs) were conducted by student members of the research team. Freya conducted a small number of student interviews, including some one-to-one follow-up interviews with people initially interviewed in pairs. Freya and John also co-led a focus group with seven members of the research team (the other three student team members observed), at the start of the data collection process. This was used as an opportunity to both gather some initial participant data from the team, and to model the process of qualitative interviewing. As student members of the team had little or no prior experience of conducting empirical research, opportunities for training and support were provided throughout the project. For instance, we had several team meetings in the early stages in which research paradigms, data collection approaches, and ethical considerations were collectively explored. The team was provided with reading materials on methodology and one-to-one support to help them prepare for conducting interviews. Early on in the write-up, members of the team attended a workshop on 'doing liberatory research', which explored the ethical demands of fighting marginalisation through empirical work.

Interviews/focus groups were recorded on smartphones and then transcribed by members of the research team. The recordings were deleted after use and the transcripts were stored on a secure cloud drive. All participants were sent an information sheet in advance, which was discussed verbally at the start of the interview, and all participants signed an Informed Consent form. Wherever possible, elements of the transcript which would make the participant individually identifiable (e.g. reference to nationality or specific events) were removed or changed to preserve anonymity. All names have been changed. In some cases, we have (with participants' permission) used pseudonyms which are indicative of a different gender identity to the one with which the participant identifies. This is because the sample overall contains so few men that, to protect their anonymity, it was necessary to introduce greater gender ambiguity across the dataset.

Where participants are potentially identifiable to members of the programme community due to, say, descriptions of a particular event, or reference to their job title, an additional pseudonym has been used. This means that some participants (six staff participants and seven student participants) have *two* pseudonyms. There are therefore more pseudonyms overall than there are participants; however, to avoid implying that particular perspectives are more widespread than they actually are, we have ensured that extracts from the same participant, under different names, rarely appear in close proximity. Where this does happen, it is because we feel a follow-up point from the same participant adds something crucially substantive to the analysis. Although we do not always explicitly state whether a participant is a student or a staff member, the formatting of pseudonyms is distinct: student names are underlined, while staff names are not.

Though interview and focus group material forms the bulk of the project data, we also draw on official BASS programme documents and, occasionally, our lived experiences as authors (for instance, when providing context for issues or events raised in the data). We have sought to make clear when we are drawing on these additional sources of information and insight. Finally, Freya kept a reflective research journal throughout the project, and a small number of extracts (four) from this have been included as project data under their pseudonyms.

Data analysis and presentation

Data analysis was done in various stages and by different combinations of team members. In most cases, initial coding on student participant data was done by those who conducted the interview. Student team members then had follow-up conversations with Freya to discuss the emergent themes in more depth. Based on this analysis, student data was divided into thematic category documents and made accessible to the whole team. Initial coding of staff participant data was done by Freya, with some further collaborative analysis done by Freya and John. Staff data was then divided into core themes and added to the aforementioned category documents available to the team. At an Away Day in April we reflected on the whole dataset and worked on analysis in smaller groups. Team members then decided which themes they wanted to focus on in their own writing going forwards.

In the write-up, data has been largely presented verbatim except for the deletion of stammers and word repetitions, which was done to protect the flow of participant narratives. However, many sections of this book also contain data presented as poetry. This was inspired by the – increasingly commonplace – experimentation with creative approaches to data presentation in social science writing (Back and Puwar, 2012). Most of the poetry has been generated from verbatim extracts of transcript[4], though sometimes small amendments and additions have been made. In many cases, the original data from which the poems are constructed is repeated elsewhere in the write-up, so that readers can get a sense of their original context and form.

Contextual factors

There are several contextual factors which shaped and affected the data collection process. For instance, while most interviews were conducted face-to-face at a place of the participant's choosing, the COVID-19 pandemic meant that ten participants had to be interviewed over video or audio call. Occasionally there were tech glitches which meant some content was inaudible, but this affected only a small minority of data. Although face-to-face interviews are the ideal, the digital format did not seem to have a deeply detrimental impact on data collection, perhaps due to the preexisting relationships between interviewers and participants. A handful of people who had initially signed up to participate either could not or decided not to due to pandemic-related factors such as illness or personal circumstances.

The pandemic also meant that the data collection process was more drawn out than anticipated – lasting around six weeks rather than an anticipated three. This perhaps compounded the extent to which events affecting the programme overtook our capacity to document them in interviews: that is, certain things which became relevant to this analysis

---

[4] The exception is *Storms of Change* and *When love entered the classroom* – these were written by Eleni Koutsouri, inspired by the project data.

(not least to do with the impact of the pandemic) happened *after* data collection had begun, and therefore were not addressed or discussed in all interviews. However, we hope that, not least because of the multiplicity of perspectives and the level of 'insider knowledge' within our research team, we have been able to reflect on such events in a balanced and constructive way, even where they are only raised by a limited number of participants.

Another key contextual factor affecting the project was the University and College Union (UCU) national strike which took place across fourteen days between February and March 2020. Thousands of HE staff across seventy-four UK universities participated in the strike in response to two employment disputes: one about erosion of staff pension rights, and another called the 'Four Fights' – regarding the sector's failure to tackle issues around pay, inequality, casualisation and workload. The strike led to significant disruption of the second semester of the programme; it was a major feature shaping people's experiences – particularly at the time of this project's data collection[5] – and is thus referred to by participants at a number of points throughout this book. Although members of the KCL UCU branch actually only voted to participate in the strike on the basis of the *first* of the two disputes (the pensions dispute) the wider aims and scope of the strike relates directly to many of the issues touched upon by this book's analysis, including the marketisation of HE, the increased reliance on casualised workers on low pay and precarious contracts, deep inequalities (particularly along lines of race/ethnicity) within the sector, and problematically high staff workloads.

Ethical considerations

This project was undertaken with approval from the KCL research ethics committee. There are some unique ethical challenges associated with doing PAR work. For instance, the fact that participants were recruited by people with whom they had a pre-existing relationship means there is

---

[5] To avoid undermining the strike we did not, of course, do any data collection on 'strike days'.

some possibility for inadvertent coercion. With this in mind, it was made clear on several occasions that participation was strictly voluntary and that it would in no way affect students' relationship with either the programme or its staff. Having 'insider status' as a team means we have in-depth knowledge of the context we are researching, and have a personal – as well as ethical – stake in ensuring its members' voices are represented accurately, and in protecting participants' wellbeing (after all, they are our co-workers, peers and friends). On the other hand, it is always possible that being an 'insider' makes us more ready to jump at the positives, and shy away from the difficult or challenging, especially when we, ourselves, are implicated. We have worked hard to try to ensure that's not the case. This project was always intended to be, primarily, a learning journey – for us to reflect on not only what we feel works but also, and perhaps more importantly, where we have hit brick walls and pitfalls, where we could do better, and what that might look like. We have therefore sought, in every chapter, to lay out explicitly and honestly not only the breakthroughs and the things we are proud of, but also where we have struggled and even where things have 'gone wrong'.

The research paradigm of social constructionism, and its attendant belief in the multidimensionality of the social world, requires "humility" (Kincheloe, 2005:332). It means accepting that capturing every angle is impossible and therefore being open about our work's inevitable shortcomings. We cannot begin to pretend that our analysis of the programme captures the 'whole'; other people could research our programme and generate a different story. But the hope is that, if our methodology has ethical integrity, others' stories would not be unrecognisable, or irreconcilable with our own. That is, that our account tells a story that is familiar – and, ideally, useful – to people across our community. As a team, we have worked together to try to ensure our writing has this 'ethical integrity'. Ultimately, the best tool for carving out truth(s) lies in reflexivity – our willingness to be honest, both with ourselves and with each other, about what perspectives, feelings and needs may be informing our analysis. Thus, we had regular team meetings to reflect on the writing process, in particular seeking to identify where our researcher role blurred into our participant role, and how this affected our analysis. We have challenged one another where we felt things needed changing, or deleting, or greater attention. We also gave a copy of our final draft to all our participants, inviting their critical feedback.

Format and research paradigm

In this text, we are not attempting to present a neat and tidy 'report', with precise delineations or clear solutions. Instead, we are trying to piece together a story of the first year of the BASS programme. And stories are shot through with "conflict and paradox" (hooks, 2010:52), not least when they are told by several different people. Our format is not far off what Denzin and Lincoln (2011) have termed 'bricolage': building up analysis through multiple styles, voices, sources of information, and media. It is part of a research paradigm that rejects the existence of a single, researchable world 'out there', waiting for us to shed light on it with the 'right' data category or the 'best' theory (ibid.). Rather, it accepts that social reality is complicated, contradictory, and partly *constructed* by the people who perceive it, and that multiple lenses – while less 'clear-cut' – may therefore do a better job of grasping at its truth(s). The upshot, though, is that this book may at times have less stylistic or theoretical consistency than is conventional in academic writing; we hope that this eclecticism – in allowing space for a diversity of voices – ends up being a source of strength, but it may mean readers have to forgive some occasional unruliness.

One of this project's participants (Rosa), when asked how they would describe the BASS programme, provided a detailed analogy of a garden. We felt that the analogy – including the strengths and weaknesses it describes – helps to capture not only the ontology of the programme, but of this book as well:

> For some reason the first thing that came to mind
> Was a garden. Why a garden?
> I think it's something to do with different elements that together work:
> Some of it's edible, some of it's beautiful, some of it's both.
> Some things will be surprises –
> Seeds will come down and grow up that you didn't even plant

That just flew in with the birds.

And sometimes, you know, something might happen
that disrupts or gets in the way
and that might be difficult and need challenging –
it might be a fox comes and digs it up and you think
 'Well, the fox is beautiful, all part of nature but it's dug up
 the plants.
   What are we gonna do?'

One more thing about the garden thing is
It's valuable in its own right,
It's got intrinsic value
And it doesn't need to do anything else
 Other than be there.

But maybe if it's somewhere where it's seen by other people
someone might walk past and think
 'Oh I never thought how beautiful
 a beetroot is next to a daffodil'
and it might inspire other people
and then the seeds from those plants
might get blown all around the place,
 And we don't know where it's gonna go.

Chapter 1.

Relationships and recognition

Freya Aquarone

We're living in a society
Where things are very *un*democratic
Where education is not democratic
Where there's huge pressure on students,
The pressure for success – and what counts as success?
It's getting A*AA on those tests.

We're living in a society
Where the mainstream ideal
    –well maybe I'm getting a bit too political–
but it's neoliberalism.
Where everything is labeled – given a mark
and we know that's in the school system too.

There's a lot of damage to undo.

    These approaches have not been normalised
    People are just not used to engaging in things that aren't
    credentialised

    I still can't let go of the fact that I'm coming from a school
    setting where I was told what to do, *every time.*

So no wonder it's about where about where the money lies
That's how we've been incentivised
Especially when the cost of living is so high
And with the diminution of the welfare state
And other educational resources
It's like
    If we're not being assessed on it, then it doesn't really
  matter
    It's not important to our lives.

We're living in a society
Where we're not taught that we are equals with our teachers
So maybe it's not surprising people haven't got used to the idea

that it's a different kind of relationship we are able to have here.

I reckon some people come in with a set of expectations
about staff and authority and institutions
and they see the community meetings as glorified feedback forums
They put out complaints but provide no solutions

They don't see it as a thing between humans.

And maybe that's why there have been so many times
Where I've come home and gone:
we're trying to do something *really* big *really* late on
in people's educational journeys-

To model a sense of collective obligation and community
In a society which doesn't have much time for
the unmeasurable and the unquantifiable
And how we do this in the confines of the neoliberal university is
questionable.

A world of individual customers and service providers
£60 worth of lectures for someone to inspire us
Or a refund.

As if it's about the money and not the way
The university continuously treats its staff like they don't
matter.
As if as students we're nothing more than the amount we pay
and not what we can do for each other.

And yet-
I do feel like we're doing something meaningful.

That the majority of us
are not trying to just get a degree and a job
but are actually trying to change the world.

That we're not doing it to have the highest grades
          we're doing it for ourselves

That some of us see the strike as an example of what this *course* is
trying to do:
Fight for people's rights
Put yourself in someone else's shoes

That there's an intrinsic motivation
To carve out a vision
Which is distinct from the culture and practice of the rest of the
institution.

From this society we're living in.

Higher Education: 'a community of learners'?

Research literature on the state of Higher Education tends not to paint a very encouraging picture. There is a general consensus that the marketisation of the sector has ushered in an era of overwhelming workload and oversight pressures (Leathwood and Read, 2020), of decisions made primarily in the name of profit and efficiency, and of 'transactional' framings of identity (Gewirtz and Cribb, 2020), which don't leave much room for the 'human'. So, relationships and community suffer (Clegg and Rowland, 2010; Gewirtz and Cribb, 2020).

In their critical analysis of the way HE has transformed over the past three decades, Cribb and Gewirtz write that the period has been characterised by "various forms of instrumentalism" (2013:344), whereby the sector is judged by its outcomes rather than its ethics:

> "In other words, it would appear that the university as an institution with a distinctive [...] social purpose [...] has been replaced with the idea of the university as a generic large-scale social organisation – what we are calling *a hollowed-out university* – that can increasingly be seen *less as a community of learners* and more as a [...] site that can be engineered to serve any social function." (Cribb and Gewirtz, 2013:344, emphasis added).

The data from this project show that our programme, too, grapples with this "hollow[ing] out" of the sector whereby various instrumental goals such as the delivery of an educational 'product' or pursuit of quantifiable 'research outputs' take precedence over other visions for HE (Clegg and Rowland, 2010). Such visions might include the age-old idea – highlighted by many contemporary commentators but envisioned as far back as 1810 by Wilhelm von Humboldt, the founder of the University of Berlin (Curran, 2017) – that universities should be, first and foremost, *communities of learners*. Our dataset highlights the significant challenges involved in enacting such a vision in contemporary HE. Yet it also indicates significant forms of resistance – an attempt to emphasise human relationships *despite* contextual constraints. This was present not only in participants' descriptions of specific aspects of the programme (such as love and kindness or equality and partnership – as explored in the upcoming chapters) but also their descriptions of the programme's ethos overall:

> Simon: I guess [the programme's philosophy] has to do with the way students are – and the way people are – treated overall [...] in the community. And maybe even understanding the programme as a *community* [is] not something that's [normally] out there, necessarily. It's not something that's considered a key part of education.

> Luke: [H]ow do you learn about the social world and the social sciences without a kind of robust and meaningful engagement with the idea of community? Like, relationships are at the heart of everything.

Indeed, the third line of the programme's 'ethos' document states:

> "The programme's philosophy is that learning is best achieved in a collaborative, friendly and supportive environment characterised by caring, committed, respectful and trusting relationships."

Such an emphasis on community and relationships is by no means unusual in HE. Initiatives have sprung up in recent years attempting to embed ideas of 'students as partners' rather than 'consumers' (Curran, 2017; Marquis et al., 2016; Streeting and Wise, 2009), including attempts to create atmospheres of emotional wellbeing and "connectedness" (Stephen et al., 2008:454). There is also widespread evidence of individual practitioners resisting the trend towards atomisation and bureaucratic indifference – choosing to prioritise care and kindness and relationships "despite the institutional setting" (Clegg and Rowland, 2010:732). But there is an evident need – given the "rather bleak picture [...] of contemporary HE" (Levy et al., 2010:2) painted by much of the literature – to document countercurrents. To exchange stories of what goes right, and what goes wrong, when you try to build a "culture [...] which sort of says that [...] we can, you know, do things slightly differently [...], we can start afresh, we can think about redefining relationships" (Luke). As bell hooks writes, "to engage in dialogue is one of the simplest ways we can begin as teachers, scholars, and critical thinkers to cross boundaries" (1994:130). We would like to contribute something small, but hopefully useful, to that dialogue.

Recognition: a theoretical lens

"Recognition is not just a courtesy we owe people, but a vital human need." (Taylor, 1994:26)

The concept of recognition in social theory is quite different from its 'colloquial' meaning – for instance, of 'recognising' someone you know in the street. Rather, recognition as a theoretical concept is to do with *social justice:* it's about recognising others as human, as equals, as esteemed and appreciated. Recognition is "an expressive gesture of affirmation" (Honneth and Margalit, 2001:120) which says not just 'I see you', but 'I *value* you'.

In trying to make sense of what our data was telling us about the programme, theories of recognition kept fighting their way to the forefront of our minds. This is perhaps unsurprising: as identified above, the programme places a heavy emphasis on developing meaningful human relationships. And recognition – in all its myriad articulations – is a well-established lens through which writers have tried to tell a story about what meaningful relationships look like, as well as why they matter. Recognition is thus a concept used both descriptively and normatively – that is, to not only tell a story about how the world *is,* but how it *should be.* In the pages which follow we hope it will be quite obvious why human relationships based on recognition should be a desirable part of education. But we are still making some assumptions about first principles here, so we'd like to briefly outline one of the core philosophical voices which has attempted to explain why recognition is so important – that of G. W. F. Hegel.

According to Hegel (and many of the later theorists he inspired) recognition is a primary human 'good' – something fundamental to our existence. This is because, argues Hegel, humans exist *in relation to one another* (Anderson, 2011). We are, in other words, intersubjective – our sense of 'self' is deeply intertwined with our relationships with 'others' (Bates, 2019; Taylor, 1994). Such a perspective is in stark contrast to the implications of the Cartesian[6] paradigm which defines so much Western thinking around identity and being – not least in education and academia (Clegg and Rowland, 2010; hooks, 1994). This paradigm claims that we are separate, atomised (and primarily *cognitive*) creatures for whom existence is predicated not on any form of emotional attachment to others, but on the mantra 'I think, therefore I am'.

For Hegel, recognition demands that we let go of this assumption that we are islands, and instead acknowledge that 'I' is to a certain extent 'we' – a collective. And it is precisely because human 'being' is so intersubjective – so predicated on relationships – that our lives are "characterized by [...] [the] desire for recognition by others" (Russon, 2011:57). To be recognised is to be acknowledged as a human being – to be fully self-actualised – something which, according to Hegel's theory, is basically impossible to achieve alone. Descartes may have thought he could sit in a room and *think* himself into certainty about the truth of his being, but this was an illusion; anyone who has ever struggled to cling onto a self-defined identity in spite of alienation, whole-scale social rejection, or overwhelming loneliness surely knows this only too well. There are echoes of this sentiment in the work of some of the most influential contemporary writers on education. bell hooks, for instance, suggests that her purpose as teacher is "humanization, the creation of a learning community in the classroom" (2010:35). The implication in this simple commitment is that recognising one another *as humans* is contingent on *community:* on the relationships we build.

Thus, our basic desire for recognition can only be fully realised through a commitment to our interconnectedness – and, accordingly, prioritising human relationships. This strikes us as the resistant antithesis

---

[6] This means derived from the ideas of Descartes, who famously posited the split between the 'body' and the 'mind' – a 'dualism' which places the emotional/physical on one side, and the rational/intellectual on the other. This Cartesian 'split' is also associated with a kind of individualist way of thinking about humans. This is because Descartes is famous for the claim that, because a person can 'think', their identity already exists. Not much attention was paid to how identity might be shaped by other factors – not just factors which go beyond thinking (like feeling!) but also wider social contexts or, indeed, relationships with *other people*.

of the 'hollowed-out university' described earlier – where collectivity is reduced to instrumentralised, commodified exchange (Curran, 2017; Levy et al., 2010; Gewirtz and Cribb, 2020). An education space which grounds itself in the pursuit of recognition is an attempt to refill the void with shared meaning-making and emotional bonds – to recentre Humboldt's original idea of 'the community of learners'. As Luke puts it (emphasis added):

> Luke: Higher Education has become so individualised and [...], you know, the marketisation of education has kind of promoted a sense in which individual customers are receiving services from an institution and the service providers that work at that institution. And if there is any way in which we are going to escape and transcend that model [...] it's through establishing a *community of learners*.

Beyond the fact that an attempt to embed meaningful relationships was a core part of participants' perceptions of the programme, there was one further reason that theories of recognition felt fitting for our analysis. As noted earlier, the programme explicitly defines itself as seeking to enable students to pursue social justice and social change in the world outside the university. Given the programme's commitment to social justice externally, we felt that it made sense to use a core part of social justice theorising – the concept of recognition – in analysing its *internal* world. As one participant (Kate) put it, it is crucial to reflect on whether the programme is "walking the walk" of its stated principles, because "we can sit round and have all these lovely debates about inequality, and discrimination [...] and how awful that is, and how much we need social justice", but it needs to also "manifest in the way that students engage, in the relationship between students and teachers, in the activities that are done" within the programme *itself.* There is a strong tradition in activism and activist-academia of 'prefigurative politics' – in being the change you want to see in the world (Leach, 2013). To ask to what extent the programme is managing to practise within its own community what it calls for in the wider world felt like an ethical imperative.

It is worth noting that the concept of recognition can be applied in many contrasting and often competing ways; as Anderson writes, "we are far from anything like a consensus as to its meaning" (2011:2). In many ways, this is good for empirical research: real-life stories do not always fit neatly within theoretical taxonomies – however helpful they may be in abstraction (Cribb and Gewirtz, 2005). A certain flexibility in the application of theoretical lenses can sometimes be the best way of grasping at truth(s). With this in mind, we jump around a bit throughout our exploration of recognition, embracing a kind of theoretical 'pick and mix', rooted in the ideas of Hegel[7] but also drawing on contemporary recognition theorists such as Axel Honneth, Frantz Fanon, Nancy Fraser, and Charles Taylor – as well as writers who do not explicitly invoke recognition as a theoretical idea but whose work has deep relevance, such as bell hooks and Paulo Freire.

Structure of the text

In the next two chapters, we will explore the way that the programme seeks to prioritise recognition through two core commitments: in chapter 2 we explore 'recognition as love, care and kindness'[8] and in chapter 3 we explore 'recognition as equality and partnership' – manifested as democratic decision-making structures (3a) and participatory, engaged approaches to learning and teaching (3b). In outlining these themes, we also explore the varying associated challenges. As Derounian writes, all attempts to dance to a different tune involve very regular "stumble[s]" (2011:91); often, these provide the richest opportunities for learning. These challenges should not be viewed as lists of negatives to weigh up against the positives: it is not as simple as challenges cancelling out the programme's attempts to realise recognition. Rather these challenges

---

[7] Hegel provided much inspiration for starting points in our analysis. But there was far too much irony for our liking in basing our entire theoretical framework on recognition around the ideas of a person whose work overtly upheld sexist and racist discourses (Anderson, 2011). This was one of many reasons for bringing in other theoretical voices.
[8] This highlights yet another reason for the theoretical focus on recognition in this piece: it is wider in scope than perhaps more commonly-used concepts in HE literature such as 'partnership' (e.g. Curran, 2007; Levy et al., 2010), which we feel only tell part of the story. Partnership tends to focus on issues of equality and collaboration but is less attendant to concepts like love/kindness, which Clegg and Rowland (2010) suggest are still seen as somehow slightly embarrassing or inappropriate in discussions of HE practice.

coexist with the programme's ideals – sometimes dominating, sometimes receding into the background. Many of them relate to the themes identified above regarding the wider context of HE and factors affecting its transformation – including but not limited to the effects of marketisation. Some challenges, however, are more general – such as how to deal constructively with conflict. In chapter 4, we will briefly consider two contextual factors which we believe make the realisation of recognition much *easier*: the ethos of the staff team, and the size of our programme community.

Finally, in chapter 5, we will consider experiences of and debates around how to oppose marginalisation within the programme, drawing on a different articulation of recognition grounded in what Charles Taylor calls the 'politics of difference'. The final chapter deviates from the structure and content of the rest of the book in several ways. Firstly, while the whole book contains critical reflection on the experiences and challenges of the programme, to some extent this builds up through the text, culminating in chapter 5 as a particularly critical chapter. Chapter 5 seeks not only to more overtly challenge participant data, but also to explicitly problematise the framing of recognition implicitly used throughout much of the rest of the book (namely, a definition of recognition resting on 'universalist' assumptions, which see justice as about treating everybody the same, rather than considering the specific needs of particular – namely, marginalised – groups). Thus, the first four chapters lay out positive experiences of the programme, as well as challenges, whilst taking particular definitions of recognition at face value. Though critically analytical, these are in some ways more descriptive. Chapter 5, meanwhile, asks difficult questions about whether these definitions are sufficient – it is thus more discussion-oriented. Chapter 5 is also written more explicitly from the individual perspectives of different authors on the team. Each subsection begins with an outline of the authors' positionalities and how this influences their standpoint and analysis. Section 5c, specifically, is composed of three opinion pieces which offer subtly different perspectives on 'recognition in the classroom', particularly in relation to freedom of speech and marginalisation.

Chapter 2.

Recognition as love, care and kindness

Laura Nehéz-Posony, Propa Rezwana Anwar and Freya Aquarone

I was constantly stressed literally my whole life

I had panic attacks in high school

I was extremely anxious and
    It was extremely intense
            And it didn't seem like they cared.

When I was at school we knew we were inferior
    I hated the fact
that I was basically powerless.

And I think usually,
in a big institution like a uni,
I think as a student you might feel quite
        small.

But here staff actually ask how power can be challenged, and I'm
not used to that.

I'm not used to that at all.

            They're open to hearing disagreements
            Don't emphasise being referred to by their titles –
            by their academic achievements.
            It breaks down the boundaries
                    Between   us.

    *At my old uni I only had three meetings with my personal tutor
    in the whole year.
    I don't actually remember his name anymore.*

So something as simple as the fact
That you actually know our names
And parts of our lives

Something as simple as the fact
That discussing mental health is normalised

Something as simple as the fact
That she guided me to get professional help through the NHS

That I'm able to have conversations with staff about my interests

Something as simple as the fact
That they say 'you can speak to us'
That the staff are genuine and they want to help us

Something as simple as all this
Can humanise
    the entire
        process.

And I feel like I'm actually a person.

I feel like I'm actually a person.

2a – Love, care and kindness on the programme

Laura Nehéz-Posony

Mainstream Higher Education is generally thought to place value on utility and cost in order to serve the interests of academic capitalism (Slaughter and Leslie, 2001; Clegg and Rowland, 2010). Yet this does not take into consideration other significant human values. To promote the importance of this change in how we think about education, Lincoln argues for a reimagining of "academic collaboration" (2000:244) as a way of learning that operates on the basis of 'love' and 'care'. Generally speaking, people do not attribute much to these words, and they believe it to be unprofessional, unrigorous and overall useless to consider applying such ideas as love in the context of Higher Education (Clegg and Rowland, 2010). From a historical perspective, it is quite understandable why this approach feels unnatural for many people working in and researching Higher Education, since such concepts have "bec[o]me associated with [...] domestic rather than working life, and thus feminised" (Clegg and Rowland, 2010:722). Patriarchal assumptions see the expression of emotions as necessarily 'feminine' and view feminine traits as 'not serious' or 'not intellectual'.

It is always hard to unlearn elements of society that have been prevalent for centuries; therefore, it is difficult to rethink and reframe education as well, in a way that it is based on love, care and personal relationships. Many often believe that placing human values in the centre of educational relationships means leaving rational thinking behind; however, others have argued the opposite. Clegg and Rowland (2010), for instance, suggest that using kindness is in fact a highly rational act, as it involves setting boundaries and actively listening to the concerns of others, which ultimately contributes to healthy and productive working environments.

As outlined in chapter 1, the programme's attempts to emphasise human relationships can be understood through the theoretical lens of recognition. Recognition theory is a key element of German philosopher Axel Honneth's work (strongly inspired by Hegel) who distinguishes between 'cognition' and 'recognition' in personal and broader societal relationships. The term 'cognition' refers to "the act of individual identification of a person" (Honneth and Margalit, 2001:115), which entails solely the perception of another human being. Recognition, by contrast, is about much more than the mere (and generally internal) *perception* of one another (e.g. 'I see that person'); it is about *valuing* a person – *recognising* them as a worthy human being, through overt, "expressive gesture[s] of affirmation" (Honneth and Margalit, 2001:120). Honneth develops this definition of recognition and attendant 'acts of affirmation' into further component parts. The first, and arguably most important, of these is 'love', which Honneth defines as "an emotional concern for [a person's] well-being and needs" (van Leeuwen, 2007:182). Love is particularly core to Honneth's taxonomy because he considers loving relationships to be the precursor to all other forms of recognition (Honneth, 2014), including those based on Hegelian ideas of mutual respect and equality. It is the idea of 'recognition as love' which forms the primary focus of this chapter, as we explore our data around emotional relationships.

In addition to using Honneth's general idea of recognition as 'love' we also refer to relevant literature on 'kindness' and 'care' in HE, drawing on the work of Clegg and Rowland (2010) and Lincoln (2000). We therefore use the terms love, care and kindness somewhat interchangeably. Although they can evidently be conceptually differentiated, there is insufficient time here for a detailed treatment of each and, moreover, the themes in our data felt best illuminated by avoiding restrictive terminology. What holds these terms together, though, is a focus on the *quality and emotional depth of relationships.*

One of the most prevalent themes in our dataset related to participant descriptions of the programme as a space which prioritises emotionally meaningful human relationships. For instance, student participants emphasised the care they felt on the part of staff:

> Maya: The staff, like, actually care about you as well. So it's not just the students but the community feel comes from the staff as well, like

being able to kind of say how you feel, or if something's wrong, you feel comfortable doing that.

Rachel: The staff on our course, they actually really care about us. They genuinely care, not just because it's their job, but they want us to do well.

Rebecca: I mean just like something as simple as the fact that [on my old course] I didn't even- I think I only had like three meetings with my personal tutor in the whole year and I don't actually remember his name anymore. And so there was [...] none of that relationship building that this course tries to do.

There were also several participants who referred to the programme community as a 'family':

Bea: [It's] a big family, like everyone puts efforts to pull together to build up our community.

Rachel: I'm really glad that I'm a part of kind of, like, this big family that I didn't expect to get [...] at uni.

Tia: It's like a small family you know? [laughs] A small Kings family [laughs]

These accounts were echoed by staff in their descriptions of their feelings towards students:

Joe: I also just, like, genuinely really care about everyone on this programme [...]. I remember in the CCM[9] one of the student facilitators said 'You know, we're in this space because we all care about each other' and that really resonated for me, and I was like, 'Yeah, you're so right. [laughs] 'You're just so right'.

---

[9] CCM refers to 'Course Community Meeting' – these are the quasi-democratic meetings which students and staff use to discuss issues and make decisions about the programme. They are explored more in chapter 3.

Belle: I feel there's lots of commitment and care from lots of, like, staff members and also students, right? And that's also very much [something] I feel on a daily basis. [...] Some members of the staff really care about the programme and really care about the students and they really also, like, put themselves forward, like you know for [...] supporting [them] in different kind[s] of ways.

Rosa: I hope we keep that specialness every year that we've got this year, but I do feel very much like these students are really sort of special and will remain- have a place in our hearts? Because they're our first group and I hope all our students that come along will have a special place in our hearts but, you know, I think there is something particular there. [...] We've got such a cool group of students.

Although Lincoln believes that the ever-changing field of Higher Education (and, arguably, education spaces in general) could be transformed into a positive learning community through love and care, it has been noted that these factors are too often missing from people's experiences of education (Clegg and Rowland, 2010). Our participants (with a handful of exceptions) cannot compare their experiences of the programme to other HE spaces, because the programme is their first experience of HE. Thus, in laying out our data below, we are not suggesting that a focus on "emotional concern" (van Leeuwen, 2007:182) makes the programme distinctive.

Nonetheless, there are three ways in which it has analytical significance for this research: firstly, 'recognition as love and kindness' is integral to other aspects of recognition on the programme which arguably *are* relatively distinctive – such as its attempts to structurally embed forms of democracy (explored in chapter 3). Secondly, and connectedly, throughout the book, as we explore various challenges – for instance to do with conflict resolution or pedagogy[10] – the importance of love and kindness emerges as a recurring theme. Thus, for both these reasons, kindness can be seen as a foundation stone to the broader project of recognition on the programme. Thirdly and finally, student descriptions of kindness and care was simply one of the most prevalent and consistent

---

[10] Pedagogy refers to the approach or method of learning and teaching.

themes in our data[11], and this has inherent value even if it cannot be compared to 'the rest of HE'. We were struck by how many participants compared their experiences on the programme with those of their schooldays, a time when – for many – love and kindness was either lacking or much less in evidence. There was a strong feeling on the research team that previous experiences of education had not led people to *expect* caring relationships – particularly between students and staff – to be foregrounded in institutional spaces. The fact that the vast majority of participants strongly emphasised themes of love and care in relation to the programme – in contrast to negative experiences in school – indicates that this is of deep significance to many people in our community.

Beyond the general emphasis on caring relationships outlined above, participants also spoke about examples of love and kindness in relation to specific themes like 'lack of hierarchy' or 'emphasis on mental health' – we outline each of these below. We then explore a series of challenges to realising 'recognition as love, care and kindness' on the programme which were raised in our data.

Lack of hierarchy

Hierarchy between students and teachers is the foundation of how education works in many HE institutions (Levy et al., 2010). However, we might argue that in order to build an open and inclusive community where relationships are based on love and care, it is essential to let go of the idea of hierarchy. This is because hierarchy is based on unequal power dynamics and ideas of superiority and inferiority which may seem at odds with a commitment to caring for others as fellow human beings. As explored more in chapter 3, participants referred in our data to relationships on the programme being more equal between students and staff, often comparing this to their previous experiences of education:

---

[11] Of course, there are also examples of problems with relationships and of conflict, and these are explored at various stages throughout the book. But there was a prevalent overall feeling that relationships – particularly between students and staff – are fundamentally characterised by kindness and care.

Heidi: When I was in secondary school [...] I felt they had a lot of power over us, and they treated us [...] like we were really young, and I feel like here we're treated like the same level.

Maya: And also teaching as well, it just feels a lot more natural, like the staff-student- like power relationships, I don't think it exists as much, if it exists at all, whereas in school it's really present 'cos it feels like they're [laughs] I dunno what the word is but it feels like... you're kind of... I dunno, like, instructed to do things.

Crucially, many explicitly linked this sense of egalitarianism to feeling "safe" approaching staff, with clear implications for wellbeing:

Selena: I just feel comfortable talking to people, and I'm not scared, which I was when I talked to my teachers back in high school, because [...] [it was] based on power relations and [...] [they] want[ed] to execute [...] power by punishing us or by making us fear [them]. [...] [On this programme] I just feel like I am not gonna be judged the second I open my mouth, and I just feel very safe, and I feel heard, so I really- this is the thing that we appreciate, [...] because I hated the fact that I was basically powerless and I couldn't do anything about my education, back in high school.

Ryleigh: I would go to [staff] after seminars, there was a lot of times I went to ask, like, maybe a question, which sounds stupid for the [...] assignments, or other tasks, just to be, like, sure that I got it right. So, yeah, I really feel safe. I don't mind asking a teacher. They never make me feel stupid for asking even stupid questions.

Marla: [At] schoo[l] the students saw the teacher as a monster – not as a monster but someone who would- who they wouldn't be able to talk [to] if they had an issue because they were the students, they were inferiors and on top you had the teacher who had all the power. [...] That simple step [of calling staff by their first names] also makes it easier for the student not to be scared about the teacher, so not to be scared about if there's anything they don't understand or if there's anything they need to talk about – which might not be related to the stuff they are actually learning.

Marla and Selena's accounts above suggest that their previous institutional experiences were oriented around hierarchy, which made them feel "powerless" and "fear" teachers. This may seem for many teachers as the only approach that can work effectively in education; however, it is based on unequal power relations. Students' subsequent feelings of inferiority – and anxiety about "judge[ment]" (Selena) – can make it impossible to build healthy educational relationships based on trust and love. Reducing hierarchy on the programme – through what participants describe as "comfortable" (Selena) and informal relationships – seems to have facilitated a degree of openness in the way students relate to teachers, as they are less afraid to raise concerns with staff and ask questions – including about issues which, as Marla suggests, go beyond the academic.

Lincoln suggests these kinds of "caring" relationships are fundamental to the idea of "community" in HE (2000:246). Yet, they point out that true "learning communities" can be hard to attain because of the prevalent approaches that are currently shaping ideas around pedagogy – approaches which would render education the delivery of a commodified product within a competitive market, rather than about partnership and emotional – as well as intellectual – "connectedness" (Lincoln, 2000:246-247). Lincoln argues that this detached, objectified approach generates a level of "fear and estrangement" (2000:247, citing Ignatieff, 1985) between students and staff. When mutual relationships with teachers are negatively affected in this way, there is a double impact: students might be severed from the knowledge teachers provide, but also feel unable to address that or address *non*-academic needs as well (Lincoln, 2000). The participants above suggest that they do not feel "fearful" or "estranged" from staff – rather they see them to some extent as approachable equals, which means they feel safe asking questions and seeking out help.

Emphasis on mental health

Many participants described how their mental health has improved on the programme compared to previous experiences of education:

Sarah: I was very mentally fragile during my previous education experiences, like I was extremely anxious and I was, like, under extremely high, intense emotions, like, the entire duration of my A levels [...]. And I have to say [on this programme] I haven't experienced- like I've been very stressed for, like, short periods and for deadlines, as you probably expect. I had a hard time but it was very much more, like, decreased and, like, very much marginal compared to the mental health [impact] that I had [at school].

Susan: When I had [...] panic attacks in high school I was a hundred percent supported by my schoolmates, my friends and my teachers as well, but at the same time I still felt a little bit weird about it, and [here] I know if I had this problem I wouldn't feel weird. So it's I think [...] [because] mental health – everything around mental health – is normalised in this course. Which I think [is] very important [...].

Susan's account suggests that part of participants' relatively positive accounts of mental health may be to do with the way discussions around mental health are "normalised". This was echoed by several participants, who referred to the way they feel staff make explicit an emphasis on wellbeing and on reaching out for support:

Maya: [There's] like a constant message [from staff] that 'you can speak to us', sort of thing? [...] Yeah, it's just the fact that the message is reiterated all the time.

May: From the get-go, all the staff have been very clear that we [can] talk to them, whenever we want, about anything.

Rebecca: [S]o, like, before every seminar we do, like, check-ins normally. [...] Which again, it's just like, you know, reminding us that- that you see us as [...] full human beings and not just, like, you know, 'We're students for an hour and then you go about your business', and that you understand the context – that we're studying this in a context of, like, our lives as well.

The importance of making such a commitment explicit was described by one staff participant, reflecting on their experience of being a PhD student in the department (supervised by other members of the programme staff team):

> Marnie: As a PhD student, Audre and Cleo said to me [...] 'This isn't just an academic exchange, you know, you can use this space to talk about other things too.' And when I did, I didn't feel like I was breaking a rule or being weird, you know. [...] [O]nce that happens enough times people start to trust that it's real and that it's not just chat.

Interestingly, both Susan and Marnie used the term "weird" to describe how talking about mental health *could* feel in a different educational context. Naturally, as discussed before, it is difficult to unlearn ways of thinking about educational spaces and relationships, so it is understandable why students feel "weird" when talking about their anxiety and other mental health problems, if that hasn't been previously normalised. But, in Marnie's words, such an explicit emphasis on talking about mental health can help overcome this – people start to "trust" that the commitment is "real", as opposed to being superficial "chat". Indeed, as demonstrated by Emma and Susan below, students did describe feeling they can reach out to staff members to ask for help or raise concerns in relation to specific mental health needs:

> Emma: When I got ill last semester, I couldn't come in for the seminars, so I asked my tutor to record the classes and they really helped me to catch up. When the deadlines I've mentioned came near to each other, I was feeling stressed. I went to talk to my personal tutor, [they] told me to focus on myself and my wellbeing first. That was a very positive experience.

> Susan: We have, like, a very nice support network behind us. I think that really contributes. So, like, I know when I have problems, which is... almost always [laughs] then I can just go talk to [my personal tutor] and, you know, she kind of guided me to get professional help through the NHS [...]. So that's really nice that we have this system

where I can trust the person- because Audre, we don't see Audre as much as other teachers but I know that I still- like, I can trust her because she's my personal tutor and she would do anything for us [...].

Another feature of the programme mentioned by participants in connection with mental health was the approach to assessment. This is quite unusual compared to other courses. For instance, there are no exams throughout the three years of the programme; therefore, the emphasis on written coursework is more prevalent. A number of participants referred to this having a positive impact on their wellbeing:

Maya: [H]ow we're assessed on this course is quite different. But in a good way. And having no examinations works for me [...] in terms of my mental wellbeing.

Kima: I think another thing that I like about this course that makes me relatively less stressed is the frequency of assessments, so the fact that not everything is done at the end of the year, so obviously there's the coursework versus exam aspect, but also the fact that we're assessed for the final thing on a regular basis, you know, makes us less stressed because we're always adding up to it slowly as opposed to all at the end of the year.

Although the different types of assessment such as essays, media articles, portfolios and group presentations are still marked similarly to HE exams (e.g. a number out of 100), participants suggested that staff de-emphasise the 'grades' element of assignments, and focus more on the pedagogical value. Participants also described a generally relaxed attitude towards work. They referred to all of this as having a significant impact on their mental wellbeing (though did acknowledge that it took some degree of 'unlearning' from previous educational experiences where certain expectations had become ingrained):

Susan: So I know I was kind of curious when the stress would kick in, and so far it hasn't [laughs] [...]. I was constantly stressed in high school, I used to have very severe panic attacks and at some point I just collapsed in my school and that was because of the lack of sleep and the constant worrying about my grades and everything. [...] And this [was] within the setting of a very liberal and very nice high school with very understanding teachers, and they helped me a lot. But I know that still, my expectations were higher because [of] the primary school I was raised in and everything. [M]y previous experiences really added up to this, you know, very unhealthy, stressful environment [...]. But this [programme] is completely different, so I don't feel stressed at all. I'm definitely not collapsing in the corridor. And it's just really nice to have a very healthy [...] environment. Where it's okay to make mistakes and to not always have good grades. Which I had to really get used to.

Paul: [H]aving personal conversations with some of my personal tutees who've basically said how much they're enjoying it and [...] how stressful [...] their previous educational experiences were, because of a big emphasis on exams and [...], you know, teaching to the test and working really long hours and all that feeling of stress and basically saying how- appreciating the more relaxed nature of the course, so [...] I was quite pleased about that.

It is interesting that some participants attributed their lower stress and anxiety levels to the programme's de-centring of grades and assessment. Perhaps this is because using a number to determine a person's academic worth can be seen as a quintessential example of what Lincoln calls "the objectifying and alienating effects" of much mainstream HE practice (Lincoln, 2000:247). There is extensive evidence that grading has profound effects on people's sense of self-worth; for instance, studies have suggested that a focus on 'exam success' contributes to the deterioration of student health and wellbeing (e.g. see Roome and Soan, 2019, Putwain, 2009) and, connectedly, that low grades can lead to an enduring sense of "worthlessness" (Maguire, 2012:249). As Foucault puts it, examination practices – and their attendant classifications – are about rendering people visible for objectifying judgement:

"The examination [...] is a normalising gaze, a surveillance that makes it possible to qualify, to classify, and to punish. It establishes over individuals a visibility through which one differentiates and judges them" (1977:184).

Hence why Joe points out the importance of the programme trying to offer a resistant discourse:

> Joe: [B]ecause we are the powerful ones in the room in terms of, like, providing a perspective on what this educational journey means. So for us to say, actually, you know 'Those numbers are, like, kind of meaningless, 'cos it's a really problematic way of doing things', I think that has a really powerful impact, or certainly that did for me when I was a student.

'Knowing' one another

We might also argue that love and kindness are deeply dependent on the extent to which we 'know' one another. This is crucial to resisting the "estrangement" Lincoln refers to above as a barrier to care and kindness (2000:247). Estrangement as a concept strongly suggests an element of not knowing – of literal 'strangeness'. Arguably we can be caring and kind to strangers, but it is surely limited if we don't have a meaningful knowledge of the person's life – of their needs, priorities and interests. We might argue that the term love – in particular – relies on this depth of connection and understanding. Yet Clegg and Rowland (2010) connect this to kindness too. They argue that kindness and teaching are connected acts in that both "require the actor to identify with the concerns of the other" (2010:724) – and identifying with someone else's concerns relies on having sufficient knowledge of their life to meaningfully and empathically put yourself in their shoes. This was echoed by participants who, in describing their relationships with staff, emphasised the importance of familiarity, and of knowing things about one another's lives:

> May: [The staff] asked us about our life – it's not like school. They tell us about their lives, we call them by their first names. So yeah, I think the student-staff relationship is probably, like, one of my favourite aspects of the course.

Susan: We have a personal relationship and stuff, like, you actually know our names and you know parts of our lives, and- and I don't feel like I'm just 'one of them'. I feel like I'm actually a person.

Rebecca: I think, like, I'm able to have conversations with staff members about, like, my interests and they take a genuine interest. And also hear about, like, their research and that sort of stuff and that- I don't take that for granted.

One participant specifically referred to how informal time spent together as a programme community, in which we learn about one another's lives and interests, is not only "enriching" to our mutual relationships, but – bringing us back to an earlier theme – also contributes to breaking down hierarchy:

Marnie: There's about ten minutes before [the lecture] when everyone's standing in the corridor [...] and the conversations that happen in that space are really interesting because [...] there is this feeling that I get, [of] [...] people feeling very comfortable, and, sort of talking about things like what films they've been seeing, or asking each other questions about stuff that's going on in their lives, that feels really enriching to our collective community. And it's really, like, reassuring in the sense of actually thinking, yeah, we have made some progress to breaking down these assumptions around student and teacher identities that I think a lot of people do bring [...] into the room with them in ways that can be quite challenging.

Resolving conflict empathically

Honneth's theory helps to understand the importance of "expressive gesture[s] of affirmation" (Honneth and Margalit, 2001:120) for achieving mutual recognition. Honneth also claims, drawing on their interpretation of Hegel, that recognition – because it involves accepting and respecting a person other than oneself – is a form of "self-limitation" (2013:247). This is, in essence, the acknowledgement that recognition is accompanied by certain social and mutual responsibilities, such as respecting the boundaries of others or core values in interaction. Grounding one's relationship with oneself and with others in these principles, while we might call it self-limitation, is in fact a liberating and freeing experience for all.

On our programme, this idea of freedom in parallel with self-limitation formed at the beginning of the academic year, in the first Course Community Meeting, where students and teachers collectively wrote the Working Agreement – a set of principles which serve as a written consensus of what we expect from each other in our relationships. Participants during the interviews described the Working Agreement as a way of normalising expectations of mutual respect, listening, and trying to deal with any disagreements in a constructive, empathic way. This is both limiting, because people are obligated to hold back natural instincts when it comes to frustration and disagreements, while at the same time it is also freeing, as people have a clear guideline for inclusive and open communication. A number of participants highlighted the significance of the Working Agreement (which Susan refers to as "ground rules" and Tia as a "list of values"):

Tia: I remember the first week, the induction week, when we all sat down and we wrote this, like, huge list of [...] values that we're gonna go by throughout the years that we study at Kings and [this] particular course. I was very surprised and that was definitely the day that I was uncomfortable, in the sense that, 'What is this, why do we... do this?' like 'How- why do we care so much about this?' [laughs] [...] [And] everyone was like 'Oh my god we've been sitting here for like an hour and a half and we've been talking about how we have to be nice to each other, isn't that like... like, isn't that normal anyway, isn't that [something] we should do anyway?' But then going home and thinking about it I was like, no, [...] I mean it *should* be normal, but that's not how it works, 'cos you know, we've all had experiences from academia and high school or whenever, when students were not kind to each other, or the members of staff were not kind to the students, or you know, the other way round.

Susan: [W]e know that it's uncool to hate on people on this course. [...] This [principle] started very early on in this course – [...] [that] hating on other people, it's not acceptable. So I think very early on...

even like- even those people who would tend to, like, hate on people more, they still, you know, they learnt, like, different ways of coping with their anger or their, you know, difference in their opinion or whatever. So I think that was, like, communicated really from very early on [...] by the teachers, and also [in] the first Course Community Meeting [...], you know, when we [built] the ground rules.

Working agreements are quite unusual in mainstream education since it might be considered obvious to treat each other with respect. Therefore, the idea to put these basic principles in writing might seem pointless to many. The significance of the Working Agreement, however, lies in its explicitness; expectations of how we imagine conflict resolution is usually not enough, there has to be something that serves as a clear guideline, and normalises certain approaches which can help effective communication.

As we will see throughout the book, there have been many times where conflict has not necessarily been resolved in line with the programme Working Agreement, or when students and staff alike have felt frustrated or upset by conflict. In other words, laying out participants' descriptions of the significance of the Working Agreement is not to suggest it has always been applied, nor that it means conflict will always be non-harmful or constructive. Rather, it is to point out the importance of its existence; as Tia and Susan point out above, it starts a process of communication and reflection on our relationships with one another, and in doing so generates an explicit foundation for interaction on which the community can build. Moreover, the Working Agreement normalises the fact that people might not always agree with each other, and that disagreements could easily result in frustration. Stating explicitly that people do not have to feel ashamed for having these natural emotions is important, because every healthy human community will encounter difficulty and conflict.

2b – Challenges to recognition as love, care and kindness

Propa Rezwana Anwar and Freya Aquarone

In the previous section, we explored participants' perceptions of relationships on the programme in relation to concepts such as love, care and kindness. However, participants also identified a number of challenges to building these emotionally meaningful relationships; these are explored in various subsections below. In many ways these challenges are more wide-ranging than the scope of the positives laid out in the first half of this chapter. For instance, there is a particularly strong emphasis on time constraints towards the second half of this section. This was a strong theme in our data which has relevance for various articulations of recognition on the programme (and is consequently referred to in other chapters too). Nonetheless, we felt that the connotations of these concerns have *particular* relevance for the programme's attempts to build relationships based on recognition as love, care and kindness. Many of the challenges explored in this section can be linked to contextual and wider constraints (for instance, institutional context or sector marketisation). However, some are also well exemplified by specific events which occurred during the year. We therefore begin our exploration of challenges with a case study about some events which took place towards the end of the year's second semester.

Case study: the strike, the pandemic, and student concerns

In early March, following the disruption to learning caused by the strike and the extreme anxiety and uncertainty generated by the COVID-19 pandemic, a number of students on the programme began expressing concern and frustration to the student representatives (reps) about the impact on their learning and the fact that they felt they were not receiving sufficient information and clarification from either programme staff or the College. The student reps compiled a document detailing student

---

concerns, including anonymised comments from the cohort's WhatsApp group chat, some of which were quite emotive and mentioned specific staff members (who were anonymised, but in many cases identifiable due to reference to their pronouns or professional role). Within 48 hours, staff wrote a response document addressing each of the student concerns, in many cases explaining how practical action would be taken. However, some staff brought the matter to a 'Course Community Meeting' (CCM) and expressed concern about the tone and content of the anonymised comments, some of which they felt did not take into account the constraints of the context in which staff were operating, nor the principles of the programme's 'Working Agreement' which emphasises kindness in communicating during times of difficulty or disagreement. Some students also expressed concerns about aspects of the document, and the tone of some of the student comments. The student reps – who had felt caught in the middle of staff and student frustrations when they decided to compile people's concerns in a document – felt targeted for their role as 'messengers'. Although the CCM discussion was calm and constructive, it was nonetheless difficult and emotional, perhaps in particular for the student reps, who felt that not all peers who had contributed to the document shared in taking responsibility for it in the context of the CCM.

Consumer identities (and one perspective on the case study)

The idea of 'students as consumers' can be seen to create obstacles for building and maintaining relationships built on mutual care. It is widely acknowledged that "the discourse of consumerism is a powerful element in the mix of structural factors that shape [...] HE" (Levy et al., 2010:2), and accordingly, 'consumer identities' featured clearly in some participants' narratives:

> Michelle: I feel like I'm paying for the course and I'm not receiving much...like my sister, she paid the same and my sister had like fifteen hours [per week], and she was doing, like, sciences but still, like, they say like, 'Oh eight hours is for humanities' but my friends are doing war studies, that's humanities and they're still doing twelve hours.

And I feel like they're just mocking us, like I'm just paying and [...] eight hours, I feel like that's not enough.

Erica: Oscar said in one seminar that we felt like customers, [he] asked us if we feel like customers and, like, all of us did. Like we literally- we pay ten thousand – for those who have home fees – to get eight hours a week and not even during the whole year, you know?

These narratives were perhaps most apparent when participants discussed the strike action, and the university's response to the COVID-19 pandemic (which first peaked in the UK shortly before the strike ended):

Sarah: [T]he matter of the fact is the university has clearly breached its contract especially with regards to the strike and now this bloody pandemic that no one could see coming. Like if we are consumers – which the university seems to think we are – then we are entitled to at least some sort of fund back! [...] [W]e've lost, like, about two thousand pounds' worth. Which obviously for some people that we've spoken to doesn't seem like it's a lot. But certainly for my family, that is a massive amount of money. [...] And obviously, like, I understand the strikes were necessary and I was one hundred percent supportive of the strike as I have said from the very beginning. But [...] if you are paying nine grand for something you obviously want your money['s] worth. And I honestly don't feel like this year I've received an education that can be valued at nine thousand pounds.

It is important not to responsibilise students for buying in (quite literally) to consumer discourses. The structure of contemporary HE arguably encourages this, not least through the charging of – in the case of international students in particular – extremely high fees. It is thus understandable why many students feel inescapably positioned as consumers, even if they reject this logic, as Bea's comment below suggests:

> Bea: I don't think [the] School is a service provider and we are not customers. However, we paid for our education and we don't receive it. I think [the] School should give us back our tuition [because of the strikes].

Another participant reflected on the way they feel students are conditioned by wider societal norms – beyond just HE – to implicitly see themselves as customers:

> Maya: I think one of the big things, kind of the mainstream ideal, well maybe I'm getting a bit too political, but, like, neoliberalism? [...] I was [thinking] about the strikes but, like, this whole focus on money and value for money and [...] I don't think students feel like they're customers, but implicitly in their heads it's about money. 'I have not been taught, so where's my money going?' 'This is £60 worth of lectures. I need a refund.' So in a way we're implicitly taught to kind of feel like that.

Nonetheless, consumer narratives, by framing interaction through the lens of financial exchange, can risk undermining other ethical or emotional aspects of human relationships (Gewirtz and Cribb, 2020; Clegg and Rowland, 2010); these include the forms of recognition explored above, based on building relationships grounded in consideration for one another's needs and wellbeing. This issue was highlighted in a dialogue between two student participants, who raised concerns about some students' attitudes towards the strike:

> May: I think the staff need to enforce the ethos more onto the students and let them know, like, everything we're studying is 'pro' this strike. [...] [O]ur module is literally called 'social justice' and whatever. And students are [...], like, calculating exactly how much money they are going to lose.
> Rebecca: As if it's about the money and not about the fact that the university continuously treats its staff like they don't matter.
> May: It's funny, that we are [studying] things like how capitalism affects us. And then we're actually like- in the real world we're like, 'Oh as students we're nothing more than the amount we pay and

not what we can do for each other'. They don't see it as a human-like a people thing, everyone's very individualistic. It's not a community in that sense, because we can't even stand in solidarity with our lecturers because it impacts money or whatever.

May and Rebecca's concerns suggest that, when things get difficult, people can easily fall back on consumer positionings; this perhaps re-centres the forms of "alienati[on]" in HE that Lincoln warns against (2000:247), obscuring our capacity to frame challenges as a "human" (May) problem, with an attendant responsibility to enact kindness and support. Rebecca went on to suggest that the intensity of the strike and the pandemic – and especially the events detailed in the case study – highlighted the "cracks" in programme relationships, exposing how – despite well-intentioned attempts at emphasising "support[ing]" each other" – students and staff are nonetheless positioned very differently in relation to the institution:

> Rebecca: [W]ith the strikes [...] and the coronavirus that's been happening right now, I think the sort of cracks in this community- I don't know, this- this feels a bit too cynical but [...] some people have written like a four thousand word complaint or something [...], and I'm just like, you know, if we're this community- this strong community that we claim to be- then now is the time to be, like, really coming together to support each other, rather than just complaining about things that aren't really in our control, if that makes sense.
> Researcher: Yeah. Why do you think people are responding [...] in a way of sort of moving towards complaint rather than... maybe coming together in a different way?
> Rebecca: I mean I think it's- it's all we know. [...] Even though this course really doesn't feel like we're consumers, we are consumers in the context of Higher Education, [...] 'cos that is how we're viewed by the university. So when things aren't going as smoothly- 'cos it's very easy to have a community when things are really nice and, you know, and we're all 'getting [...] our nine thousand pound[s'] worth of education', quote unquote, but when that's not happening, people sort of, like, go back to what we know, and what we know is that,

you know, 'We're on this course and we deserve to get a certain amount of education, and we're not getting that anymore'.

Strikes are unusual — they are not something most programme communities have to contend with on a regular basis. Nonetheless, the events detailed above are helpful for highlighting some of the tensions involved in building relationships based on mutual care in an educational context in which people are commonly positioned as 'consumers' and 'providers'. Calculations about financial value do not tally well with attempts to humanise education. How can we, for instance, put a price on building meaningful relationships when that manifests in ways which go well beyond specific hours of contact time, and are related to difficult-to-quantify phenomena like kindness and emotional support? How can we square a desire to receive 'our money's worth' with, as May highlighted earlier, the employee exploitation on which that 'service' may be based? At the same time, students *are* paying a lot of money for their degree. Most will be in tens of thousands of pounds of debt for decades as a result, and many have to work alongside full-time study just to cover basic living costs. Thus, in a context like the strike, students arguably end up caught between the competing aims of getting what they have paid for — in a system which makes considerable financial demands on them and does ultimately treat them as consumers — and broader ethical commitments to building meaningful, mutually caring relationships with staff.

Despite this significant tension, many student participants demonstrated powerful forms of resistance, explicitly problematising and challenging consumerist renderings of their identity — including in relation to the strike:

> May: I think in terms of the strikes, the lecturers are doing way more than they should need to do. Like babying everyone. They're striking. Let them strike. [Students shouldn't] be like, 'me, me, me, me' — you didn't get your pensions cut. Asking about money when people are losing out on paychecks. These are their lives, these are their jobs. [...] [T]he students need to stand in solidarity with the staff. It's our responsibility.

Other participants pointed to how the strike helped them to better understand the position of staff – to move beyond considerations of financial impact and link up the course's ethos of justice with the aims of the strike itself, thus suggesting the strike actually helped work to override consumer narratives and build bonds between students and staff:

> Tia: What you guys [staff] did [in striking], it was important because we understood what the strike is, and people stopped complaining about their money or whatever [laughs] [...]. Like, complaints are normal, but at the same time, [...] we should understand. [...] Like it was a good [...] example of, like, what we're trying to do [on the programme], you know? Like, fight for our rights, all this sort of thing, and having [...] this, like, community experience that we're all in this together and like giving the teach-out [was] really nice, like it was good that students got to participate in the picket line and things like that. [...] Because you kind of put yourself into someone else's shoes and then you understand the situation from a different perspective.

The idea that the strike facilitated a process of mutual humanisation and of bringing alive the course's own social justice aims was echoed by staff:

> Rosa: The engagement of the students [in the strike] [...] and the widespread support of the students is really cool. [...] I think that will strengthen [...] many of the good things about the feelings between the staff and the staff and the students, of kind of cooperation and knowing each other in all our humanity and thinking about the politics of what we're learning and [the] politics of education itself.

Lincoln warns against the notion of the "learning community" becoming a "nostalgic" ideal, detached from the "objectifying and alienating" realities of HE (2000:247). While it is important to consider the challenges generated by these realities – such as the prevalence of consumer discourses – there is strong ground for maintaining faith in practices of resistance. Many participants' opposition to reducing student identities to that of consumers, coupled with the themes of mutual care and kindness outlined in the first half of this chapter, surely demonstrate that while contextual challenges may *complicate* the programme's attempts to prioritise recognition, they do not necessarily counteract or undermine them.

Conflict and communication (another perspective on the strike)

Above we suggested that, for some participants, the events outlined in the case study highlight the way people fall back on consumer identities in times of difficulty. But these events highlight other challenges for building relationships built on care and kindness. For the student reps, for instance, the strike brought sharply to light what happens when "there aren't sufficient lines of communication in place" (Rhonda). This is strongly connected to the analysis of 'time and relationships' considered later. For instance, Rhonda identifies a root cause of communication issues being the sudden drop in *time* which students and staff were spending together (which also perhaps exacerbated the extent to which students turned to reps with their problems, rather than taking responsibility for raising them themselves):

> Rhonda: [S]o the reps, [...] our job was to convey to staff the fact that students were struggling on the course as a result of... lack of communication from kind of both sides [during the strike], and students feeling very unsure about what to do. And [...] as I said, the fewer contact hours [...] means that students aren't really communicating with staff because they're not comfortable [...] so then students thought that reps were in a position in between students and staff to therefore kind of amend things, and that put unreasonable pressure for a prolonged period of times on the reps because we felt that [we] were basically trying to do the job of staff but also protect staff [...]. So as reps we found it very difficult to kind of stand in this middle ground.

Again, the strike cannot be considered as an example of 'normal' programme experience. Yet the events do highlight just how important lines of communication are, and how these can be damaged by a lack of face-to-face contact. When people do not see each other, it can damage the efficacy of their communication – people feel they can't reach out to one another in the same way. This is perhaps why many participants described feeling less comfortable with staff that they see less often (not just during the strike, but in general):

> Selena: I find [it] quite hard to, well, bond with my personal tutor, as I barely see her. [...] 'Cos I never have actual classes with her, apart from a few lectures. So [...] because with some teachers [I] have more classes and I guess I see them more, so I feel more comfortable around them.

Another factor to bear in mind is that, when people don't see each other very often, they understandably fall back on (usually written) electronic communication. Indeed, the student reps explained – when asked at the CCM why they had opted to raise their concerns in a document, sent by email – that they had felt two weeks (until the next CCM) was too long to wait given the time-sensitive nature of the concerns. There is a considerable range of literature suggesting that inherent features of written electronic communication – such as lack of body language, facial expression and verbal nuances – can make it more difficult to resolve conflict constructively (e.g. see Friedman and Currall, 2003; Byron, 2008). Rhonda herself suggests that the written medium by which the conflict was handled may have led people to be less thoughtful in their communication than they might otherwise have been:

> Rhonda: I thought that that was the right approach – to make an anonymous form with my other rep, so that we could get opinions that we weren't seeing – 'cos we knew people had lots of opinions, they just weren't saying them in public. But then [sighs] what we soon realised, soon after making that anonymous doc, is that a lot of those comments, instead of being very open and honest and pleasant and just things people wouldn't want to say in public, it turns into... quite insensitive things, which even we as reps struggled to read.

Strong lines of communication also help with building a shared understanding and solidarity about institutional realities; this could ensure that everyone has a better awareness of people's positioning within the institution, and thus what can be practically expected of them in an HE context. Max Weber advocates for 'verstehen' – an effort made by researchers to understand the perspectives of those whose behaviour they are analysing, by empathically putting themselves into their shoes. This approach provides us with a foundation for understanding the relationships between students and staff members in the institution. Though participants suggested students do try to understand the position of staff members and vice versa, because students and staff *are* in different positions, sometimes it is important to build on one another's understanding:

> Rhonda: I think there's a lot of respect, a lot of effort to understand? [But] we [students and staff] both have quite different positions -even if we're trying to get rid of those rhetorics, they're still there.

For instance, it is understandable that if students are not clear on the positioning of staff members within HE, then it may be difficult for them to know what level of communication with staff should be considered 'normal.' As we saw above, as a result of the strike, students felt less comfortable in communicating with staff overall; frustration arose seemingly because students felt staff had the power to answer their questions and provide greater clarity. Yet staff were not in a position to solve the problem, even though from a student's perspective it may seem like staff on any level have 'all the power'. For instance, although students were particularly frustrated about uncertainties around tuition fee refunds, teaching staff on the programme have no control over tuition fee policies.

This links into the importance of building awareness around wider inequalities within KCL – for instance, the way that teaching staff are themselves subject to forms of hierarchy and differential levels of power due to the institutional structures of the College. As one staff member pointed out, not all students are aware of the significance of this, especially when it comes to the differences *between* staff:

> Marnie: I might teach, but technically my role is described in other ways, but most of them don't know what GTA[12] means and they've

---

12 GTA stands for Graduate Teaching Assistant – the term generally refers to hourly-paid teaching staff who are also doctoral students.

never heard that language because we use 'seminar tutor' on this programme, [...] so maybe a lot of them are quite surprised when they realise these realities and inequalities of HE.

According to a University and College Union (UCU) report about precarious work in HE, 54% of all academic staff and 49% of all academic teaching staff are on insecure contracts (UCU, 2016). In the UK, undergraduates are *particularly* likely to be taught by someone on an insecure or precarious contract (ibid.). Many students may not be aware of these realities when, for instance, making complaints or filling out feedback forms. This is a matter worth raising as staff on insecure contracts may struggle to meet the high bar of professional service they strive for in the face of working conditions that leave them underpaid, vulnerable and constantly facing the possibility of unemployment (ibid.).

Perhaps staff ought to have more discussions with students about the realities of HE (including about the strike, so much of which was predicated on sector inequalities), to build shared understanding. Not only would this potentially bring students and staff together at times of uncertainty and increase mutual empathy, but it would also be beneficial for students to expand their critical understanding of their learning context, and for them to gauge where staff are positioned in relation to the institution – both in relation to the context of the strike and pandemic, and in general.

Institutional culture

Following on from the discussions above around institutional context, another challenge identified in the data relates to the way the university often operates in ways which are arguably not conducive to promoting love, care and kindness in student-staff interactions. For instance, while above we described how some staff were upset by the way students raised their concerns about the pandemic and strike, students themselves were distressed by the wider institution's apparent lack of care for them and their needs. Indeed, this was seemingly the core of many students' frustration:

> Sarah: [W]e are also entitled to some care as students. Like it's not right that we have sort of been left in the dark by the university and are not being [...] treated by them very well?

For another participant – Fran – this "detached" non-concern became particularly apparent when a group of students tried to lobby management for a change to assignment requirements in the wake of the disruption of the strike and pandemic:

> Fran: It was disheartening because myself and the other student rep both went to different meetings. We asked all the questions and we got very limited information from, like, the university itself. It was disheartening because I thought as a student rep I was in a better position to maybe make a change of the situation that students are in right now. [...] [But there was] such a lack of concern, like, for their students, like it's so detached. [...] Like, I don't even know who the Dean of our university is, like, it's so detached. And alien. It feels like such a foreign and distant body where, like, you feel like you don't even stand a chance because there have been like physical walls that have been put up in between. I feel like ... so distant from the university.

The institutional context generates obstacles to recognition in other ways too; for instance, due to the institutional requirements of their employment position, staff can be required to "side with power structures" (Kate), despite the harm that they might cause. Some staff pointed to the enduring reliance in HE on quantitative grading as an example, which they suggested could be viewed as a form of "symbolic violence" against students in which they are complicit:

> Luke: [F]or example, marking assignments when, [...] the marking criteria sort of becomes this standardised tool [...] [and] the symbolic violence of getting a number, like, from the essay that you've written and you didn't quite get the grade that you wanted, and the number comes back and that's all that you see, and it's like this kind of institutional thing which is sort of unavoidable. [...] If we had the opportunity on this programme *not* to assess our students for

59

particular modules, I think a number of us would be really interested in that idea, but it's not the kind of thing that we can do. [...] I think that sort of interferes with [our ethos]. Like, in what other [context] would you feel like you had a meaningful, engaged partnership with someone and then you ranked them or [...] quantified their [work]? I mean I suppose that happens in some areas of life but it just feels really odd, like, to be building on like a meaningful relationship through conversations with people and then, like, you give them this- this- this *mark*, you know?

Marnie: I was talking to students on Friday about [...] these module evaluation forms, kind of as an example of how, like, ridiculous and shallow university education can become when it's about consumers and service providers. And in that moment I forgot that we basically do the same thing to them! [...] And it made me feel awful afterwards 'cos I thought, like, 'Hang on a minute, now I'm on the other side of the table I can think about this way students objectify *me'*... but without remembering that we do the same thing to them when we give them a number out of a hundred to, like, tell them what their work is worth.

As touched on earlier, there are times where the differential position of students and staff in relation to the wider institution can place them on opposite sides of the table, in ways which don't necessarily lend themselves to recognition in the form of love and kindness.

Interpersonal conflict

Earlier we explored indications in the data that participants value the emphasis on handling interpersonal conflict in ways that foreground care and kindness – for instance, by establishing a working agreement. However, a small number of participants did describe occasions on which staff members behaved in ways which, they felt, were not rooted in these principles:

Susan: I only had one teacher [who] I really felt like wasn't working out for me. And I think [they were] a good teacher [...] I really love them, I truly love them and I'm not lying [laughs] [...]. The only thing is I didn't really feel comfortable in their seminars in terms of like, when I tried to explain a concept, or when they asked something, and [...] we tried to explain something, I kind of always got this [...] feeling that I was dumb? [...] I know that this probably wasn't on purpose, [...] [so] I didn't take this personally, mainly because other people had the same feeling.

These concerns were limited compared to the data describing positive experiences with staff, but they are important to include. For one, they demonstrate that even in a community in which positive relationships are widely considered a core feature of interactions, interpersonal conflict is unavoidable, and people are always capable of being unkind in their behaviour towards others, even if unintentionally. The key question is how these concerns are handled. The programme's guidelines around dealing with interpersonal conflict recommends that students raise concerns with their personal tutor or a member of staff in the first instance. The Course Community Meetings (explored more in the next chapter), which offer a space for collective deliberation and decision-making about the programme, have a remit which explicitly *excludes* matters of concern between specific individuals, on the basis that quasi-public spaces are generally not the ideal space to deal with such matters. However, there was some indication that students did not always feel that approaching staff informally about matters too sensitive or specific for a CCM had actually led to change:

Tia: I was unhappy to some extent with, like, [the] seminars, for instance? And I heard that from many people actually, it wasn't just me, and when we were going to Oscar to talk about it and saying, 'Well maybe [the seminar tutor] should do this and this to change that', like I don't think that- I don't know, maybe he did get back to [them], like maybe he did give [them] some feedback but [they] didn't change anything.

The question arises, then: where and how can these more specific concerns be effectively addressed? Many established democratic education settings – e.g. democratic schools – have spaces for conflict resolution which are separate from their main, collective decision-making forums[13]. Given the programme's time constraints (explored more below), and the fact that interpersonal conflict in *particular* can be complex and time-consuming, it's hard to know how the programme could maintain separate spaces like this. We don't have clear answers, but we wanted to flag this because it strikes us as difficult to democratically navigate the practicalities of day to day life in any community without acknowledging the fact that many of the most important aspects of those practicalities will be bound up in interpersonal relationships, as Rosa points out below:

> Rosa: [I]f there's something maybe a bit difficult to bring up [at the CCMs] [...] – and it often might be difficult because it relates to certain staff or students [...] – that maybe is just tricky to bring up because maybe it could be seen as an implied criticism of someone else. [...] [T]hen that can be tricky because, you know, we've decided well we won't, kind of, do [interpersonal conflict in the CCMs], but a lot of tricky things in education *are* to do with people.

---

[13] For UK examples see *Sands School:* https://www.sands-school.co.uk/policies-and-paperwork/ and *The New School:* https://www.thenewschool.org.uk/documents

Another barrier is time
yeah, time is a big one.
I often think
what would this be like if people had more time?
What if we were able to spend double the time together?
That would make–
it would change everything.

The amount of time we spend together just changes everything.

So even though I think that we have a community
that runs a lot deeper than most universities

Mutual care and respect and–
people feeling comfortable

if I'm honest
if I'm really honest
the reality of Higher Education is
that it's quite
a fragmented thing.

You know.

We don't have enough time to be together
to *be* together
In the messy day to day sense
of muddling along
making mistakes and getting it wrong
being shown to be human
and reflecting on

what we're doing here.

People have got too much on.

To be getting teas and coffees in a shared communal space
To create a real sense of–
I don't know.
Pace?

I really value face-to-face
relationships and I'm struggling.

And in the ideal uni, a utopian world–
part of that would be
the collective self-care
of saying 'let's not overdo it'.
Let's not exhaust ourselves by expecting
always to be undergoing
multiple multiple multiple
pieces of work
as we lurk
at our desks
eating sandwiches at our desks.

I'm constantly horrified by the level of burnout.
People are *so* overworked. I'm literally–
I'm in shock.

If the ethos of the programme is having a strong community
then why do people go home
and feel lonely?

Isn't it better to be at uni and change the world together?
That's the point, no?
That's the point?

Time: its significance for emotionally meaningful relationships

In our data, time – or to be specific, *lack* of time – was a constant, ever-ticking through line. In Higher Education (especially UK humanities courses) limited contact time is fairly standard. In its best light, it's part of an educational paradigm which values individual study and exploration – time for people to find themselves intellectually, and dive into the things that interest them, without being guided constantly by a teacher or structured, formal learning. We don't have to reject that logic and go to the opposite extreme, driven by some kind of authoritarian urge to force people to invest in being part of a compulsorily collective approach to learning. Some people love university precisely because they are freed from what they see as the horrors of institutionalisation and year group batches! But we do have to consider the constraints on building meaningful relationships based on recognition when people simply spend very little time in the same room. Some of this is less to do with educational paradigms and more to do with institutional constraints – not least the marketisation of the sector. For instance, participants expressed frustration at the difficulty in pushing back against the College's "business" priorities in terms of the distribution of "resources", including contact hours:

> Maya: I know that contact hours were mentioned, [...] that's a constraint in itself. Like how many contact hours do we get as a humanities slash social sciences course. Like it's typically supposed to be eight to ten. We can't have any more, but do we want any more and why do we want any more- like it brings up so many questions. So I think, yeah, bureaucracy as well is a factor in kind of not being able to implement certain things.

> Luke: I mean there's lots that we could say about, you know [...] the institution being run as a business which is concerned about, you know, profit and turnover and that might have an impact on the way that resources for example are available or not. This is the reality that we face, this is how Higher Education operates in the UK.

There is a stark reality to what Joe describes below as the "fragment[ation]" of Higher Education – the way in which staff are required to spread their time more and more thinly across multiple programmes, growing student populations, and a plethora of institutional demands (Stephen et al., 2008; Times Higher Education, 2016; Gewirtz and Cribb, 2020; Leathwood and Read, 2020), arguably leaving little in the way of time or energy for building meaningful relationships with students:

> Joe: I think that we have a community that runs a lot deeper than most universities, or even most- even full-time schools. In the sense of, like, all the things I've mentioned before around sort of, mutual care and respect and, people feeling comfortable. [...] [But] I still feel that it's [...] fragmented- it's more fragmented than you know, than in my ideal university. [...] What if we were able to spend double the contact hours [together]? [...] That would make such- it would just change everything. Because, you know, the amount of time we just spend together changes everything.

This was echoed by students discussing the lack of opportunities to build relationships with peers, even citing feelings of loneliness – which raises an important and troubling counterpoint to the programme's emphasis on mental health explored earlier:

> Erica: To be honest I don't feel like we're really a community yet in the course [...] because we lack hours. [...] I feel like if we had more hours we would have more opportunities to, like, I don't know, go have a lunch with someone or, you know, create a real sense- or talk more or I don't know.

> Tia: If the ethos of the programme is having a strong community, then why do people go home and feel lonely after? Is it better to have like- to be at uni and like- like change the world together? [laughs] That's the point, no? [laughs]

Below, based on participant narratives, we go into greater depth on various sub-themes around time and how it affects building meaningful emotional relationships on the programme.

Academic contact time: quantity versus quality?

Academic contact time is a fundamental facilitator of relationships which go well beyond the academic. Yet it's important to consider what that time actually entails. When it comes to building relationships, quality of time spent together is arguably just as important as quantity. On the programme, academic contact time takes place largely in two contexts: a) large group lectures consisting of the whole cohort, and b) small-group seminars. In lectures, students may be spending an hour with one another, but there is less opportunity for interaction, and the large group setting arguably makes in-depth exchange more difficult. On the other hand, seminars are an invitation for an exchange of opinions in a more intimate setting. Participants described seminars as having particular significance for building meaningful relationships. For instance, they suggested people have an opportunity to engage in discussions and express standpoints and perspectives to a much greater degree than in lectures:

> Carl: In the seminar[s] I feel safe in expressing my opinion. In lecture time, because we are very [many], like fifty students, I do not like it because it's intimidating to speak in front of a large group.

> Ryleigh: I feel seminars, like, it's much more helpful and worth it. 'Cos in the seminar firstly, I can ask a question. [Because it's] not in front of everyone, we are in a small group. Secondly, I can discuss and give my opinion. [...] In lecture[s], I wouldn't be as open to express myself, because there is a lot of people, it's quite...so [...] 'cos I would be kind of like of afraid to say something wrong, or something that sounds stupid.

Participants also suggested that the depth of discussion in seminars helps people to learn about one another's backgrounds and lives in a way that enriches not only learning but also mutual understanding:

67

Rhonda: Like I remember [...] when we studied the like Haiti and, like, the earthquake and how the earthquakes happen in Bangladesh and I was able to [provide some] input, and I know that there are people [...] from Eastern Europe, you know, they bring in really interesting ideas into the seminars? So there was actually a seminar last semester where [someone] actually gave us a poem from [their] language, like a translation of it?

Crucially, participants highlighted the seminars as key for facilitating open *emotional* exchange, suggesting that when people have spent time together in an intimate small-group learning context, it is easier to discuss "personal stuff" or "problems" both within that space and beyond:

Helena: [L]ike in seminar groups [...] I think everyone felt comfortable sharing their own experiences at least [...] that was what it was like for me. Because in smaller groups I feel that it's easier to share personal stuff.

Kima: Seminars are the place where we really talk about our thoughts and actually get to know each other's opinions [...] so if I haven't had those conversations with people, then [...] it's maybe difficult for those people to openly talk to me about their problems?

Some participants suggested that the familiarity afforded by the context of the seminars affects not only their openness with one another, but also with staff. For instance, one participant suggested that they felt "closer" to seminar tutors than lecturers, and more comfortable opening up about "personal stuff", because seminars enable staff to get to know students in greater depth:

Erica: I'm feeling like [lecturers] don't have time to deal with my personal stuff you know. Even if [seminar tutors] might not have time either, I feel like [they] would be more open to it because in seminars it's small groups, they've all heard our voices, they all know kind of what our opinions are. [...] Lecturers they're just here talking to a class and no one is really answering actually in the lectures, every time they ask questions. I think that's why I also feel closer to seminar teachers.

Recognising the significance of *quality* of time spent together on the programme, rather than just quantity, means that even if we do consider an increase in academic contact hours to be significant for strengthening relationships in general, this would arguably only have its full effect if the *right kind of* hours were increased, rather than a mere increase in the number contact hours overall. There are also questions to be asked about how quality of time spent together connects with issues around community size – this is explored in more depth in chapter 4.

The significance of physical interaction and space

Several participants pointed to the crucial importance of space and physical interactions for human relationships. Kima, for instance, explained how this became particularly apparent to them once lockdown measures were implemented in the wake of the pandemic, and they noticed how a connection to 'place' and to passing physical interactions with people in the programme and beyond had become integral to their day to day experiences of the community:

> Kima: I just think physical connections with people are something I really value. [...] There are so many [aspects of that] that I think go unnoticed? [...] For example, I remember, every morning when I'd walk through the doors, there was a specific [security guard] [...] who I used to see every day, and he used to give me, like, a massive grin and he never used to check my ID card and he would always raise his hand and wave at me, and I'd do the same back, and we've even high fived on some occasions – so, like, these people, I just really miss [them], [...] because now I'm not seeing them at all [due to lockdown], and I don't have any excuse to virtually connect with them, which hurts because that was also part of my education experience. Like when I think about King's I don't just think about the books and the Zoom webinars, I also think about all the [people] [...] [laughs] that I was forming relationships with, who are just not in my life any more?

So far, we have explored the significance of time for building emotionally meaningful relationships, and in the previous section we briefly touched on the significance of group sizes. This might lead us on to wider considerations of the significance of space and physical context for time spent together. Indeed, the significance of space for quality time has been so widely acknowledged that some theorists have suggested that time and space should not be separately theorised (Lingard and Thompson, 2017). As Leathwood and Read write, "we cannot think about time without also acknowledging spatiality, materiality and embodiment" because time is always "context specific" (2020:2).

As Kima's account above highlights, human relationships are so often about organic moments of physical proximity or contact – high fives and bumping into people in corridors. Part of facilitating these interactions is about having access to communal spaces for spending time together. Issues around space have significant relevance for our programme community and were picked up on in the data. Even before the onset of the pandemic and the necessity of a newfound reliance on virtual communication methods, there was not a physical communal space solely dedicated for the use of the programme community. A departmental common room did exist – however, it was relatively underused (this could be for a number of reasons: e.g. it is at the end of a corridor on the second floor – not exactly a 'central hub' of the building – and the space has been described as not especially comfortable). Moreover, it is sometimes dominated by large groups of people from other degree disciplines – for instance, in-between teaching sessions; there was never a space that students from the programme could 'put their stamp on' and feel was their own. One participant suggested that this is partly an effect of the sporadic nature of HE timetabling, whereby people drop into educational spaces for an hour or so at a time, and it is less normalised for people to spent large chunks of time in the same space collectively:

> Tia: If we had to stay in the School for, like, I don't know, four or five hours instead of, like, one [...], then we'd have a chance to, like, you know, meet up, study together, talk about things – which we still do, but it's more [that] we do it personally, individually, like from home

where we can, you know, [or] on WhatsApp or something like that. We don't do it at, like, the university campus.

But timetabling aside, if there is no communal space you can go, where you feel comfortable and can expect to see familiar faces, it is perhaps unsurprising that people just head straight home after class rather than opting to spend the day on campus. This was exemplified by one participant, who indicated that they felt other campuses at the College had more of a community feel, with students staying on campus to work together (they also made specific reference to aesthetic concerns, describing the Strand campus as a "nicer" space):

> Ryleigh: Personally, I just finish class and I leave. And to be honest, it's because of the campus. [...] Maybe if we were in the main campus, the Strand, for sure, I would have stayed more. [...] If I have, like, I don't know [an] assignment, essay to write, I would rather go home, and do that. [...] Whereas, if you were in the Strand, I feel like there are much more people from other courses. The area is nicer. The building is much nicer, the library is much nicer. I'd stay there and, like, I spend you know, much more time around. Meeting all the people from other courses and doing my work there in uni.

Indeed, one staff member, Paul – when asked about the main obstacles facing the programme – referred explicitly to "material constraints" around space. They referred to how a better-functioning community space – such as a shared "cafe" – would create greater opportunities for "develop[ing] relationships":

> Paul: I think the main [obstacles are] [...] material constraints. So, for instance I think what we really need is, like, our own common room with a cafe attached to it [laughs] [...]. Maybe again I'm romanticising about when I was at university – [...] my brother and some of my friends [at a different department] [...] had their own space and their own social space with a cafe that did toasted cheese, you know, toasties and it was all really kind of friendly.
> Researcher: [...] [W]hat would that change? Why would that be a good thing?

Paul: [...] I think it would just- it's just more opportunities [...] for students to socialise amongst themselves but also for staff-student socialisation, so, I mean, it wouldn't even have to be just for this course, 'cos it could be for the whole School, but I just think if people would just be in there more, there'd be [...] more opportunity to talk and develop relationships [...].

This was echoed by another staff member, Joe, who described an "imagin[ed]" alternative HE in which departmental spaces were more cooperative and communal:

Joe: [S]o recently I found myself imagining redesigning the physical space so that it's a shared environment with different spaces for socialising, working alone, working in groups, creative brainstorming, and eating etc. – a space we share, clean together, work in together. [...] This would change so much, like if we actually shared the space with our students rather than hiding away in [...] places that literally delineate 'us' from 'them'. I wonder whether it needs to be this way? Is it necessary [...] to have such stark divides between us all? [...] Yes, of course, staff meetings still need to happen for the sake of administration, safeguarding, professional solidarity and so on, but [can] we cut all the rest of the bullshit professional distancing and relate to one another more like humans, in spaces that we share together?

Joe's description also raises important questions for how physical "delineat[ions]" can reinforce 'us and them' mentalities within education; this has connotations for the attempts at mutual humanisation so fundamental to recognition, as explored earlier and – later – in chapter 3.

Looking ahead: COVID-19 and the era of digital learning

It is worth noting that challenges around electronic communication and lack of physical contact have become especially apparent in the new academic year as we adapt to the fall out of the pandemic. There are, understandably, concerns over our ability to sustain a substantial sense of community in the context of digital/virtual learning. Obviously, some people find it easier to access learning remotely and there is much to celebrate on this front (e.g. there may be particularly promising connotations for access to HE for dis/abled people or those with caring responsibilities). At the same time, though, we need to consider the impact of fully digital/virtual learning on other aspects of community – including the nature of relationships. Our limited data on the impact of the pandemic suggest that virtual learning could have a negative impact on programme relationships as – among other things – frequency of communication is reduced, and contact is more confined to 'formal learning time'. This was noted by Kima, in reflecting on the digital learning which took place towards the end of the second semester at the height of the first wave of the pandemic in the UK:

> Kima: [W]hen we suddenly [...] went digital [...] I felt that if... a big part of my success and happiness is my contact with staff and that's not happening. [...] Once students have kind of [got] accustomed to this online way of learning, I fear that- and I have even had friends say that, 'Why can't uni just carry on like this?', and that makes me sad because I really value face-to-face relationships [...] and I'm struggling [laughs] with this whole virtual thing.

Time and staff wellbeing

As seen above, students and staff alike frequently refer to time constraints as a major challenge faced by the programme. These time constraints have significant connotations for the programme's capacity to build meaningful relationships based on emotional concern, and there was some indication of consequences for mental health. Yet, while we saw at the start of this chapter how student narratives around mental health in general were quite positive – in spite of the various constraints the community faces – *staff* discourses made frequent reference to compromised wellbeing, often in quite strong terms:

> Robbie: I mean people are so overworked. I'm literally- I'm in shock. I don't think I've ever seen people working so much and doing so much teaching before.

Luke: I sort of had anticipated that it was going to be a lot of work [...] but I think it's sort of taken over my life a bit. [...]. I think on a personal level I think I probably worked- well I definitely worked too much [laughs] towards the end of last year so, you know, I wasn't well towards the end of last year and [...] I think that was in part a reflection of, you know, like, stress from the programme.

Joe: Yeah, time's a big one, people's energy levels [...], I'm sort of constantly horrified, by yeah, the level of burnout. [...] Even though [...] this is, like, honestly one of the most open, emotionally intelligent working environments I've ever [been in]- probably *the* most [...] – and yet still, like, we're facing these really big hurdles as a team in terms of keeping ourselves well. And that inevitably has an impact on how this programme operates, in terms of trying to model something to our students that we're only barely able to model ourselves. You know, we're trying to create [an] emphasis on wellbeing [...] and then, like, as a team [...] it's quite hard to do that in relation to ourselves, let alone in relation to our students.

In a way, 'time' was used as a proxy by staff participants for discussing broader challenges, not all of which would necessarily be resolved simply by adding more hours to the week. For instance, a well-documented instrument of public sector marketisation is what is called 'the new managerialism' – a strategy for increasing service "efficiency and effectiveness" through the proliferation of varying forms of "imposed external accountability, including the widespread use of performance indicators and league tables, target setting, benchmarking and performance management" (Deem and Brehony, 2005:220). Thus, HE staff are increasingly subject to demands that they 'deliver' teaching and research in a way which pleases a plethora of top-down quality frameworks and satisfaction surveys (Gewirtz and Cribb, 2020; Leathwood and Read, 2020).

These forms of oversight subject staff to varying forms of "terror" in their own right (Ball, 2003:215): one study suggests that academic staff are increasingly expected to be "'super-hero[es]''- that is, "multi-talented, always ready and available worker[s] [...] capable of being everything to everyone" (Pitt and Mewburn, 2016:99). Nonetheless, such pressures are very often – including by this project's participants – described through a *temporal* lens. Indeed, the Times Higher Education's most recent University Workplace Survey (2016) frames its findings around the claim that academic staff *work extremely long hours*[14], often at the expense of their health and wellbeing, and the University and College Union's 2016 workload survey opens with the claim that HE staff are increasingly "expected to do more in less time" (UCU, 2016). Similarly, in our data, participants often described institutional demands as problematic primarily because they *limit time* to dedicate to other core aspects of HE practice, such as teaching and building relationships with students:

> Paul: [My ideal university] would be a cooperative university. So you wouldn't have [...] senior management who are sort of market-oriented, who are completely disconnected from what's going on at the chalk-face. [...] You wouldn't [...] be wasting a lot of time with stupid research assessment exercises. Not everyone would have to be publishing the whole time, if they didn't want to be. It'd be more like you'd publish something if you had something to say and you wanted to. So there'd be more, like, democratic evaluation of what we do. [...] [Y]ou wouldn't have like one-size-fits-all metrics to evaluate what you do. [...] I think you'd be able to spend more of your time doing your teaching, [...] you'd have the space to develop the relationships that are necessary for good learning to happen- and good research as well, 'cos I think you need that for good research. [...] [T]he kind of infrastructure would just be more conducive to developing strong relationships. And you wouldn't have other distractions getting in the way of that.

Connectedly, staff indicated not having "enough time to be together" (Rosa) – for building and maintaining their relationships not only with students, but with one another. If we believe that meaningful social interaction is part of supporting wellbeing, then this compounds the concerns already highlighted in the data around staff mental health:

---

[14] And, importantly, many more hours than they are contracted to. The 2016 University and College Union workload survey found that, on average, HE staff work the equivalent of two days per week unpaid (UCU, 2016).

Robbie: We don't really get to see each other all that much. [...] Like there's people that I'd love to be, like, meeting for lunch and stuff [...]. I'd love to see people more. Talking to people around the strikes has been really eye-opening, 'cos it's been like [...] 'Oh how are you doing?' [...].

Researcher: Yeah it's that thing of during the strike people being like 'Oh let's go out for lunch! Why don't we do this normally?' [laughs]

Robbie: No one's got time. People eat sandwiches at their desk[s], you know.

Audre: It's all to do with the intensification of work, because a few years ago, you know, we'd always go out at lunchtime. [...] Yeah definitely things have become more... like, the space has been squeezed for things like that.

The focus on time in discourses around HE (both in the literature and in our data, above) is in many ways unsurprising: strict temporal control is a core feature of market logic, because it's fundamental to maximising financial 'efficiency'. As sociologist of time Barbara Adam writes, theorising the relationship between time and market capitalism, "when time is money, then faster means better" (2003:67). If Higher Education institutions can get away with cramming more activities and responsibilities into fewer hours in their workload modelling, then what's to stop them[15]? As Leathwood and Read write, in a marketised sector, "time is decontextualised, seen as an abstract standardised unit, a neutral exchange value, and any time that does not equal money is wasted time" (2020:3). That is, other values – such as human wellbeing, or first principles around what Higher Education 'should' prioritise – are decentred by a logic which sees financial efficiency as the main end goal.

Interestingly, almost every staff member pointed in some way to the fact that realising the programme's philosophy and ethos – not least its

---

[15] As demonstrated by the staff cut backs which happened across the sector, literally as we wrote this book, in the name of 'necessary cost savings' in the wake of the pandemic (UCU, 2020), one inevitable consequence of which is that remaining staff have to pick up the shortfall in already overloaded working weeks.

emphasis on building meaningful emotional relationships – is *particularly* time- and energy-consuming:

> Robbie: I do wonder how much of that stuff is feasible within the kind of structures and strictures of the contemporary university and, like, neoliberal university, and I think that applying some of this stuff is great but [...] the workloads are too great. [...] You know, there's an attempt on this BA to actually live the ideologies of, you know, a radical educationist and ideology and living those politics through the teaching, and I think it's really difficult. [...] We really need to think about the feasibility of all of this.

> Luke: For me I think the best way to contribute towards social justice and social change is through education by changing the way people think, changing the way they act, the way they engage with, you know, the projects of our lives and with other people [...]. So it feels rather than something like an intellectual exercise, which Higher Education can be- can be a fascinating intellectual exercise, but this is [...] not *just* that. [This is] also like a political, and [...] emotional engagement with students as people, you know [...]. [A]nd that is emotionally [laughs] it is emotionally engaging and emotionally draining [...].

Realising the programme's commitments – not least to meaningful emotional relationships with students – is clearly important to staff. Yet, as one staff member put it, "there's that danger [...] [that] we do it at the cost of our [...] mental health" (Audre). As noted earlier in this chapter, empathy is crucial for building meaningful educational relationships. Some commentators (e.g. Ecclestone and Hayes, 2009) have argued that too much emphasis on the emotional is inappropriate in educational contexts. Such critique is very often rooted in a problematic dualism which splits off the rational from the emotional and assumes that education rooted in emotional care necessarily damages student self-sufficiency or the pursuit of knowledge (Clegg and Rowland, 2010). But aspects of this critique are rooted in (important) concerns around sustainability and the danger of asking too much from practitioners[16] (e.g. McAllister et al., 2014, Constanti and Gibbs, 2004).

bell hooks' work has pushed back against this, suggesting that the idea that love "renders us unable to set healthy boundaries" is a misnomer, because love actually gives us an "enhanced understanding" of the classroom and of our students which makes us *better* able to set appropriate boundaries and exercise discerning judgement about our practice (hooks, 2010:161). Nonetheless, teachers must undoubtedly be cautious about the extent to which they let the emotional needs of students affect their *own* mental wellbeing; they need to be able to look after themselves before they can help their students. Getting the balance right can be difficult, as Joe acknowledges below, noting how the emphasis on care for students on the programme sometimes makes it difficult for them to "attend to [their] own boundaries and needs":

> Joe: Maybe to, like, a problematic extent [...] I can never really just, like, go home and switch off and stop thinking about everybody. Because these are people that I work with quite closely and I really care about them and I, you know, sometimes know quite a bit about them, and therefore I wanna always be doing everything I can to be there for them in whatever way they need, whilst still sort of attending to my own boundaries and needs... which is an interesting one to navigate.

The issues around staff wellbeing raised by the analysis above provide an interesting point of contradiction in the data in terms of the programme's attempt to emphasise recognition based on care and wellbeing. Among other things, this contradiction highlights the different positionality of students and staff in relation to 'time' and the associated issues of workload. Although students face workload and 'performativity' pressures too, and – as explored above – are certainly short on time in the sense of opportunity to see one another, they do not refer to being time-starved *in general*, in the sense of facing workload demands that have a directly

---

[16] There are also gender equality implications, given evidence that female staff do a disproportionate share of pastoral care in universities, potentially at the expense of their career progression on other counts (Ashencaen Crabtree and Shiel, 2019).

detrimental impact on their health and wellbeing. The university's demands on students' time are set primarily by institutional norms. Their work output does not directly contribute to the university's efficiency and rankings except as a commodified final grade. And because a student cannot produce more than one degree qualification for the university in the space of a single course, there is little 'surplus value' which can be gleaned by working them harder[17].

Staff, on the other hand, are university employees, and their workload is directly linked to the institution's competitiveness in the HE market. If they can do more with the time available, the university can make 'efficiency' savings (which it can reinvest in such 'vital' areas as real estate development or competitive management salaries). For both students and staff, the lack of contact hours on the programme is concerning, for all the reasons explored above. But for staff, the problem of time goes beyond wanting more contact hours on the programme: they need the professional context and its attendant demands to change. So while everyone feels the results of time-shortages in terms of the impact on relationships and community on BASS, staff also feel it as exhaustion and burnout[18]. This, in turn, has troubling implications for the capacity of staff to sustain their commitment to being emotionally available and supportive to students. As Rosa notes, the programme's ethos of social justice includes a commitment to self-care – which should include everybody, students and staff alike:

> Rosa: [The programme ethos involves] thinking about how can we do [things] in a way that's thoughtful, that [...] contributes to a fairer,

---

[17] Except perhaps some kind of warped public perception of academic rigour. Though we might cynically suggest that unless KCL decides that upping its workload demands is going to greatly improve its market appeal (rather than, in fact, damage student satisfaction survey ratings), things are – thankfully – unlikely to change on this front.

[18] As noted earlier, many students also face the impact of broader marketisation trends in ways which affect their use of time. And students who are working to fund their degree are surely also grappling with some of the same themes around economic precarity and neoliberal pressures. Nonetheless, no participants mentioned this in the data (perhaps precisely because of which students had enough time to engage in a voluntary research interview). And students are still not subject to the particular market logics and institutional pressures of being university employees, which is what this section examines.

more equal world in whatever tiny way [...] and part of that would then [be] the self-care or the collective self-care towards ourselves and our students of [...] 'Let's not overdo it, let's not exhaust ourselves by expecting staff and students to just be doing multiple, multiple, multiple pieces of work'. [...] It's important that an ethical practice would also take into account people's kind of energies and time.

Chapter 3.

Recognition as equality and partnership

Freya Aquarone

Equality and partnership on the programme

In chapter 2 we explored how recognition can be theorised as 'love, care and kindness' and how this is reflected in participant data – in terms of both how this form of recognition manifests, and how it is challenged. Another core recognition theme we identified in our data relates to perceptions that the programme actively pursues *equality* between students and staff; that it seeks to challenge the typically "hierarchical nature" of HE (Levy et al., 2010:1) through forms of educational partnership:

> Sarah: [The programme is] designed to sort of flip Higher Education on its head and break down the boundaries that normally are very in place with [...] university courses.
>
> Oscar: We see them as partners in a strong sense [...]. [W]e are learning together and we are trying to address these questions together [...], from different positions and different perspectives but through something like a partnership. [...] [It] is, like, fundamental to the way that we think about education on the programme.

The idea of recognition as equality is, again, deeply rooted in Hegel. For Hegel (1807), recognition is dependent on foregrounding not just human relationships *per se*, but human relationships based on mutuality and equality. Hegel's thought experiment on recognition (sometimes called the 'master slave dialectic') is notoriously complex to fully unpack so we are just going to touch on it here. It goes something like this: Two people encounter one another, and in a 'struggle to the death' one defeats the other. The 'master' (the victor) sees the 'slave' (the loser) as inferior. Although the master desires recognition from the slave, the slave cannot actually grant it; because the slave is seen as inferior, their recognition 'doesn't count' in the eyes of the master. Thus, the master's failure to recognise the slave as fully human is precisely what, in turn, ends up damaging their own humanity.

For Hegel, then, recognition is impossible when it is predicated on inequality, because inequality is rooted in denigrating the humanity of 'the other'. One might argue that the dialectic somewhat foregrounds the master's inability to feel recognised. However other writers, such as Paulo Freire, have more strongly emphasised the consequences for the 'slave', specifically (and helpfully for our purposes) in the context of education. In analysing Hegel's dialectic, Freire writes · that when inequality characterises education, those in the position of 'slaves' – which he labels 'the oppressed' – can *also* never properly develop a subjectivity; they are "dehumanise[d]" as both agents and as learners (1970:26). The solution, for Hegel, is for the power holder to enact a moment of 'sublation' – of 'lifting up' – which breaks the cycle of misrecognition and sees the other as a true equal. Freire has written in very similar terms: "if what characterises the oppressed is their subordination to the consciousness of the master, as Hegel affirms, true solidarity with the oppressed means fighting at their side" – it means the power holder "stops regarding the oppressed as an abstract category and sees them as persons" (1970:32).

This has quite significant connotations for HE practice. As Rosa describes, treating each other as "human beings" who are part of a community of equals means challenging fundamentally hierarchical categories of institutional 'difference' – categories, indeed, such as 'students' and 'staff':

> Rosa: [Here] there's a kind of [...] mutuality [...] where staff and students treat each other as human beings [...] – which sounds kind of obvious but I don't think that always is the case [in Higher Education]. I think sometimes students are seen as this mass body of students who are just students.

Freire's educational philosophy is based on creating a different kind of pedagogical space in which learners are not disparaged as "just students", but seen as partners, who have "the right to [...] engage in dialogue with teachers, and to fully participate in the educational process" (Kellner, 2010:57). This commitment was echoed in our participant data:

> Helena: Usually in a big institution like a university I think as a student you might feel, like, quite small [...] – [that] the relationship between students and lecturers is not [based on] co-creation. [...] But with our course [...] teachers ask a lot about how power structures can be challenged.

Of course, realising this connects deeply to the commitment to love and kindness explored in the previous chapter. In Hegel's dialectic, there is a strong element of disregard and contempt which is the *foundation* of the asymmetry between master and slave, and Freire himself has argued that the move towards equality requires "risk[ing] an act of love" (1970:32). But we think we need to go further than this. Love and kindness are powerful, but they do not necessarily place people *on a level*. Love and kindness can exist between people who nonetheless retain fixed assumptions about 'us' and 'them' – about students and staff, superiority and inferiority. We can care about students but still perpetuate mechanisms which relegate them to a lower status within the community – whether that's through paternalistic discourses, the denial of their capacity for 'responsibility', or structures of decision-making. We might then consider love and kindness to be a necessary but not sufficient condition for recognition, and equality the same; both are different sides of the recognition coin.

How might 'recognition as equality' be realised, beyond a mere commitment to the idea? In answering this question, we believe we need to attend to institutional *structures and processes*. Questions around 'who gets to make decisions' – whose 'voice', to use Freire's language, gets heard both in the classroom and in the community. This is close to Pateman's classic theory of participatory democracy which they describe as "built round the central assertion that individuals and their institutions cannot be considered in isolation from one another" (1970:41). That is, that our individual *relationships* are mediated by the institutional *structures* around us. It is institutional set-ups, and not just interpersonal dynamics – such as positive or friendly relationships, or good intentions about partnership – which are key for realising equality and partnership in a meaningful way.

Our data indicated how the programme attempts to realise *recognition as equality and partnership* in two core ways, both of which relate to institutional structures: firstly, through embedding forms of quasi-direct democracy as a central mode of community decision-making. And secondly through a classroom practice based around engaged, dialogue-based pedagogy.

3a – Participatory democracy: Course Community Meetings

"To have a democratic course, we need to have democratic structures." (Rosa)

One particularly unusual aspect of the BASS programme is in what is called the 'Course Community Meetings' (CCMs). A quick practical summary is as follows:

> *The CCMs provide a quasi-democratic discussion and decision-making space for raising and negotiating issues relating to the programme. They happen two to three times per semester and are open to all students and staff. The CCMs are led by a group of student facilitators, supported by a member of staff – known as the 'facilitator group' or FG. The FG changes each semester and members are determined by voluntary appointment or nomination. The FG collates the agenda (to which any community member can add an item) and decides how to run the meeting between them. The space is governed by the principles laid out in the programme Working Agreement which was co-created by students and staff in the first cohort's induction week; changes and additions to the Working Agreement is the only aspect of community decision-making which is based on consensus. All other decisions are made by majority vote. Decisions made at the CCM – except for those relating to CCM procedure – are considered 'recommendations' until ratified by the staff team[19].*

'Student voice' is an increasingly trendy term in education circles (Cook-Sather et al., 2014). However, it is all too common for student participation to be cordoned off into relatively marginal, limited spaces

---

[19] So far, all decisions made by the CCM have been ratified in this way; none have been overturned.

where the capacity for real contribution or dissent is diminished (Fielding, 2004). Examples might include student rep systems which, while laudable, are still only creating spaces at existing, staff-dominated tables for a small number of students to sit. This is no less the case in HE. As Cook-Sather et al. write, "there is a growing public interest in student representation and student voice [...] in university governance systems. [...] [But] while we welcome these initiatives, partnership is too significant to be limited to student representation on committees and through the brokerage of student unions" (2014:140). With these concerns in mind, the CCMs aim to provide a regular, open deliberative space for *all* community members. Below we lay out how participants described the CCMs and consider their significance for recognition as equality.

Student participants spoke about the CCMs contributing to a feeling that their voices genuinely matter on the programme. Often, this was contrasted with perceptions or experiences of other educational spaces where student perspectives are either not taken seriously or not elicited:

Selena: It's where the students can actually have a voice, and how if we want to change something, we can actually do that and discuss it with other people [...]. [W]e actually can co-create the course.

Helena: I think it really is a nice representation of, like, how co-creation works on our course because I do think, like, everyone who attended the CCMs felt it was a, like, good and welcome space for making your voice heard.

Bea: I did [a] foundation [course] from [another university] last year. The main difference is that no one provided students, us, opportunity to express our opinions. At this School, we have [the] CCM and it is very convenient.

Rachel: On other courses I've heard that it's like whatever [the staff] say, you just do it, but for us it's kind of like, we negotiate and discuss the things we want and don't want to do. I think that makes the course quite special.

Student participants also expressed a feeling that the CCMs contribute to the deconstruction of traditional educational power structures, helping to build more equal working relationships between students and staff:

> Ali: The fact that students like can actually be facilitators alongside staff. So again, that power dynamic doesn't exist as much. [...] [T]he fact that we have staff and students [together] makes it comfortable. Like that we're kind of on a similar level. Like a similar playing field.

> Susan: It just- it makes the whole community stronger. It actually makes sense because the whole course is about, you know, teachers and students working together to some extent and [the CCM] is a very good, like, tool for that.

Connectedly, students described the CCMs as a place where students and staff can recognise one another's common humanity and even vulnerability:

> Rachel: I think we actually need them [CCMs] because I feel like it [...] gives us, like, a chance to kind of like talk to our lecturers, and kind of see them [...] as people instead of, like, teachers.

> Sarah: [It] shows vulnerability from both staff and students so I think that's essential for, like, making those meaningful relationships [...]. [I]t's quite an eye-opening experience.

Following on from students' emphasis on the role of staff in the CCMs, Joe points to how a sincere commitment to the CCMs by staff is fundamental to them being seen as legitimate by the community as a whole:

> Joe: I've often been pleasantly surprised by [...] [staff] letting go of power and letting go of being the final say on things. And obviously we have this thing where, you know, as a staff team we have to approve the decisions of the CCM but by and large that's happened and I think it's so important for people to buy into the idea that even if [...] they don't personally agree with something, it has legitimacy,

because it was a collective process. [...] Yes, it would be easier for us not to do it – it would be way easier, in a practical sense, to not take the risk or have to undergo the feeling of like 'Oh no something's happening that actually we wouldn't have done ourselves as a staff team', or whatever. But it's so important to follow through on the decisions that space makes.

It is arguable that one of the most important effects of spaces like the CCMs is that they change the context of interaction, shaking up previously fixed and normalised distinctions between people's roles (Pateman, 1970). But it may not be enough to hope that these spaces emerge organically, of their own accord. In a sector facing severe time and human resource pressures and in which hierarchy is institutionally normalised, it could be necessary to carve out explicit spaces for this 'disruption' to occur. Indeed, participants noted that one of the most important features of the CCMs is that they occur in a structurally recognised space:

> Paul: In all the things that I've taught on [...] that sort of presumption of equality between students and staff [...] has always been part of the ethos. But the idea of having a structured Course Community Meeting I think is quite distinctive.

> Rosa: [O]f course also, you know, everyone will be talking about the Course Community Meetings [...] and I think that that is a key aspect of what's very different from other courses that I teach on, or that exist in [...] most of the country, you know, most of the university [sector]. [...] I do hope that I would practise [democracy] anyway, in any educational endeavour that I do, but [I do it] more in this one, 'cos there's a structure for it.

> Hester: [When I was an undergraduate] we were constantly fighting for lecturers to listen to us when we had problems. [...] [W]e had to go through the whole organisation [...] saying, like, 'How can we talk to our lecturers about this?', like, 'How can we make them come to this space where we were discussing these problems?' And I think

the fact that they *have* that space [on this programme] is very important.

Freire warns against the dangers of "affirm[ing]" a commitment to equality without doing anything "tangible to make this affirmation a reality" (1970:32). There are widespread commitments to notions of 'partnership' in HE (Curran, 2017), manifesting in myriad laudable ways – such as involving students in curriculum-design (Bovill et al., 2011) or research projects in which students and staff work together as co-investigators (Marquis et al., 2016). Yet these commitments seem to rarely manifest in the form of regular, open decision-making and problem-solving spaces, a perception echoed by the participants' comparisons above with their wider experiences or perceptions of education.

Despite the broadly positive descriptions of the role and impact of the CCMs above, our data also highlighted a number of related challenges. We explore these below.

Engagement and collective responsibility

Participants pointed to the need to improve engagement with the CCMs. For instance, one of the CCM facilitators (Leanne) pointed to the variable rates of attendance (which are often around 40-50% of the cohort, but at times as low as 20%) and suggested this damages the extent to which the space can enact truly collaborative change:

> Leanne: The attendance rate is quite low still. So that's a bit disappointing [...], but other than that I feel like we do get stuff established in the Course Community Meetings, so [...] I'm glad and proud about that. [...] [B]ut then I just feel [...] imagine, like, if everyone comes, like the more change and, like, the perspectives that we'll get. But unfortunately we can't force people to come, so... that's that [laughs].

Another participant suggested many people still fall back on student reps to convey concerns on their behalf, rather than seeing the space as a place for *collective* deliberation:

> Rhonda: As a rep I found a lot of people personally messaging me what they feel instead of actually speaking out in the CCMs, which defeats the point of the CCM.

One explanation for non-engagement with the CCMs may lie in people's priorities in terms of their university experience – including how they define the purpose and value of Higher Education. For instance, there was some evidence in our data of students demonstrating – or feeling that others demonstrate – instrumental attitudes, whereby education is judged against its applicability to future careers:

> May: [Some people] don't see [the course] as something that affects them or [is] something important to their lives. They think this is just a stepping-stone in their life, 'Something I need to do, so that I can work in the future and make money', and stuff like that.

> Ryleigh: [B]ut some of [the things we study] I found them, like, as I told you, useless. Like, I wouldn't use them in my career later on.

Instrumental attitudes are increasingly prevalent in HE (Muddiman, 2015; Tomlinson, 2017) and are deeply connected to the marketisation of the sector and the attendant paradigm of 'students as consumers' (Tomlinson, 2017). When education is rendered a product, notions of inherent value more easily fade into the background (Tomlinson, 2017); thus, some people may come to see spaces for collaboration and partnership as extraneous or irrelevant to the 'purpose' of education. Indeed, Leanne suggests that such instrumentalism could be at the heart of people's lack of engagement with CCMs:

> Leanne: [T]rying to get people to care [about the CCMs] is, like, a big thing [...]. I just feel like sometimes people see this course as... like just a course? But we're so much more than that, we're trying to actually like do things, to make it like better, like we're just not- like

some people see it as [...] somewhere they wanna get their BA and kind of just like wave goodbye to everyone else after that. But I feel like we're so much more than [that].

Of course, it is important to understand these attitudes in context. For instance, some participants pointed to the way instrumental attitudes – such as a focus on grade outcomes – are conditioned from very early on in people's educational journeys:

Leanne: I feel like it goes back to [laughs] when we're in like elementary school, [...] [education] was kind of like labeled, like given a mark, like obviously when you do like your A levels and stuff as well, like, [laughs] okay you get like- you need like AAB to get into King's [...] so it's just, you've kind of always seen it as a grade.

And, as other participants pointed out, the university itself continues the trend. Its focus on metrics and outcomes (like grades) may mean that other valuable aspects of education – including "extracurricular" community activities like the CCMs – get more easily "missed":

Rebecca: You know, Higher Education has turned into this thing where, like, you know, it's a means to an end. [...] It's just about getting a degree and getting a good job. [...] Like the way in which university's framed it's natural that this is going to happen. [...] And we see that also with, like, you know, the extracurricular stuff that isn't compulsory, [...] like the depletion in the people that come because it's like when we're not being assessed on it, then it doesn't really matter. And [...] I do it as well, so that's not, like, a judgement it's just more of like a... you know, that's just how [...]- it's hard to care about everything in uni, especially when we're not incentivised to care, by the university itself.

Luke: Most of the things that appear in the [...] programme ethos [...] don't really lend themselves very well to metrics. You know, they might in fact be unquantifiable and unmeasurable. And so I think if an institution values things which can be measured and is, at best, indifferent to things which can't, then, you know the value of those things may be missed [...]. [I]t's that culture that we're trying to push back against.

In addition to the institution encouraging students to frame their educational journey in instrumentalised ways, it is arguable that, as Rowland writes, "students, with their concern to find employment, [are actually] more vulnerable to forces of the market and globalisation than their teachers. Perhaps they cannot so readily isolate themselves from the pragmatic imperatives of a degree course" (Rowland, 2003:94). Thus, as Rosa identifies below, many may feel forced to prioritise outcomes such as grades; it can be understood as an act of self-preservation in a system which places a premium on certain definitions of 'success':

> Rosa: The wider world is always just a challenge as well, just the kind of wider landscape of Higher Education in particular, students [...] having to pay ridiculous fees [...], the general costs of living being so high and the sort of diminution of the welfare state and other educational resources and so on, I think there's such a huge pressure on students, and then I think that's also partly to do with the pressure for success and what counts as success and the pressure for high grades and we know that that's in the school system, and that creates a whole amount of anxiety [...]. So I think for students they have limited time sometimes to engage with things which might be seen as extra, like the Course Community Meetings, [...] [which are] not credentialised [...]. Yeah that's a challenge to the system.

Some participants suggested that, even when people do attend the CCMs, the space is too often viewed as a vehicle for simply making demands without any attendant commitment to collective responsibility for initiating change:

> Robbie: The CCM[s], these are a form of politics [...], a form of radical politics, aren't they? [...] So we need to find out a way of doing it, that [...] doesn't get co-opted back into a kind of neoliberal consumeristic- 'cos you know, I think the CCMs are changing now but there is [still] a lot of, like, 'We want this and we want that'.

Joe: Sometimes I'm concerned that some people come in with a set of expectations about staff and authority and institutions and they see [the CCMs] as, like, a glorified rep feedback forum – they put out concerns but provide no solutions.

Robbie explicitly links this problem to the broader "consumeristic" culture of HE. Interestingly, 'student as consumer' narratives are often couched in empowering language around placing students at the heart of institutional processes by taking into account their perspectives as service users (Levy et al., 2010; Tomlinson, 2017). But the crucial difference between this and the vision of recognition as equality outlined earlier is that the former is a one-way system (Bunce et al., 2017; Tomlinson, 2017): the consumers (students) make demands of the provider (the university and its staff). It is not necessarily attached to ideas of students and staff working together (Giannakis and Bullivant, 2016). Recognising one another as equal partners, with shared responsibility for a learning community, is quite a different institutional vision from one in which one party pays for the services of another and makes attendant demands as part of that 'transaction'.

Joe, meanwhile, seems to locate the problem in broader educational attitudes and expectations, which rarely normalise partnership and equality between students and staff. As Cook-Sather et al. write, most people come to university after spending years in institutions which frame students as subordinate and passive (2014). This perspective was echoed by, Rosa, who suggested these wider currents limit the extent to which initiatives like the CCMs can push beyond a "minimum" level of resistance to the status quo:

Rosa: [W]e're living in a society where things really are very undemocratic, where education predominantly is not democratic, where our democracy is not democracy – as in what I would mean by democracy, which is [...] about the people who are affected by decisions having a really big involvement in making those decisions. If that's not what happens in the wider world, then yeah, what we're doing is challenging – is exciting, but is challenging.

Moreover, as a number of participants pointed out, the wider university of King's is heavily oriented around hierarchy and top-down decision-making – something many linked to the university's marketised position as a "business" and its attendant need to control its "image" and "reputation":

> Luke: So King's is very ambitious but in a sort of- I would say in quite a conventional sense. So it sees itself as, like, an institution guided by ambitions for 'academic excellence' for example [...]. That kind of approach doesn't lend itself to experimentation or kind of devolving decisions, you know, beyond a certain point [...] [because of] a concern with image, a concern with reputation.

> Researcher: How much flexibility do you think we have to resist [...] institutional limitations?
> Sarah: [laughs] Not as many as we thought we did! [...] We think we have so much choice but, like, actually we're still very much confined by institutional limits and I think they start to show when we push for things like changing the assessments due to strikes[20]. [...] [L]ike it just ties into the fact that uni is a business.

The power of broader educational norms was arguably borne out in the way some participants described the programme's emphasis on equality and partnership as "weird" or uncomfortable (a phenomenon echoed in literature on similar 'partnership approaches' in HE – e.g. see Marquis et al., 2016 and Felten et al., 2013):

> Susan: I still cannot let go of the fact that I'm coming from a school setting where I was told what to do. Every time. And it's just- like even after these months it feels... weird to- to have a say [laughs] in these things.

> Simon: I think a lot of [students] have adapted very well to the dynamic of not being hierarchical, like 'You are the lecturer up here

---

[20] Sarah is referring to when some students tried to negotiate with the College to change its assignment requirements in the wake of the disruption of the strike and pandemic.

and I'm the student down here'. [...] But I see some of them... struggling with that. [...] [B]ecause I think some of them – and I might include myself in that – didn't have an education that taught them that they were equals with teachers. [So] I feel like maybe [...] they haven't got used to the idea that their education is different from the kind of relationship they are able to have here?

Staff attitudes and engagement

Some participants highlighted the significance of *staff* attitudes towards the CCMs for determining the extent to which they are truly a space of equality and partnership. For instance, some staff acknowledged that they inevitably retain "vestiges" of conventional assumptions around educational roles which may be at odds with viewing students as equal partners in processes of discussion and deliberation:

> Joe: There's always more to learn or unlearn, right, around the way we just talk about students. So I'm sometimes really fascinated by how easy it is to slip into the language of 'us and them', and [...] [I'm] slightly horrified by that. [...] You know, we all have vestiges of attitudes around, like, students and what student identity means. I think it's so important that we are constantly critically reflective around the language we're using and asking ourselves 'Would I talk about colleagues in that way? Would I make suggestions like that to colleagues?' And that's not always easy in the context that forces us into specific roles.

Connectedly, Rosa, referring again to the challenges of wider conditioning, noted that much of the programme's core philosophy goes against the grain of many staff people's personal and professional experiences of education, with the result that the certain approaches may feel "risky" or "whacky" to staff:

> Rosa: [T]here are some elements of the programme that I think sound quite whacky or 'out there' to some people? [...]. [N]ot because of any deficit on their part, but just [because they] haven't experienced it or- or maybe they've got objections, I don't know, but like, [...] we

might be talking about doing Course Community Meetings and nobody's against it or anything, people are interested, but sometimes people do think 'Oo that sounds- that does sound risky', or 'Are the students gonna cope?' or 'I'm not sure about that' and maybe that's a good... creative tension? I don't know. But I suppose what I think is [...], none of it should be unusual [...]: students being listened to, staff and students trying to know each other and understand where each other are coming from [...], taking into account and challenging inequalities and oppressions, students and staff having say over what they're learning, how they're learning it – [...] I mean *none* of that should be outlandish or weird. That should be normal and the fact it isn't normal then again is a challenge in itself because it's kind of, we're starting from... you know, we're starting from a point of seeming to challenge something [laughs].

A connected concern regarding staff engagement was that, although there are always a number of staff members present at every CCM, there have been times when a minority of the staff team has attended, something which some students expressed disappointment about:

Leanne: [Y]eah, and I noticed at the last CCM there wasn't a huge amount of staff attendance either, so we were kind of disappointed about that... yeah because sometimes the staff inputs are really important as well.

As discussed earlier, staff commitment matters: if staff don't appear to take the CCMs seriously, it's likely to undermine their legitimacy in the eyes of students, particularly given – however much we may strive for equality – the relative power of staff in educational spaces. It is important to note that attendance at the CCMs is not factored into workload models for permanent staff, nor into the contracts of hourly-paid staff. Thus, reasons for staff non-attendance may be more to do with difficulty balancing competing workload demands than a lack of support for the principle of the space. Nonetheless, there was an indication in the data that some staff do perhaps see the CCMs as a space primarily 'for students', or that the CCMs would be better if staff were not present:

Belle: I mean I think the CCM is [...] a very valuable space, I think for students, or at least I'm not sure, that's my feeling [...]. [R]eally, I mean, students are [in] the best position to [talk about the CCMs] because in a sense the CCM is there for them.

Robbie: They need to be having their own thing like [the CCMs, without staff]. That just *they* go to. Like, that would be a really radical space.

It is entirely understandable why the CCMs might be perceived as primarily for students' benefit, or why having a student-only space, free from staff-student power dynamics, could be important. Nonetheless, as explored earlier, the CCMs are unusual precisely because they create a space where students and staff come together, on a more equal-playing field, to address issues collectively – not as 'teachers' and 'students' but as members of a shared community. It is this which enables the CCMs, at their best, to start breaking down us/them distinctions which would reduce students to passive 'consumers' and staff to responsibilised 'providers'. But this difference of perspective on the purpose of the CCMs perhaps simply reinforces the importance of participatory democratic process – part of the purpose of which is to create spaces for exploring contrasting viewpoints and building shared understanding about community priorities and values.

Both subsections above focus primarily on the enduring power of broader social and institutional attitudes – whether around consumer identities, the instrumentalisation of education, or conventional ideas of hierarchy and authority. As Foucault claims, the power of normalisation can never be underestimated; its 'disciplinary power' shapes our perception of the *parameters of what is possible*. It is designed to make certain behaviours feel like the obvious, easy choice (Foucault, 1977). That is why 'doing things differently' can feel so difficult, slow and painful.

And yet there are strong grounds for hope. The simple fact that a substantive proportion of students and staff do attend, co-organise and engage with the Course Community Meetings, and believe in their value, should warn us against overly defeatist conclusions. Moreover, Rachel (below) describes their perception that the programme community is characterised not only by a rejection of instrumentalised logic but also by a commitment to meaningful, non-transactional relationships and to collectively working for change, both on the programme and in the wider world:

> Rachel: We're trying to be [...] a community. And we're actually trying to, in a way, as students, [...] help create the programme, as we're going through it, with the staff members. So we can [...] help the next few cohorts to have an even better programme. [...] [A]nd, like, especially during the strikes I think, our course did, like, the most teach-outs[21]? Yeah so I thought that was really interesting to know that, like, people who are studying social sciences – they're not only trying to like, get a degree and get a job but they're actually trying to change the world. And I feel like the majority of our course feels the same way? [...] [A]re trying to change the world in some way or another.

Scope and conflict

Another core concern raised in the data related to the scope and purpose of the CCMs as a deliberative space. Some participants expressed a concern that the CCMs deal with relatively trivial matters (such as personal tutorial timetabling):

> May: Everything we do in [the CCMs] is so formulaic [...]. [A] lot of the people there, they don't actually seem like they want to make a change. It's just like 'I don't want to wait for my personal tutorial longer, so then let me go first'.

---

[21] 'Teach-outs' are workshops, sessions or talks which take place on the picket line during industrial actions. They are not a replacement for learning and teaching that is missed due to strikes, but an alternative way of engaging in a collective learning process. Teach-outs often engage with social/political issues of relevance to the strike and/or the sector, such as activism, wellbeing, community work, and employment inequalities, and can be run by anyone – students, staff, external strike supporters etc.

In a similar vein, participants suggested that the CCMs ought to engage more with social and political issues beyond the programme:

> Researcher: In your ideal world, what would they look like, the CCMs?
> Robbie: [...] [T]hey would be about more than just the BA. The BA would be the base but they would be about the university, the world, 'Let's go out and protest'...

Hester specifically compared the CCMs to 'student assemblies' in their national context, where it's commonplace for deliberative fora to address contemporary political issues:

> Hester: So I think I really like that space here [...], but my heart [...] makes me feel that those spaces should be also for political discussion. So, for example [...] a part of me thinks that we should be talking about the strike in the Course Community Meetings. I know the space is not for that originally. But sometimes I feel like that's very different from what I learned in my university, where these spaces were meant for people to discuss political issues as well – in a more wider sense, not only based on your programme but on what's happening outside the university or at a national level.

What may seem "formulaic" on first glance may have a significance which isn't immediately apparent: if someone lives far away from campus, or has work or caring responsibilities to fit around their study, then being able to choose their personal tutor appointment – rather than having it assigned to them – could make all the difference to their ability to attend. And given that personal tutor meetings are about checking in with students and their wellbeing and needs, they do matter.

Nonetheless, the concerns above raise an important question: is the CCM a space for making decisions about daily life on the programme, or a space for also seeking to discuss injustices going on in the wider world? One could argue that the space for discussing these wider issues is in seminars and lectures. But what about when those issues *cross over* with the practicalities of the programme? An important case study on this front relates to a CCM which occurred in the first semester of this academic year, outlined briefly in the box below.

Case study: the CCM about violent content and trigger warnings

A CCM was held which focused on concerns raised by members of the course community about a video shown in a student presentation which depicted the attack on Muhlaysia Booker, a Black trans woman from Texas, by a group of men in the street. The attack (and the video) generated international media attention – in particular, highlighting the violence and prejudice experienced by Black trans people (e.g. Martinez and Law, 2019). Some members of the course community felt that the decision to show this video highlighted the need to generate a course policy on the platforming of violent or potentially harmful content. A difficult discussion followed around what content should and should not be given a platform in the context of the programme. Some people – and one student in particular, Neve (who is one of a very small number of Black students in the programme community) – raised concerns about the dangers of voyeuristically consuming violent video content, and the fact that such videos tend to display violence against particular groups – most often Black people. They pointed to the way that members of the Black trans community have asked people to stop circulating the video so as not to reproduce the platforming of violence against an already marginalised minority group. A number of students strongly disagreed, and suggested that the Booker video was important because it was educational and opened people's eyes to problems they may not be aware of.

Evidently, the discussion incorporated themes of deep relevance to the programme both practically and ethically. However, questions were raised by participants about the extent to which CCMs are equipped to deal with such issues. This was primarily due to concerns that the CCM in question actually reproduced exclusion; some felt that there was a lack of willingness on the part of the vocal majority to listen to the voice of a student speaking from a position of knowledge and lived experience (though Neve is not trans, they are Black, and also involved in queer communities and social justice activism):

Dan: Yeah, I mean I think that [CCM about trigger warnings], it turned into a massive pile-on. Against one of the most vulnerable- not in terms of that person's voice because that person has a voice, but their voice is a matter of their survival, they've, like, fought for that voice. [...] [T]his is one of the most vulnerable students that is on our programme and so it was just [...] so worrying [...]. I was just really pleased they didn't drop out, and so that's what I mean about sometimes not letting students have the opportunity to do harm to each other [...]. I personally don't think that I would approach the CCM to deal with an issue like that. I don't think it is ready for that shit yet.

It is a sad irony that a space designed to promote recognition in one way may have inadvertently damaged it in another. This raises important questions about the suitable ethical limits of democratic deliberation and decision-making. Few democracies are a majoritarian free-for-all[22]; there are usually principles underlying them, such as human rights or democratic values to do with respect or harm-prevention. The programme's Working Agreement could be considered one such source of underlying values and, indeed, the discussion in the CCM above concluded with the addition to the Working Agreement of a series of temporary guidelines around difficult content and trigger warnings as an interim measure while a working group decided on a long-term approach. But some students, echoing Robbie above, suggested that staff should have stepped in from the outset and made clear that the programme's commitment to justice – including the principles outlined in its Working Agreement – rule out the platforming of content showing violence against members of marginalised groups. In other words, this debate was beyond the scope of democratic deliberation:

May: I think lecturers should have some input [at the CCMs] too. I mean, I understand they want to make this, like, a student-led thing, student-led course, whatever. But, like, when it comes to stuff like

---

[22] Debates around the role and limits of free speech in relation to recognition and marginalisation are explored in depth in chapter 5.

this, they need to stand their ground and say, 'Hey, like, we shouldn't be showing videos like that', not like, 'Oh, let the students decide'.
Rebecca: ...I don't know, like where is the line between letting the course be student-led and also enforcing the ethos?
May: I mean, students should lead stuff that affects the students. When it comes to stuff like showing violent videos [...] it should be from the start like – 'This is what we're going to do, this is the course, it's not open for discussion whether we show videos of people dying. We aren't.' – done. [...] The ethos should be clear and shouldn't be up for debate. And things like [...] trigger warnings should be part of the ethos if we're talking about social justice.

Perhaps another problem lies in the fact that, as Neve suggests below, the CCM became a polarised and personalised debate about a specific video, which – for many – was a particularly clear-cut example of content that simply should not have been shown. But, as Neve suggests below, there was nonetheless a "wider conversation that needed to be had" about the representation of content in education settings *in general*. This incorporates considerations of how we address and frame potentially triggering content in group discussions, and what we believe are the limits of free speech. Arguably this wider conversation would have been ethically within the remit of the CCMs, but only if the discussion had been framed and developed differently by the community:

Neve: I think when you're not sort of used to having accountability processes- [...] 'cos, like, in the communities that I'm in, if I do something wrong I expect to be called out like straight away, and, like, we'll have a conversation about it and then we move on. [But] I think for a lot of people, you know, these processes are very new [...], so people become very defensive when they're criticised on something, and then that sort of tension is what carries through. [...] So like in the Course Community Meeting, [when we raised the issue about] Muhlaysia Booker [we] weren't personally criticising anybody – even though it was one group that like showed the video, it wasn't a personal critique of them, because it was more like a wider conversation that needed to be had. But I feel like it was taken as, like, a personal attack.

The trouble is, as Neve points out, engaging in these discussions ethically relies on practices of community accountability whereby people are open to being critically challenged and to moving beyond feeling personally attacked to engage in broader collective processes of reflection. Neve implies that these practices – among which we might count 'non-violent communication' and forms of 'transformative justice' – are not commonplace in most people's daily lives and communities, nor most educational institutions. We might add to this that these practices *also* rely on people actively reflecting on their positionality, on the ways that they may be complicit in perpetuating structures of inequality and discrimination, and on how they can work to challenge them. Again, though, this form of "self-awareness" is far from universal, as Robbie points out:

> Robbie: [W]e need to think about who [our] students are? Like where they come from, and what they might have understood about the world, because the stuff we're sort of assuming that they should fit into knowing how to do, are forms of like mobilisation and action and self-awareness and [...] accountability that we cannot assume exists everywhere.

The accounts above suggest that a major challenge for the CCMs' capacity to deal with more 'radical' subject matter lies in the fact that forms of community accountability are deeply unfamiliar to most people. Thus perhaps, as Robbie says, the CCMs "are not ready"; a deeper collective learning process is necessary before their scope can range beyond the practicalities of the day to day into more political territory. Some participants did explicitly call for more in-depth training to facilitate this collective 'learning' or 'unlearning':

> May: [T]there needs to be more sensitivity. But how do we control that? [...] I mean with academic staff, it's cool because they have a degree, they understand how to talk about race in a way that's, like, important, but I guess letting students carry these topics without giving them sensitivity talks as well, it's leading to disaster. If you're not giving people, like, anti-racism training, or training on how to facilitate discussion.

Rebecca: Asking people to deal with these topics, then there should be, like, mandatory 'How to deal with topics sensibly' training kind of thing. [...] [I]f we'd all had the training like at the beginning, and that was compulsory, that would have made things very different.

The programme hosted a workshop in January 2020 with external facilitators from Resist+Renew, specifically to support conflict resolution and participatory practices on the programme. Unfortunately, student attendance at the workshop was minimal (perhaps bringing us back to the challenges of encouraging collective engagement explored earlier). However, partly because those who did attend found the workshop extremely helpful, the programme community voted at a recent CCM to integrate similar training into the formal curriculum for 2020/21.

Difference and critical dialogue are core to healthy democracy. As one of the great democratic education advocates, John Dewey, writes, "the expression of difference is not only a right of the other persons but is a means of enriching one's own life-experience, [and] is inherent in the democratic [...] way of life" (Dewey, 1939:252). But we must work towards building skills that ensure "expression[s] of difference" can be negotiated without reproducing harm. Indeed, Dewey also writes that democracy is a "faith in the capacity of human beings for intelligent judgment and action" but only "if *proper conditions* are furnished." (1939:251, emphasis added). How to furnish those conditions is a question of paramount importance to a programme which seeks not simply to make space for deliberation *per se*, but to do so in the name of social justice.

Greater critical reflexivity or skill in community accountability practices are not necessarily all that is needed for the CCMs to constructively resolve conflict. If face-to-face spaces like the CCMs exist, but people don't always feel comfortable using them to raise difficult issues, then the crux of the problem remains. For instance, to return to the case study outlined in chapter 2 about the student 'concerns document' related to the strike and pandemic, the student reps felt their peers remained silent in the subsequent CCM discussion, leaving them alone in responding to staff:

> Rhonda: [T]he CCM then becomes a place where people [...] say what they [think] [...] staff want to hear them say, instead of what they actually are saying to the reps and constantly bombarding us with.

If people don't raise their voices in the CCMs, then this places the onus on certain individuals – such as the reps – to respond to and resolve conflict. This is problematic not only for the wellbeing of those individuals, but also for the integrity of the CCMs as a space for students and staff to deal openly and honestly with programme concerns as equal partners in a 'community of learners'. It may be that greater clarification is needed about the distinction between the role of the student reps and the role of the CCMs as a space for broader student-staff partnership. And it may also be that part of the problem stems from issues around lack of collective responsibility, as explored above.

But it has also been argued – to return, again, to our discussions in chapter 2 – that much of the success of conflict resolution practices relies on the quality of the *underlying relationships* (hooks, 1994; 2010). As Rhonda suggested, in reflecting on the conflict around the strike, "the solution is for staff and students to be more comfortable with talking to each other. Because that just means that all the relationships are more meaningful" – including when those relationships are placed under strain. Feeling comfortable raising difficult or sensitive matters in a democratic forum relies in large part on the extent of collective trust between community members (Mills and McGregor, 2014) – trust that we can raise these issues without backlash, that people will listen and take seriously what we have to say, that it will be handled with honesty but also due care of everyone involved (hooks, 2010). And doing it in a way which is as non-violent and compassionate as possible – what bell hooks calls "positive dissent" (2010:87) – relies on the extent to which we can empathise with one another's positions and perspectives on an issue or problem, the extent to which we understand one another's needs – the extent to which we know one another's stories.

Time

As is surely evident from the above discussion, engaging in collective deliberation and decision-making is a complex and time-consuming thing. It requires work to normalise and develop systems of decision-making. It requires investment in self-reflection, training, and relationship building. As one staff member wryly observed, "I mean, it's so much quicker if you tell everyone what to do!" (Kate). Indeed, a final challenge identified by participants in relation to the CCMs was time constraints. Some participants pointed out that if meetings were simply more frequent, it would be easier to tackle problems meaningfully:

> Joe: It struck me, as it always does, that if we had a weekly meeting, then each of the items on our monthly meeting agenda could be addressed in depth, one at a time. Or even a fortnightly meeting. Instead, we have to allocate 15 mins to each [issue] and hope we can get somewhere. Is this better than nothing?

The time constraints in which the CCMs operate have quite direct relevance for both case studies of conflict explored so far. For instance, the student reps felt they had to compile a document of student concerns about the strike and pandemic, rather than discussing the matter in person with the community, because they felt the next CCM was too far away to be relevant for tackling the matter in a timely manner. They also felt that the lack of time spent with staff *in general* exacerbated the extent to which students expected reps to deal with the problem on their behalf, rather than raising it at a CCM. In the CCM in which the matter was discussed, the community voted to enable emergency CCMs for when matters like this require urgent communication, so as to avoid the need in future for concerns to be raised via email, and for reps to have to take on the role of messenger between students and staff on difficult topics. Nonetheless, this can only go so far in resolving the broader time constraints within which the CCMs operate.

In the case of the CCM about the Muhlaysia Booker video, despite other items being on the agenda, the meeting became almost entirely about this single issue, and lasted over an hour and a half. The discussion raised several ethical concerns, but a *practical* concern highlighted by participants was that (even if the conversation had been handled differently) there was simply not enough time to address it in the depth that it deserved:

> Maya: I did also share the frustration about like, this is going on too much, 'cos I'm someone who kind of likes to stick to an agenda? [laughs] So I felt like that kind of [the] point that was being made should've been, like, a separate discussion that should've gone really in depth and not kind of [...], like, rushed.

Other participants suggested that time is not only short in the CCMs themselves, but also in terms of following through on what they discuss and decide:

> Rebecca: I'm not saying I don't see the point in them, 'cos I see the point of them, but I don't think that they're always doing what they're supposed to be doing, and I think not everyone engages in them, and then we end up, like, having a really long discussion and then there's [...] very little follow-up and very little, like, resolution. So if we go back to that example [of the CCM about Muhlaysia Booker] [...] to my knowledge, there's not been resolution to that, so, it was almost like what was the point of having those long discussions when nothing's come of it? And that's for like various reasons and that's no one's fault in particular, but I think there should be more of a follow-through.
> Researcher: What [do] you think the cause is of that lack of follow-through?
> Rebecca: Yeah I just think people don't have the capacity.

> Joe: Investing in the kind of background work around the CCMs [...] [means] just having time to think. [...] Time that's not, like, caught up in emails or tasks just to, like, do that free-floating thinking around like, proactive things that can be done to support and nurture that process. Because I don't think it would... it doesn't just flourish on its own. Well, not yet.

One thing the programme community decided to do, in response to some of these concerns, was to assign the task of supporting the CCMs to one member of the staff team whose job it is to provide consistent support and follow-through on the CCMs decisions and development – to do that "free-floating thinking" and proactive support that Joe mentions above. But this is not an easy task in the context of the pressures of HE explored already. The question that faces us all, presumably, is where our priorities lie.

3b – Learning and teaching: engaged pedagogy

"Throughout my years as a student and professor, I have been most inspired by those teachers who have had the courage to transgress those boundaries that would confine each pupil to a rote, assembly-line approach to learning. Such teachers approach students with the will and desire to respond to our unique beings, even if the situation does not allow the full emergence of a relationship based on mutual recognition. Yet the possibility of such recognition is always present." (hooks, 1994:13)

In section 3a we discussed recognition as equality in relation to participatory democracy. In doing so, we referred to the work of Paulo Freire. Yet Freire's work really focuses on how educators can promote equality through a participatory and egalitarian approach to *pedagogy*. We therefore turn now to how the programme seeks to embed recognition as equality in its approach to learning and teaching. The term 'engaged pedagogy' actually comes from bell hooks, though their work is strongly influenced by Freire's writing on 'critical pedagogy'. We prefer hooks' term 'engaged pedagogy', partly because it better foregrounds the "interactive relationship between student and teacher" (hooks, 2010:19) (another reason is for its attendant emphasis on *emotional* engagement – explored more below). It is important to note that while hooks and Freire's educational visions both strongly emphasise teacher-student equality and partnership, they also consider 'criticality' to be fundamental: in other words, true engaged pedagogy is not just about including the voices of everyone in the room, it's about equipping people to be critically reflexive about *what they express with those voices*. This is explored in depth in chapter 5. Below, we focus on how the programme can be seen to embed aspects of engaged pedagogy through an emphasis on foregrounding the active participation of students, as well as their ideas, voices and needs, in learning and teaching.

Learning and teaching on the programme is oriented strongly around student contributions and participatory discussions. Though large-group

111

lectures do form part of the timetable, these are often structured around inviting student contributions or smaller-group activities and discussions (rather than simply involving listening to teacher-led content). In addition, participatory workshops and small-group seminars (generally containing up to a dozen students) form a large proportion of the week's contact time. Seminars are oriented around collective discussion of the week's set reading and lectures. Sometimes seminars include a short activity – which may involve working alone or in even smaller sub-groups – designed as a springboard for students to actively participate and even direct the discussion. In the past, these activities have included discussing critical questions – either about the specific readings or the issues surrounding them; exploring policy problems; doing thought experiments or games; writing short reflective paragraphs or bullet points; and drawing posters or mind maps. Although these activities tend to be set in advance by the module leader or seminar tutor, sometimes they are led by students, or seminar tutors create activities based on student suggestions. As noted earlier, assessment on the programme is all coursework-based, and students have a high degree of autonomy over the subject focus of their assessed work.

Participants strongly foregrounded the programme's commitment to students' active engagement with their learning, often comparing this to what Freire might call the "banking" model of education (1970:75) – in which students are seen simply as passive recipients of teacher-led 'content':

> <u>Rachel</u>: I guess previously we were just kind of fed information? [...] Like we would sit in the classroom and then there would just be, like, a teacher talking to us and preparing us for an exam. But then on the course now, we're [...] given the material, [and] then we're given, like, an opportunity to kind of navigate it and figure out what it means and kind of come up with our own ideas from it.

> <u>Tia</u>: We have a lot of choice, like we get to choose the topics that we want to talk about or, like, topics that we're gonna write about, so we are very independent. And I don't think that other courses are like that because they're very, you know, directed from the tutors and the seminar leaders [...] and our course is not like that.

Michelle: Like, it's really, like, it's not like other courses [...], like 'You have to study this and you have to do an exam about this and this'. It's more like if we wanna do something else then [...] we can make it happen, the students can make it happen. [...] We have more, like, a say in how the course is run and what we can do, and we have, like, more freedom.

Luke: This is partly about trying to get students to develop a kind of sociological imagination, like [...] beyond the classroom, and to see the material as a set of tools for engaging with the world, and I think there's a sense in which that transcends a lot of typical undergraduate teaching, which is more focused on you know, students learning a curriculum – learning content – and being able to recycle that in an exam or in an essay or something like that.

An emphasis on student engagement was also raised in relation to assessment practice specifically. Participants pointed to the level of choice and autonomy afforded to students, including – as Selena refers to – a module in which students were actually involved in co-designing marking criteria:

May: I love the assessments. I love that it's not fixed, like 'You have to do this, you have to write about this'. Letting us decide what lens we want to focus on, letting us decide what issue we want to talk about, I think it's a very- people will find something [they're] passionate about, and they're going to research that very well. They're going to focus and I think that's one of my favourite parts of the course.

Neve: [W]e're able to take the theory and do what we want with it [...], so even if we haven't explicitly been told about prison abolition in the course, for example, I can write an essay on that if I wanted to.

Selena: [F]or example in the first semester when we actually all sat down and agreed on the terms that we're going to be assessed on, for the assignment for one of the modules, I really like that because we discuss and no one would feel left out, I think. That was really helpful for the first big assignment.

As noted above, hooks' definition of engaged pedagogy emphasises not only partnership between students and staff, but also the importance of *emotion*. This contrasts with the pervasive assumption in educational philosophy (rooted once again in Cartesian dualism) that the rational can somehow be separated from the emotional (Clegg and Rowland, 2010). It implies that we can launch into definitions and theories and 'pure' intellectualising in a way which is disconnected from our lived experience, from our feelings about ourselves and the world. For anyone who has ever felt truly liberated by academic pursuit, the fulfillment of reading work that truly resonates, of putting words to the page in a way that feels like it has meaning and integrity, such a claim is surely a "philosophically thin account of what it means to be human" (Clegg and Rowland, 2010:722). People don't learn in a bubble in their heads called 'thinking'; learning is as much *felt* as it is *thought*. Thus, hooks argues that love is vital to engaged pedagogy; without it, we are cordoning off a section of our humanity, and cannot participate as full partners in the learning process (2010). For hooks, then, educational engagement is rooted in emotional engagement.

The idea of the interrelationship between the emotional and the intellectual was touched on by a small number of participants. Although not a dominant theme, we felt it was worthy of note, not least because there are significant consequences for pedagogy. Joe, for instance, suggested that the most meaningful moments intellectually are those in which taught "material" is linked to personal and emotional experience:

> Joe: I find it very hard to put into words, but sometimes there's this feeling that just something has clicked, and that people have walked away from that space not only feeling that they have engaged with the material [...] but also that they've [...] had some degree of personal discovery, even often in quite small ways, and that something that on first glance has seemed very remote or abstract has suddenly come home for people in a way that is, like, palpable.

[...] Before the holidays there was a particularly good session [...] like I came in and everyone was [...] just being really relaxed [...] – I think it's always a good sign when people start sort of swearing freely in your presence [laughs] and also feeling like they can talk about quite personal things in a way that's [...], like, relevant, and that's not actually turning into some kind of quasi-therapeutic space where that's maybe asking more of the space than it can deliver. But actually using personal experience in a really, like, honest and relevant way. And that's hard, right? Because personal experience is messy and it's not like I would want people to do it in a kind of perfect neat kind of way. But, when it happens well, I think [...] something quite magical can happen.

Joe refers here to two ways in which emotion matters for learning: one is the idea that people feeling "relaxed" and able to be themselves in the classroom is core to their ability to engage. The second relates to connecting up abstract content with "personal discovery" – of rooting taught "material" in what is personally meaningful to the learner. Crucially, Joe suggests that – although the balance can be difficult – this *can* be done in a way which doesn't "ask more of the space than it can deliver". hooks has noted the problem of expecting teachers to become therapists, or of emotional expression being reduced to competitive "exhibitionism" (2010:57). Nonetheless, hooks maintains that when we "share personal experience in a manner that illuminates assigned material, we help lay the foundation for building an authentic learning community" (ibid.:56–57); not only does it "help us understand one another" (ibid.:49), it brings academic content to life.

Joe went on to suggest that bringing the personal and emotional into the classroom can also help strengthen the process of 'mutual humanisation' identified by Hegel as fundamental to all forms of recognition as equality:

Joe: I feel that when I have [shared personal experiences] [...] it has enabled students to do the same. So the first time I sort of mentioned something about mental health in a seminar, immediately three other students talked very openly about mental health, experiences of mental health, and I was sort of emboldened by that. [...] [A]nd then

115

> I sort of linked that [...] to the theory in the readings to sort of show how personal experience can be bridged to content in a theoretical sense. So, I think it's really crucial [...] [for] just humanising this entire process, you know?

Crucially, this mutuality is at its best when staff attend not only to students' emotions, but also their own. As hooks writes, "empowerment cannot happen if we refuse to be vulnerable while expecting our students to take risks" (1994:21). Thus, a commitment to 'engaged' classroom practice often requires educators to place themselves on a level with students in terms of demonstrating their own vulnerability – taking care to acknowledge their *own* emotional needs and experiences, as well as those of their students.

Evidently, much of this analysis connects to the earlier iteration of recognition as love, care and kindness in chapter 2. Though being loving and kind to one another *in general* is subtly different from emphasising the personal and the emotional in *pedagogy*, hooks – at least – considers them so deeply related that she advocates a commitment to love in education to cover both bases. This interconnection of emotional recognition with rationality was touched upon earlier in relation to Honneth who considers recognition to be a precursor to cognition (2005). That is, that when we feel affirmed by acts of love and care (which we could say includes having our personal experiences and emotions recognised in the classroom) our capacity to fully comprehend and cognize the world is strengthened. Delineating different versions of recognition has its analytical uses – they are different angles on a problem, emphasise different ways of 'humanising' one another. And they are not always mutually co-occurring, as we suggested earlier when arguing that love and kindness may not be enough for realising equality. But these forms of recognition are nonetheless deeply interrelated, as the above analysis demonstrates in suggesting that a commitment to love, kindness, and care for one another's emotional needs in the classroom is integral to engaged pedagogy. Such a commitment strengthens our capacity to participate fully in intellectual exploration. It humanises teachers and learners. In short, it can only work to strengthen educational partnership.

As with participatory democracy above, the programme's attempts to embed engaged pedagogy are far from straightforward. We explore some core challenges below.

Concerns around student engagement

There was an indication in the data that some students have struggled with adapting to a less directed mode of learning and teaching. Perhaps unsurprisingly for a programme whose pedagogical approach is oriented around equality and partnership, there is limited top-down monitoring of attendance or workload. Student absences tend only to be followed up if they are long-term or if a staff member is concerned about a student's wellbeing. And there was widespread indication in the data (for instance, highlighted in chapter 2) that students see staff attitudes to work as relaxed. This was cited by some participants as precisely what enabled them to feel safe 'engaging' in class:

> Maya: So the seminars that I've been in, a lot of people say that the seminar lead [...] makes them feel included? So it's not like, 'Oh, you need to do the readings, and you come in, and if you don't understand the readings, like we're gonna assume you understand the readings' [...]. Because it's like a common understanding that, 'Yeah, you might not understand the readings, and let's start from the basics and let's go from there'. I think that's what makes people comfortable enough to talk to the staff?

Yet, other participants suggested that this relaxed approach can be "misunderst[ood]" (Tia) as a license either not to engage, or not to attend:

> Tia: Yeah I've noticed some people being... too relaxed, about the course [...]. And then [...] sometimes we don't take it that seriously? [...] Yeah, it's easy to misunderstand that individuality and that freedom that we have in the course and take it for granted and be like, 'Oh yeah I don't have to do anything'.

> Rachel: I feel like with the readings, everyone tried to do [them] in the first week? But then when we kind of realised that, 'Oh if we don't

do the readings, we can still go to the seminars because the tutors will kind of adapt to whoever didn't [do it]'. [...] So everyone just kind of went, 'Okay so, if the tutor's just gonna do that then I don't have to do the reading', well that's- I'm guilty of that as well [laughs] sometimes.

Susan: I think it's mostly- people really love this course, like I can really tell that [...] but at the same time if it's not- like if attendance is not, like, you know, regulated, or it's not, you know, punished if you don't come in, [then] at some point – even if people love the course [...] they're just [laughs] not gonna go in.

As Clegg and Rowland argue, it is easy for kindness to get misinterpreted as leniency, but they are not the same thing (2010). Kindness includes taking into account the needs and wellbeing of everyone in the learning space (ibid.); but while that – coupled with a commitment to equality and partnership – means respecting others' priorities and choices, and rejecting authoritarian attempts to surveil students' learning, it surely also includes generating forms of collective responsibility for the learning process. Because when some people consistently do not engage, it damages the extent to which the learning process can be truly intellectually and emotionally fulfilling for everyone. Luke, for instance, pointed to the simple fact that if people don't show up to class, it's difficult to see them as partners in any meaningful sense:

Luke: [T]he absence of students I find sort of disappointing on another level and it's [...] to do with this idea of being partners and being in a community with people who are learning together – it's really hard to do that when people are not showing up, right?

This was echoed by student participants who described how, even when attendance is good, some people's disengagement has a detrimental impact on the overall quality of discussion and deliberation:

Rachel: I feel like sometimes in the seminars, we can't really go in depth into what we're discussing, because people don't do the readings! [laughs] And [...] the seminar tutors are all really nice because they'll adapt to the situations of like whoever comes to the seminars but I just feel like because people don't do the readings, sometimes it can kind of feel like [in] the seminars we're just kind of... chatting.

Kima: I personally think there's not enough discussion of the actual readings in the seminar. And I've felt this pretty much throughout the year, because even in the seminars where we do have two hours, it's been more of a case of some people do the readings, some people don't, so then if we start discussing the readings specifically then if someone hasn't done the readings, it's difficult for them to take part in the conversation, so [...] we discuss the readings less.

Hester echoed this, suggesting that people doing inadequate prep generates an imbalance whereby the seminar tutor ends up doing all the talking to fill in the knowledge gaps. This undermines the possibility for foregrounding students' perspectives *and* for breaking down teacher/student hierarchy:

Hester: [T]here's been some particular seminars when people engage more. I'm [thinking of a particular seminar which] was very good because [...] everybody [was] attentive to give an opinion and to respond to something and I feel like in that seminar, [...] they all did the readings. Which is not something that always happens [laughs]. I think I was quite emphatic in saying they should do the readings the week before, so that week everybody did the readings [...]. And that week I felt like it was working very well, because I felt like people had, like, a fully realised reflection on the topic and at the same time even when they didn't agree, they were able to have a dialogue, and I didn't have to intervene as much [...]. I felt like it was good because I wasn't responsible for the conversation, in a way? [...] I think that's the way that it should be every time.

In a similar vein, Joe acknowledged that sometimes their frustration around student non-engagement gets the better of them, leading them to fall back into problematic 'us and them' narratives around students and staff, with explicit consequences for recognition:

Joe: It's incredibly easy to fall into that trap of seeing students as a homogenous mass. When just one or two students really give off an air of not giving a damn about the reading [...], I end up thinking, 'Hey, why do I bother to get up at 6 a.m. and do this reading and put all this thought into trying to make the session engaging, only to have people show up to take advantage of the fact that I don't police their work or put them on the spot?' But then I realise that I'm employing that 'us and them' language and I'm falling into the trap of seeing students as somehow 'different' [from myself] [...] and that's just incredibly ironic in the context of [this] course.

Participants themselves had varying perspectives on the roots of – and attendant solutions to – problems around lack of engagement. Despite positive accounts of the programme's approach to assessment, a number suggested that the lack of exams means there is insufficient external incentive for people to engage with a wide range of curriculum content:

Neve: There's no like incentive to, like, learn more about any topic we've studied. [...] [I]f we took an exam we [would] have to keep going over stuff but, with the coursework we can just choose, and even with the reading, like, if we don't do the readings there's no way of being check[ed]. So I guess that's sort of the barrier, in that people can opt in and opt out of engaging.

Some participants suggested that a solution might be to return to conventional top-down pressures and incentives, such as forms of regular testing:

Rachel: Yeah I think to help people to care [...] maybe doing some like maybe weekly quizzes? And stuff? [...] I think it will help people like kind of stay on track because they know that it will count. [...] Because the readings are not assessed, people don't do them [...]. I think that regular check gives a good push to people and would make the course work better and the teachers and students more comfortable.

As before, it is important to understand problems in relation to the broader context of education. When mainstream paradigms emphasise quantifiable outcomes like grades, and the idea of education as a 'product', it's perhaps unsurprising that many people feel disincentivised from engaging in work unrelated to that product/outcome. Similarly, bell hooks writes that engaged pedagogy is premised on the notion that true joy and fulfillment in learning comes from people becoming "self-actualized" (2010:8) – able to let go of a reliance on the teacher as the sole source of knowledge and affirmation, and able to trust themselves and their own ideas and voices – yet points out that this is at odds with the educational approaches most people have grown up with. Thus, hooks' collaborator Ron Scapp writes:

> "To acknowledge student responsibility for the learning process is to place it where it's least legitimate in their own eyes. When we try to change the classroom so that there is a sense of mutual responsibility for learning, students get scared that you are now not the captain working with them, but that you are after all just another crew member – and not a reliable one at that." (Scapp in hooks, 1994:144).

Indeed, some participants explicitly referred to their discomfort with being expected to take an active role in the learning process, even while acknowledging that their preference may be based simply on what they are "used to":

> Susan: [I]t's just my personal preference that I like it more if I [laughs] if I'm told what to do in an educational setting, because I'm really used to that.

Nonetheless, these feelings of discomfort co-exist with strong forms of resistance to both passivity and instrumentalisation; many participants clearly stated their intrinsic motivation for studying and their appreciation of the course's 'engaged' approach to pedagogy:

Selena: I've been very stressed during my years of high school and there's so much pressure put on students, because we learn for school, not for us, and this is why teachers and the headmaster and everyone basically wants us to have as high grades as possible, and here on the contrary we're doing everything for ourselves, and I really appreciated that, and I really can choose for myself, 'What do I focus on? What [am I] not very interested in, what do I wanna do, what don't I wanna do?' And just, yeah, I really like that.

Susan: The other thing that drew me to this course was [...] I kind of got this feeling which proved to be true then, that grades are not the only thing that are important on this course, and I think for me that's a very different approach from what I'm used to, but at the same time I knew that it would probably be beneficial for my mental health.

This outlook was echoed by a staff member describing their impression of (assessed) student presentations for one of the first-year modules:

Rosa: [J]ust like the presentations in [the] 'Understanding the Social World' [module], how amazing they were, what a range of issues they picked up on, you know reading some of their media articles and how much they get it [that] we're doing something real here, this is not just an assignment for the sake of an assignment, it's writing about something [we] care about.

This resistance is not only evident above but also in our lived experience of the programme as *authors*. For instance, this project itself might be seen as a form of resistance to instrumentalism and passivity. It is not assessed, or even part of the formal curriculum. Almost half of the programme's students voluntarily participated as interviewees and a quarter as researchers. Moreover, those researchers have undertaken a considerable amount of self-directed study, including choosing and researching their own analytical focuses, and have been working in partnership with staff members on the team as co-writers and co-investigators.

In light of this resistance, we might argue that evidence of participants' discomfort with a more egalitarian, student-led approach to learning and teaching is not necessarily a reason to fall back on conventional, top-down forms of incentivisation and control. Maybe what is needed is an *embrace* of the discomfort involved in doing engaged pedagogy. Indeed, some participants explicitly pointed to their own (often challenging) journeys in coming to terms with the programme's approach:

> Rachel: I think the beginning was so rough because the course is very different to what I've experienced during the A-levels. Then, the teachers used to basically give us the information [...]. I think this change and adapting to it would be a challenge for people who come to university to do this course. But [...] I feel like I'm learning and last term I didn't feel the 'push' to work. Now I [still] don't feel it from 'the outside'. But you have to learn to push yourself.

As touched on in section 3a, staff also face challenges in coming to terms with more egalitarian, participatory approaches. Thus, Susan suggests that deconstructing conventional educational assumptions is a journey which students and staff must undergo *together.*

> Susan: I still feel weird and good with this kind of freedom. At the same time [...] I feel like if I didn't have this kind of freedom I would miss it, but it still feels weird having it [laughs] so I would- I would need to get used to it, but I would definitely not change [it]. [...] I think it's necessary and I think this is something that both students and teachers have to get used to, in a way?

Student concerns about learning and teaching

Having said all this, it would be deeply misguided – not to mention ironic – to write off all student concerns around the programme's engaged approach to pedagogy as simply due to conditioning! As explored in section 3a, taking student concerns seriously is part and parcel of a commitment to recognition as equality. With this in mind, we now turn to four further core concerns around the course's pedagogical approach, highlighted by student participants in the data.

A small number of student participants said they felt that there was too much emphasis on student opinions and personal experience, at the expense of engagement with literature. These concerns were mostly raised in relation to a specific module in which seminars are designed around student reading 'self-reflections' about the week's topic and leading a discussion. Even if we believe people learn best when they are able to learn content through personal engagement with it, it is widely-acknowledged that getting the balance right is a challenge for progressive educators (Clegg and Rowland, 2010), not least when there are stark time constraints (as noted above):

> Tia: I like the fact that we got to talk about topics but at the same time, like, the self-reflections and everything [...], like, you put your own experience out there, which is totally fine, I like that, but I think it should be a little more structured around the topics that we learn and the theories and everything. So we can understand that we're not just talking about what we think, but you know, there's been research done before us. [...] I felt it was a bit like the academic parts of the topics that we were talking about were a bit devalued in a way? That we're not paying enough attention to that, academically.

> Maya: And with the seminars, personally I don't like the structure of them. 'Cos I'd like to get more into the reading? [...] Like I don't mind hearing other people's perspectives on certain topics, but [...] I feel like if you go through the reading first and then kind of explore that, like we have with other modules, I think personally for me that works better?

A second concern related to not understanding content. Some students expressed a desire for slower, simpler language by teachers and for more structured input on breaking down difficult texts. These concerns should not be underestimated; if students feel lost or overwhelmed by course material, they are not in an empowered position to participate as partners:

> Ryleigh: Sometimes, in the lectures and the seminars [...] there were topics that, like, I didn't get a thing about. [...] Maybe it's, like, not [the staff's] fault, but, like, [the way] they were explaining it. Like first

thing the lecturer would go very fast sometimes. [...] Sometimes even talking with, like, terms I've never heard about.

Maya: One of the difficulties [...] is say, like, a key thinker like Durkheim and Marx, breaking down their readings or even trying to find their readings was really difficult for me, although I knew the general gist of what they were saying, I would like it if I could actually read their texts and actually analyse it for myself without being like 'Well, what the hell is this?' I think that would be really good, kind of sitting down with lecturers or seminar tutors and kind of really breaking down like one specific passage, because I don't think we've had that much of that.

Some participants suggested that there had been more focus on "breaking down" difficult readings in semester two, and that they appreciated having the opportunity to do this:

Selena: I mean I love [...] breaking down the readings. I kind of feel that [...] this semester we're doing this in seminars more than the first semester. My seminar tutor changed so that might be the reason. But we actually, well I feel like when there is a hard-to-understand reading we just spend an hour [...] basically analysing it, clarifying and making any sense of it. Which is very helpful and... maybe not every text but some texts maybe – it just helps me.

Connectedly, some participants referred to struggling with consolidating their learning on the programme – primarily because there is so much content to cover in so little time, and therefore minimal opportunity for re-covering ground. Although some participants, as discussed above, suggested more frequent assessment exercises to provide an 'incentive' to revisit material in their own time, others suggested that creative pedagogical techniques in the classroom would help them to better understand and engage with material. Susan, for example, highlighted a narrative-based technique they experienced in high school, whereby each week a different member of the group would be chosen to present on the previous lesson's content, by orally describing the content as a 'story'.

Susan felt this helped them to maintain "focus" and connect meaningfully with the curriculum:

> Susan: The reason why the whole storytelling thing worked out for me is because I had to sit down, and I had to practise it for a long time before it got into my head and with this kind of studying, it's like, you know, it goes in one way and it comes out the other, 'cos because I'm just- I'm really- for me it's impossible at some point to maintain my focus? [...] [It']s a good way of practicing it because it really sticks in your head, it really- it never leaves [laughs].

It strikes us that the programme could explore pedagogical techniques like this without compromising on its egalitarian ethos, for instance by discussing and deciding on approaches collectively (e.g. as seminar groups), by making them optional when they involve singling people out, and by ensuring the primary aim is what supports deeper engagement, rather than a desire to test people. Selena, meanwhile, reflected positively on a seminar in which they felt there was more structured preset 'activity' than usual (students were required to work on a sheet of detailed questions about the week's readings in small groups):

> Selena: [T]hose sheets when we were doing the questions, I think that was very helpful [...] and that helped to reset our knowledge. Yeah, I'm referring to the day when we had one hour of seminar in the lecture. [...] And so we got these questions and we worked as groups and then reflected altogether and I think that was really helpful, just doing exercises, not just discussing as we do in seminars [...].

Most seminars on the programme are oriented around some preset activity – at the very least some general questions about the week's topic. However, the activity from the seminar in question relied on a particularly in-depth knowledge of the week's readings and was more focused on critically discussing their claims than on generalised discussion of the subject matter. This more focused group work, grounded in the reading, could – like Susan's description of 'oral narrative' above – add an additional option to the pedagogical toolbox, which seminar groups could foreground to a greater or lesser extent depending on the week's readings, the interests of the group, and what best supports the learning process at a given time.

A final concern was centred around a perceived need to better connect academic content to 'real-world issues'. A core part of engaged pedagogy, and of recognising students as partners, involves making academic work feel relevant and meaningful for people's lives and values. Moreover, the programme philosophy and ethos statement suggests that connecting social science to real-world problems is part of its commitment to promoting social justice outside the academy. Many participants actually referred to what they perceived as the programme's success in this regard:

> Kima: [T]here's been a mixture of theory-based lectures and also guest lectures from organisations who are currently implementing policies in their organisations. So we can see the link – it's not just that we're studying people who have died and writing essays on them, it's [that] we're connecting their theories [...] with the modern world. And that helps me understand how this information is still relevant [...].

> Rebecca: So we're doing [...] like queer theory and like postcolonial theory but also, [...] the way in which we learn about the topics, [...] we're not just doing the theory, we're also doing the linked oppression, so we'll do like, like queer theory and then we'll do like homophobia the next week, which again is very different from a lot of other courses because we're seeing the real-world implications, in real-time [...] and sort of understanding how these theories impact people's lived experiences [...].

> Emma: I think things have changed for me. I can [apply] what I've learned in different situations, for example when I watch the news, I now know and understand what's going on. Even in conversations, I can engage more, I use what I've learned in everyday life.
> Rachel: Yes, I agree. Social sciences never go away. I analyse situations differently now, I apply things from the course into my everyday life. I feel that because I'm able to use the theories it makes

me understand what's going on around me. [...] I've learned a new way of thinking.

Yet a significant minority of participants felt that more could be done to facilitate these connections between academic content and 'real-world issues':

> Marla: I'm enjoying a lot the course but I think it's – it's especially in the last two modules, so 'Power, Inequality and Social Change' and 'Social Justice and Policy Analysis', I think we're focusing a bit too much on the issues and its complexities, making the solutions [feel] unthinkable because one realises that the issue is so complex that it's hard to solve. Even though there are of course the readings [that] mention that actions have been taken, movements have been made, but yet the issue never seems to change or never seems to be solved, so I think one thing [that] is missing or we could have more of is [...] looking more [at] the positive and the way that people through collaboration actually achieved improvements.

> May: I think the nature of our courses, it needs to be about, like, discussion, like the number one thing we need to be doing is talking about this stuff, because this is real stuff. It's not just like, academic stuff we do in the classroom, this stuff is going on around us. So, if we don't have the chance to like expand and talk about the real issues that are going on around then most of the people in the course are just going to leave the classroom and forget everything. Because they just see it as academic required stuff and not stuff that's really going on.

In many ways, these student concerns underline the importance of equality and partnership in learning and teaching; by building an environment in which people feel able to speak out about problems (and not just in the context of qualitative research projects!), the hope is that these challenges can be identified and collectively addressed. There was some encouraging evidence of this in the data, where students referred to their comfort in raising concerns:

May: I think the fact that the course allows us to criticise it, is also a strength in itself because, like, we can recognise that the course is doing amazing stuff. But we can also be like, 'Actually, you're still falling short on these things [...]'. That is a pretty good thing, that we can criticise, without feeling like, 'Oh we're going to get in trouble'. [...] On other courses, people have no voice. [...] I like the staff; the staff are good. I know that they will change the stuff, now people have raised concerns, I don't think they're the type of people to just brush stuff off, they actually care.

Michelle: In the first semester I felt like we were just going on from theory to theory without really putting them in[to] practice, without really knowing what they were for. Without having time to link them all together [...]. But, we talked about it in the Course Community Meeting, [and] they said that we're going to, like, [do] it more throughout the next years' [modules], so I'm looking forward to that.

Kima: In the first semester there was [...] an assessment where we had to write a media article, and given it was a new type of assessment for a lot of us, some of us were unsure how to go about doing it? But we as students felt able- at least I can speak for myself that I felt able to approach staff and to ask for clarification. The assessment was amended slightly, as in the marking criteria was made a bit more clear.

A useful case study on this front was provided by a staff member, Cleo, and their account of navigating a module in which students had an active role in co-creating the marking criteria. Some participants (e.g. Selena earlier) referred very positively to this process. However, Cleo also noted that it caused anxiety for some students, and that addressing their desire for clarity whilst also committing to the process of co-creation was, at times, challenging. What is interesting here is the way that Cleo presents navigating the challenges as *part and parcel* of the programme's commitment to pedagogical partnership and collective problem-solving:

Cleo: So on [one of the modules] for the first assignment we decided to co-devise the criteria with the students. And I think that was very risky because [...] it's seen as kind of an advanced thing, you know, 'Students are not able to think about this when they first come, [...] should they [...] be able to have so much freedom to choose the issue that they want to investigate together as a group?' [...] Let alone 'Should they be able to design the criteria'? And [...] I thought of doing that [...] partly as a provocation of just, like, 'Well let's challenge all those things, let's challenge who decides', but while also understanding that it could be quite anxiety-provoking for students. [...] I hope and I *think* from feedback this worked for some people although I'd be interested if it didn't work for others, in the end, but I hope that we were able to provide a space where students could say, 'This is making me anxious, I really need to know where I am with this, I don't even know the criteria' [...] and provide space for [responding], like, 'Yes, that's a [challenge] in education, isn't it? Let's talk about that'. [...] And I hope that we were able to both kind of hear those concerns [...] and to be able to [...] kind of live with that tension, live with that difficulty, discuss it together. And I still don't know [whether] we should do it again next year, and I want to talk to the course community about that [...]. [But] I think it's the way of dealing with it, [...] of [saying], 'Yeah let's think about these things together, let's not deny the difficulty or just solve the problem as quickly as possible', 'cos the quickest solution would be to have said, 'Ok fair enough we won't do it that way' or 'We *are* gonna do it that way, it'll be fine', you know. And I hope we did neither of those.

Managing such tensions is by no means straightforward. But we feel that Cleo's account highlights how navigating them is greatly strengthened by participatory approaches where everyone – students and staff – can feel heard. It is an act of mutual recognition which only serves to strengthen the quality of the learning process. The key to its success however (as discussed above) is for everyone to acknowledge their responsibility to contribute to that process. As hooks writes:

> "When everyone in the classroom, teacher and students, recognizes that they are responsible for creating a learning community together, learning is at its most meaningful" (hooks, 2010:11

Chapter 4.

The context of recognition on the programme

Freya Aquarone

In chapters 2 and 3 we explored how the BASS programme can be understood to pursue various forms of recognition – from foregrounding love, care and kindness, to embedding partnership and equality through quasi-democratic decision-making and engaged pedagogy. We also highlighted several challenges raised by participants in relation to each of these aspects of the programme. Two further, strongly foregrounded themes in our dataset relate less to challenges and more to aspects of the programme which appear to facilitate the various forms of recognition explored so far. These were: 1) the ethos of the staff team and of the wider departmental culture in which the programme exists, and 2) the size of the programme community. Although difficult to fit neatly into the flow of analysis so far, we felt they were fundamental to understanding the programme and its context and therefore deserved a dedicated interluding chapter.

As far
as it's possible to be authentic, you can be authentic.

Because obviously they're my colleagues–
    but also mentors, heroes, friends.

There are
very strong and meaningful emotional bonds

It's not just a job for anyone.

And although we have our differences
there are certain first principles
that we're kind of like
        'No
            We're not debating those'

Cos they're at the heart of what we do.

Around treating people as people,
Around wellbeing,
Around people's right to actually
Not be subject
to constant paternalistic oversight

And surveillance.

A belief that intellectual rigor need not be traded off against
    emotional engagement

And yet people are willing to listen
        To disagree
I can be an obsessive perfectionist
Really pernickety and...
maybe even slightly annoying–

Because I feel like there's a strong foundation of trust.
    It's just–
Fine to say what you think.

I don't have to tiptoe around people–
        (I mean, I hope Oscar doesn't listen to this and think 'I
    wish she'd tiptoe around me a bit more'!)

I guess what I'm trying to say is that although we have our
differences, there is a kind of a core
                    Core centre

Like an extended family
Based on shared purpose and empathy
    Trust and comfort and
The feeling of safety
Of passing on a legacy
Of what we want Higher Education to be

I think it's quite unusual, this space.
It's kind of special for me.

4a – Recognition on the staff team

So far, we have explored how the programme seeks to promote recognition through a commitment to love and kindness, and to greater equality between students and staff. Interestingly, staff participant descriptions of the programme team strongly echoed both these themes explored in relation to the programme as a whole. Staff spoke about what they perceived as a clear effort within the team to break down professional hierarchies, and normalise equality in decision-making:

> Robbie: The other thing that's really different here to other places that I've taught is that we're not just left on our own to deliver a module. Everyone's sort of agreeing on it? Like the module[s] [are] designed through a consensus. Like somebody might do most of the work but like there has to be some kind of consensus reached? [...] I'm just completely unused to interacting in that way. That [has not] been my experience historically. [I]n the course I told you about at [another university], there was just the person in charge [and they] had a veto. And [they] would just change stuff and rewrite stuff- like zero consideration.

> Rosa: I think we're cooperative, I think that's a good word, I think we cooperate with each other [...]. And that's been designed in from the beginning – that we're doing it together.

> Simon: I don't feel like it's hierarchical. I don't feel like it is. [...] The way we treat each other, like, I don't know how to explain it but there's different ways to show authority I guess, and I don't feel like in the relationships that we have, I don't feel like there's any intention to show hierarchy.

The experiences of the two most junior staff members are particularly telling when it comes to considering attempts to promote recognition based on equality within the programme team[23]. Marnie and Hester are what KCL terms 'Graduate Teaching Assistants' (GTAs) – doctoral students hired on fixed-term, hourly-paid teaching contracts. The term GTA can itself be seen as a manifestation of institutional hierarchy which has been critically challenged for its misrecognition of graduate teaching labour (Megoran and Mason, 2020). Far from just 'assisting' senior staff, GTAs – alongside other hourly-paid teaching staff – provide up to 50% of teaching at HE institutions in the UK (UCU, 2019; Megoran and Mason, 2020), and many carry out work which spans seminar facilitation, lecturing, module development, pastoral support, marking, and administration. The widespread use of teaching staff on hourly-paid, fixed term contracts is part of the general trend towards 'casualisation' in HE, which has been widely decried for exacerbating economic inequality and precarity within the sector (UCU, 2019; Megoran and Mason, 2020), particularly for women and ethnic minorities (Megoran and Mason, 2020).

Yet studies have suggested that it is not just the objective facts of contract-type or employment status (including job titles) which determine whether casualised workers feel "dehumanised" (Megoran and Mason, 2020:11). Megoran and Mason's study for the University and College Union focuses not only on material factors (such as pay) but also on casualised staff accounts of feeling denigrated and devalued in their professional relationships, seemingly *as a result of* their employment status (2020). Of course, more equal staff team dynamics cannot 'disappear' the impact of casualisation, in the same way as they cannot disappear the time, workload and performativity pressures identified in chapter 2. But teams which seek to normalise an ethos of equality and mutual respect – which include all staff in decision-making and hold them all in high esteem, regardless of their position in the institutional hierarchy – can go a long way to reducing the destructive impact of wider problems in the sector.

---

[23] It is also quite encouraging when students perceive the programme team to be non-oppressive; as one student put it, "I wouldn't be able to tell that Oscar was the programme director if I didn't know [...]. It's not that I don't see the work he's putting in, it's [that] I don't see him, like, oppressing the other teachers [laughs] you know, which is really nice" (Susan).

Marnie and Hester's accounts – particularly their emphasis on the absence of discourses around superiority/inferiority – are indicative of the extent to which the programme team has succeeded in promoting recognition in this way:

> Hester: I've heard a lot of experiences from fellow students from [another] department doing GTA work there and they were talking about a completely different experience than the one I'm having here [...]. [A] complaint I heard a lot [from them] is that they feel like they're not part of the staff. [...] [T]hey don't have a relationship with the main lecturers. [...] [Whereas] [...] I feel very included as a staff member and not just as someone who comes helping for a term. Like, even if I have a contract that ends quite soon, I don't feel like 'Okay that's done and I'm leaving'. Because I feel like I'm part of a community [...]. [L]ike for example here we have the [staff] meetings, which [GTAs] are included in, [but] the staff meetings [in the other] department don't include GTAs. So they are not part of the conversation.

> Marnie: Everyone's incredibly, like, supportive and amazing as a team. [At the start], being the most junior person in the room, if not only by status, but also by age, I felt like, 'I don't really know where I fit in here and what I'm allowed to do or, like, what is okay to say without coming across like an upstart, or like, you know, disrupting something that actually other people have been working on for years'... and then actually realising that, no, actually the ideas that I had [...] shared with others were taken seriously, and like, you know, it wasn't like I was being inconvenient. [...] Then I felt, like, safe being part of the programme.

> Hester: For [the] 'Power Inequality and Social Change' [module], we have been informally meeting Dan sometimes [...] and I feel like [...] he's actually acknowledging us, as part of the staff, and asking us what we think, and [...] not being, like, authoritarian [laughs]. [...] He *could* make the decision by himself [...] [but] there's an intention of checking with other people and, like, knowing that you just can't be right all the time, and I think that's a practical example of how

there's a movement in the whole programme about, like, checking if this is right with other people?

In addition to themes of equality and collaboration explored above, staff participants also invoked themes of love and kindness, discussing how relationships and emotional support are a core part of the programme team ethos:

> Belle: In the programme [team] there is a particularly supportive environment. That is really, I think, not something easy to find [...] in a programme or in a department. [...] [Y]ou know, having, like, a group of people that share [...] [an] ethos or these kinds of values, but also that [...] if someone needs help, like someone wants to chat, [that will happen] in a kind of a very understanding and supportive way.

> Joe: So this team is kind of special for me, because although we have differences in our opinions, there are a certain set of first principles that are kind of like, 'No actually we're not debating those, 'cos they're kind of at the heart of what we do'. Around, like, treating people as people, around emotional wellbeing, around people's rights to actually not be subject to constant paternalistic surveillance or oversight, around the idea that intellectual rigor need not be traded off against personal experience and emotional engagement.

Thus, staff described how relationships on the team go beyond professional categories of 'colleague' or someone with whom one merely shares a job, and rather extend into friendship, mentorship and even family:

> Rosa: I think, like, really, the relationships between staff on our programme are really fantastic. [...] [I]t feels like we all really believe in this programme, that we're all really excited to be involved – it's not just a job for anyone, it is *part* of our job, and it is work, that needs to be recognised, but it's not *just* a job... that we're all delighted to be involved, that we enjoy working together, that we like each other [laughs].

Luke: Some people have been here for a very long time and the relationships are kind of a reflection of the time that they've spent together but also things like learning together [...] [S]o there are some quite particular features of those relationships and, like, depth to those relationships which involve things like trust and empathy and, like, quite deep emotional sort of bonds, really, between people who [are] obviously colleagues but also friends, mentors and heroes. And, you know, I'm sure it would go the other way [...] like, senior staff would describe their relationships with, you know, more junior staff as having, like, very strong and meaningful emotional bonds.

Robbie: People are really, like... they're welcomed in as a family member.

Joe: Unless you've got a really great, like, wider extended family – and a lot of people *don't* have that – it is quite unusual to be in a space where there are like people of varying ages and levels of experience all relating to each other on, like, a common project.

Others described the trust that they feel characterises staff relationships and suggested that, crucially, this facilitates a level of openness and critical honesty which in turn supports the quality of the programme itself:

Audre: I just feel like there's a really strong foundation of trust. So [...] as far as it's possible to be authentic [laughs], you can be authentic. I suppose what's really nice about it is I don't feel like I have to tiptoe round people – I mean I hope Oscar doesn't listen to this and think 'Oh I wish she'd tiptoe around me a bit more' [...] [laughs] [...]. [I]t's fine to sort of say what you think [...] – because you've got that foundation of knowing people for a long time and, like, really respecting them and [...] that's the whole kind of reason why friendliness is so important in a working relationship, [...] because it's through the friendliness that you develop the trust and the comfort and the feeling of safety to [...] then make [the work] really good.

Hester: I feel like I can make mistakes. [...] I feel like if I have a problem conducting my seminar I can go to Dan, or to you, or someone else, and say, like, 'I have this problem, like how would you address it, or what would you suggest to do?' And I feel like if you are in a more authoritarian context where, like, hierarchies in academia are more visible, you will be afraid of saying, 'Look I think I made a mistake or I said the wrong thing', like, you wouldn't ask for help.

A number of staff noted that key to developing this trust – and to developing a shared understanding of the programme ethos in general – was dedicated time for collective reflection. Given the time constraints noted throughout this book, it's not easy to make space for this, but staff referred to the annual Away Days and their non-tokenistic engagement with reflecting on educational philosophy and practice as a core example:

Robbie: [Before the course started] I didn't get the sense that the [programme] was particularly radical [...]. I just thought, 'This mirrors the kind of general trend that I am seeing in Higher Education in this country', which [...] [is] not because of any kind of top-down institutional process, it's because, you know, young people of colour in the 80s rioted and organised. [...] [But] then I went to the teaching away day last summer [...] and I was like 'Oh, okay, it's not cynical, it's genuine', which *really* surprised me [...].
Researcher: So what made it feel genuine?
Robbie: Because we sat around for two days talking about how we felt about teaching! [...] [I]t was about people sharing experiences of teaching. [...] [Y]ou know, you don't usually get asked those questions [...]. [I]t was about, you know, [...] 'What can we put into practice here, what do we believe should be happening?' Which I thought that was great, I liked that.

Joe: And then the Away Days were the chance to sort of build that team [...] – I mean, [...] it's so easy I think in any context to take for granted what, like, hymn sheet – for want of a better phrase – people are singing from. And obviously, we're all different people with different perspectives on education, and there's some healthy differences I think in the team, it's not just some kind of monolithic echo chamber, but I think there's something [...] immensely valuable about building a shared language around what we're aiming for, and in terms of also, like, identifying [...] what priorities we have.

We believe it should not be considered a coincidence that the staff team culture so strongly echoes that of the programme. In fact, perhaps it should be seen as a prerequisite. Earlier we explored how Hegel's dialectic implies that when recognition isn't present it can generate a downward spiral of alienation and 'othering'. That when we are not recognised, our capacity *to* recognise is diminished. This has quite a troubling implication: that we often reproduce what we have been subjected to. Thus, Paulo Freire himself writes:

> "Once a situation of violence and oppression has been established, it engenders an entire way of life and behaviour for those caught up in it – oppressors and oppressed alike. Both are submerged in this situation, and both bear the marks of oppression. [...] [It] is perpetuated from generation to generation." (1970:40).

One staff participant, Joe, in reflecting on their own experiences of being an undergraduate (at a different institution), described how easily they felt staff and students fell into a vicious cycle of misrecognition:

> Joe: I think that in my experience of being an undergraduate [...] a sort of quite problematic, self-reinforcing negative cycle had built up where staff felt very disempowered in terms of what they were actually able to change in terms of the kind of teaching they were able to do and the pressures they were under, which leads to them feeling that it's very easy to hate students because they're kind of part of the problem, and their demands or their attitudes are sort of fueling your own pain and then students pick up on the sort of disregard or apparent sort of, like, derisiveness on the part of staff, so then they don't like the staff because they think 'Well they don't want us to be here, they don't really care about us.' And so [...] people start to live out precisely the behaviours that are the stereotypes, you know?

What is particularly interesting to note here is Joe's suggestion that the roots of staff contempt can be located in their own disempowerment by the culture in which they work – rather than in simply an inherent unkindness or failure on their part. Nonetheless, there is something a bit too deterministic in the theory of a vicious cycle, and it presents a problem for those of us who are interested in how to enact change. Specifically, how are we supposed to identify the *start* of the causal loop? If you cannot recognise unless recognised, how can recognition be possible in the first place? And what about all the people who buck the trend in terms of their own life experience, and do things differently in spite of how they are themselves treated? So, we want to revise this to something which feels closer to accurate: maybe it's not impossible, but just much, much more difficult to generate a culture of recognition in a vacuum. The consequences for our sector are, we feel, clear and important: staff teams can much more easily reproduce a resistant culture in their teaching practice and in their relationships with students if they feel accepted, valued, and cared for in their own workplace and professional relationships – even if aspects of the sector as a whole are dehumanising or disempowering.

This notion of positive reproduction – of a culture acting as a springboard for one's own or for collective practice – was powerfully echoed in the data; staff were clear that they felt the staff team ethos was integral for upholding the values of the programme as a whole:

> Rosa: [I] think that Oscar's leadership is key [...] and helps those relationships to work because he takes a lot of responsibility for things but he also really makes sure that we're all informed, but without putting pressure on [people] to be involved in everything and [is] just so thoughtful [in] the way he does everything. And again that kind of then hopefully becomes the culture on the course: that we all are thoughtful and cooperate with each other.

> Joe: In the past I've just spent a lot of time working in contexts where I've felt like [...] I had to sort of cling on to my own [worldview] in a way that was quite isolated because there wasn't really a lot of stuff coming in that helped me to keep that afloat – it was very much 'on me' to do that. Whereas in this space I feel that there's a lot of

collective work, often quite subtle, that's done to keep afloat something in terms of a set of principles and ways of being.

Oscar: That sense of kind of empathy and shared purpose and the sense of which we are engaging in like a meaningful [...] articulation and enactment of our kind of view about what Higher Education is, [...] I think that gets extended to students – or hopefully it will get extended to students. Like this is the idea that the local institutional culture is something students are a part of and not just staff.

Encouragingly, a number of *students* expressed the belief that the staff team ethos has significance for their own enactment of the programme's values:

Susan: I feel like there is a very trusting environment generally in the course, which wouldn't happen without the trusting relationship [between] the staff.

Tia: The general atmosphere is very positive [among staff] [...]. [T]hat helps for us too- to, you know, to create this community.

Helena: [...] [B]ecause I know that staff really care about this course and they care about the content and that inspires me to work hard because I don't know if you can say that I want to make them proud but in terms of, like, I wanna do that course justice. Because I know that they care for it and I care for it and the way that we all work together on this ... it like ... inspires me to work really hard for it.

Students building on the foundation laid by the staff team ethos is, of course, integral to the functioning of the whole community, as one staff member pointed out:

Rosa: The students [...] have also then enabled [the programme] to be what it is. Because they've really engaged with it. And they've really embraced it and they've challenged [it] and they've taken on board different things and they've challenged themselves and they've challenged us, and they've brought so much to it, so that's also part of what's making it work.

Just to reinforce the importance of 'facilitating context', it is worth briefly noting that some staff participants went beyond discussions of the programme team and invoked the importance of both the "wider culture" of the School and one of its research groups – the Centre for Public Policy Research (CPPR) – which was heavily involved in developing the programme. This included particular reference to the role of senior staff – one of whom (Nancy) does not actually teach on the programme, yet their values and behaviour were nonetheless considered crucial for "enabling" the programme ethos:

> Rosa: What's enabled [the ethos] is probably partly the people and the combination of people involved. And part of that's a lucky accident but part of it's also a wider culture that I think is created in our School, and in our research group in particular. And some of that has come from a couple of key [senior] people, as in Paul and Nancy, their kind of way of leading which is very thoughtful, very engaged. [...] They're very interested in, you know, making those of us 'early career people' who are involved feel that we can be part of shaping something. [...] I mean they – Nancy and Paul – practise that all the time so I think they're a key element in enabling it?

> Luke: The programme itself is maybe not as new as it appears because actually it *reflects* something which is quite well established, which is I think a kind of culture of working that happens – at least in the Centre for Public Policy Research but I think more broadly across the School as well. So I think the ethos of the programme – [...] like a commitment to social justice and wellbeing and to interdisciplinarity and to rigour and criticality and, you know, critical pedagogy [...] – all of that I think is reflected in what CPPR is [...] and that's obviously a reflection of the people *within* CPPR and their commitments and [...] the way they understand Higher Education to be valuable and to be meaningful. So I think what we've tried to do on the programme is try and get down onto that blank page the culture of Higher Education we believe in, in CPPR.

The challenges we have explored in this book so far should lead us to question assumptions of virtuous cycles of recognition emerging neatly in any real-life education context. In our view it is less a virtuous cycle and more often a mostly virtuous zigzag. Not everyone is ready or able to engage with or reproduce a culture of recognition. Sometimes, for all sorts of reasons, we fail to live out and reproduce the practices we value. But the essence of what has been argued in this section is that cultures based on recognition *reproduce cultures based on recognition.* That means foundations – like the working culture which underpins a programme – cannot be underestimated.

4b – Sheer numbers: why community size matters for recognition

The BASS programme is small: in its first year, there were forty-three students and eight core staff. Evidently, the fact that it is a new programme in its first year is a contributing factor. Nonetheless, a single cohort size of below fifty is relatively unusual in HE. Even when all three cohorts are present – and even accounting for likely institutional pressure to expand student enrollment – it is likely the overall course size will not much exceed two hundred students in the years to come. Only time will tell how the expansion of the programme – even if its size remains below the national average – will affect its ethos and enactment of recognition. A follow-up of this study in a few years may be needed!

Much has been written about the 'massification' of HE – the radical rise in student numbers and proliferation of courses (Giannakis and Bullivant, 2016). There are ethically important consequences of this, not least around transforming HE from a profoundly elitist space populated predominantly by the white middle classes into one with a more diverse student population (ibid.) (although there is still a very long way to go until HE can be considered anything like truly diverse or inclusive (Bhopal, 2017; Dorling, 2016)). Much of the literature, however, notes that this massification is occurring, in many cases, without an attendant expansion in staffing or consideration of impacts on workloads (ibid.), which places severe strain on the possibility of building quality relationships (Stephen et al., 2008; Curran, 2017). It is also possible that even *with* appropriate workload modelling and adequate staffing, some communities are just too big in absolute terms to allow for meaningful bonds between their members. For instance, some anthropological and psychological theories have suggested that communities of fewer than 150 people are inherently better able to maintain familiarity and emotional closeness (e.g. Dunbar and Sosis, 2018). Given these considerations, it is perhaps unsurprising that this project's participants consistently referred to the size of the programme as a core part of what makes it 'work' in terms of building relationships based on recognition, whether in relation to themes of love/kindness, or equality/partnership.

For instance, when considering the theme of love and kindness in chapter 2, we explored participant data highlighting the importance of knowing things about one another's lives for building meaningful, caring relationships. However, participants were clear that they think this would be much more difficult to achieve in the context of a bigger community:

> Marla: I think the size is one of the things I like the most for example, some of the students going to different universit[ies] they were [...] quite unhappy about how they were treated as a number [...] [that] professors don't recognise them, they have no actual interactions. In fact one of the things that most scared me- that I was most scared of going to university was that it would be so big and so full of people that you were left alone and if you had a problem [...] it [would be] more difficult to find someone who could help you.

> Researcher: Could you tell me about ways you experience that sense of community in your [...] day to day life on the programme?
> Maya: [...] I think it's the fact that I know everyone's names? And I kind of know, like, little facts about them? Whereas if I were on, like, a bigger course or even during sixth form, I wouldn't know everyone in my year group, for example, so [...] even if [...] obviously you're closer to some people, I still know stuff about [other] people so it's like I can say 'hey' and if we see each other in the library and I can actually go talk to them.

> Heidi: I guess the size of the course is so much different to other courses which makes it feel like there is more of a community 'cos you get to know everyone, whereas the bigger courses, like, well basically all the other courses, there's too many people and it just feels a lot like you just go to the lectures and that's it, and you don't really make friends with people.

The theoretical concept of recognition is (as described earlier in our exposition of Honneth's theory) clearly distinct from its colloquial meaning of recognising someone in the sense of being able to match them with a memory of a previous encounter. Nonetheless, we would suggest that if the community you are teaching/learning in is so large that you cannot actually recognise someone in even this basic sense when you bump into them in a library, then any more substantive form of recognition – such as love/kindness or equality/partnership – becomes considerably more difficult! One reason for this might be that – again, as argued earlier – love and kindness are grounded in empathy. And empathy, in turn, relies on knowledge about another person – sufficient knowledge that you can put yourself meaningfully in their shoes and imagine the emotional impact of their circumstances. In other words, to enact care and kindness in a way that is meaningful, rather than passing or superficial, we need to know one another's *stories*. In the play *The Encounter*, actor Simon McBurney describes the power of stories for human relationships:

> "Stories [...] shape everything we see and believe in. [...] I remember my father reading me bedtime stories as a child that transported me to other places and times. And that was how, for the first time, I started to get inside someone else's head, and imagine what their experiences felt like. And now I get into bed with my children at night and tell them stories in the same way. I watch them empathising with the characters, discovering what connects and separates them from other people, other worlds. It is an intimate process. It seems empathy and proximity are connected." (McBurney, 2016:7)

The idea that empathy is facilitated by proximity seems like a powerful one in the context of education, and we were struck that a commonly-used word in participant descriptions of caring relationships in chapter 2 was "close" or "closeness". What are the consequences of this for a sector increasingly characterised not by *stories* but transactions, not by proximity but the kind of massification that necessitates staff standing in front of three hundred students in lecture theatres, both literally and figuratively at a distance?

Participants also noted the significance of the programme size for building relationships with staff based on equality and partnership – pointing, for instance, to familiarity being a key element in students 'feeling safe' speaking up about issues and having their voices heard:

> Marla: I feel comfortable in emailing my lecturers saying, 'I don't understand this' or 'I need clarification for the assessment' and I think because there's not many of us, or there's not, like, three hundred people. It's easier for them to hear our voices.

A similar point was made about relationships in the classroom in chapter 2, with participants arguing that small-group learning was a crucial part of them feeling safe expressing themselves. Participants often compared this to the context of lectures, where – despite the small size of the cohort *overall* – they still described feeling intimidated by the numbers in the room. This perception was echoed by staff, who specifically expressed a feeling that small-group seminars provide space for voices which might not normally get heard:

> Belle: For instance I think, like, the size of the seminars, right? That there are just, like, ten people. [...] I saw students over time, like, you know, for instance students that at first were more disengaged or more shy to express their opinions and then they felt in a sense more comfortable [...].

Echoing this from another direction, one staff member reflected on how – when facilitating a larger-than-usual seminar due to a staff shortage – they noticed a detrimental impact on student participation, particularly among 'quieter' students:

> Marnie: [E]ven fourteen people is too many for the kind of, like, intimate dialogue and openness we can achieve with a group of up to nine, but ideally five or six. [...] There's a reason the best learning takes place in small groups where everyone has a chance to speak. [...] [With the bigger group] I was so concerned by the way that quiet people I have worked with before just didn't say anything at all – because the group was just too big for comfort. [...] I couldn't keep in mind every person in the room and their needs, because there were just too many to keep track of whilst also being, like, present myself. And these are, like, practical issues which maybe seem ridiculously trivial – but they change everything.

Indeed, hooks has written explicitly about the impact of class sizes on the possibility for enacting true engaged pedagogy:

> "Th[ese] practices are undermined by sheer numbers. Rebelling against that has meant insisting on limits to classroom size. Overcrowded classrooms are like overcrowded buildings – the structure can collapse." (hooks, 1994:160)

Drastically increasing student numbers may make financial sense for universities seeking 'efficiencies' and may even have positive social justice connotations simply in terms of access to the sector, but the trade-off, unless the sector radically transforms in other respects, is the anonymity of crowds. The impact of this on people's university experience – whether as students or practitioners – seems incompatible with recognition, whether based on knowing and caring for one another, or based on forms of democracy and equal partnership. Indeed, the size of the programme increasing dramatically was one of the most consistently voiced staff concerns when discussing the sustainability of the programme's approach:

> Rosa: I think inevitably there will be pressure for [the programme] to get a bit bigger and I [...] don't think a bit bigger's always bad but I think there- if it got really really big... could it still- how would... it might still be possible, I'm sure we'd think of creative ways, but it would be quite hard then to have the kind of democratic approach of sort of everyone having a say over everything. I mean there'd be ways of doing it but it would be different. [And] just the relationships that we [...] all, as students and staff, think are really important. That would be more of a challenge. So I- I worry about it.

> Belle: I think a thing that would be important [for the programme] is to keep a relatively small number of students? [...] [T]hat would be, like, important- would be like essential [...] for the kind of identity of the programme. [...] [It's] not just that, you know, staff are [...] caring and kind and available but also, like, the [...] small size of the programme, right, makes this kind of interaction possible. And in a sense more- more human, right?

One final note on size: we are aware that students' points about feeling safe in seminars but not in the presence of the whole cohort raises questions around how safe they feel expressing themselves in the CCMs, which are open to the whole course community and therefore relatively large in size. The size of the CCMs wasn't raised explicitly in the data as a barrier to their functioning. It may also be that the reasons some people don't feel comfortable raising concerns in the CCMs are less to do with size and more to do with other issues, explored earlier, around a lack of familiarity or motivation to engage with this kind of deliberative forum. Nonetheless, some participants did point to people feeling "shy" (see Leanne below) and, given the feelings of comparative safety associated with the small-group seminars above, it is reasonable to assume that the number of people present might have something to do with it:

> Leanne: I feel like it should be, like, a safe space for people to bring up any concerns and I feel like at the moment some people are still quite shy? So they don't really speak about what they are feeling, so I think it would be nice if we can kind of find a way to get everybody to kind of be involved and kind of say how- what they feel.

Some participants did note the problem of people not feeling comfortable speaking openly when a large number of *staff* are present. Thus, although in chapter 3, participants highlighted the importance of staff being present at the CCMs, it is important to also recognise the power dynamics inevitably at play in this space. The programme may be working towards deconstructing hierarchy, but as hooks writes, staff have institutional and structural power over students in ways that cannot be ignored (2010). Moreover, staff are used to leading and being heard in educational spaces; inevitably, they sometimes forget (as Ali implies below) not to "dominat[e] the conversation":

> Ali: [S]taff kind of coming in [is good], but not dominating the conversation, as well? [The] previous CCM wasn't like that but I think that's because there wasn't a lot of staff anyway. But I think the previous two CCMs, like quite a few staff came and it was like- personally I didn't feel comfortable... speaking out.

In response to these concerns, facilitators and other participants called for greater experimentation with "creative techniques" (Rosa) in the CCMs for making people feel safe in sharing their opinions and ideas. Some of these related explicitly to breaking into groups that are smaller in *size:*

> Ali: I think breaking into groups, like smaller groups, but not just, like, those around [you], because typically people who [laughs] are friends or [...] people who are similar to one another tend to sit together, like group together, if that makes sense, so I feel like if we split into small groups that were completely random. [...] [Because] we all talk to each other [on the programme] but, like, I['d] say there's [a] certain closeness with certain people, when you talk to someone that you don't normally talk to as much, and kind of hear their perspectives [...] I feel like you'd get so much more, like, so much more diversity in thought.

Chapter 5.

Enacting Recognition Through the Politics of Difference: a key challenge for the programme

Samira Salam, Eleni Koutsouri, Minkyung Kim, SooYeon Suh, Tope Mayomi, and Freya Aquarone

Recognition and the politics of difference

In chapters 2 and 3 we talked about recognition as love and kindness, and as equality in the form of participatory democracy and engaged pedagogy. These were focused on ideas about how we should treat *everyone*, regardless of their different positionality or identity. Charles Taylor has called this the 'politics of universalism', where recognition "is meant to be universally the same, an identical basket of rights and immunities" (1994:37-38). Yet Taylor and other writers have challenged the idea that this goes far enough in realising recognition, particularly for those who *start out* in a position of structural marginalisation. In this case, 'equal' treatment in the sense of treating people identically may actually leave marginalisation in place, perpetuating forms of misrecognition. We see this when said treatment actually disproportionately benefits particular groups: for instance, standardised employment/admissions procedures may *seem* fair, but in fact they can reproduce the advantages of those already in positions of relative power, whether due to race, socioeconomic status, gender or a host of other factors. Giving every voice 'equal' airtime might seem equitable, but if certain voices are already privileged, express harmful views, or just outnumber the rest, does this simply reproduce marginalisation?

With these concerns in mind, Taylor lays out an alternative vision of recognition, grounded in what he calls the 'politics of difference'. This approach asks us to "recognize [...] the unique identity of [an] individual or group, their distinctness from everyone else. The idea is that it is *precisely this distinctness* that has been ignored, glossed over, *assimilated to a dominant or majority identity*" (Taylor, 1994:38, emphasis added). In other words, the politics of difference asks us to attend to the lived experiences of marginalised groups, and recognise that specific forms of affirmative action may be required to ensure equitable recognition.

Just to add to the unusual circumstances in which this book was written (a national strike and a pandemic), in May of this year (2020), demonstrations erupted across the globe in protest at the murder of George Floyd. The scale of these protests – mainly associated with the justice movement Black Lives Matter (BLM) – outstrips any civil action in the name of systemic racism which has taken place in recent years. In this context, it's as urgent as ever to talk about why generic commitments to 'equality as sameness' may not be enough. There has been widespread criticism of those who have adopted the slogan 'All Lives Matter' in response to the BLM protests, precisely on the basis that it misses the point; Black people are subject to *particular* injustices that a focus on universalism fails, quite literally, to recognise. Indeed, Fanon (1952) tells us how, historically, the attempts to break the cycle of Hegel's master-slave dialectic between the oppressor and the oppressed has been rooted in the former's imposition of their history and their norms onto the latter; framed as an act of 'sublation', this actually sub*sumes* people beneath assumptions of whiteness.

The critiques of universalism raised by the politics of difference highlight important questions for recognition on the programme. It is these questions to which we turn in this chapter, drawing on participant narratives around inclusion, marginalisation, freedom of speech and structural justice – which were, in fact, some of the most consistently articulated themes across our dataset. Thus, while the previous four chapters have been, by and large, about adopting a particular articulation of recognition and describing – albeit critically – the ways in which the programme may or may not manage to realise it, this chapter seeks to more explicitly problematise how we *define* recognition. It does this, in part, by relating the programme's practice to broader social justice aims around marginalisation and inequality in education. Much of this analysis implicitly relates back to the rest of the book's themes – particularly in section 5c, in which we explore where to draw the line on a commitment to democracy and partnership, and what ethical values should underpin those processes to prevent reproducing the priorities of the dominant group. We also explore the role and limits of kindness in relation to classroom practice, especially in relation to tackling – or inadvertently reproducing – marginalisation.

In some ways, then, this chapter is more of a discussion chapter. This is also reflected in the fact that it is more personal and normative in style when compared to the rest of the text. Most subsections of this chapter are written from a particular author's perspective, often grounded in their lived experiences, and each begins with an explanation of author positionality to explain the factors informing the writing and analysis. In section 5a, Samira Salam explores the importance of critical consciousness around students' lived experiences of race and class for ensuring recognition on the programme. In section 5b, Eleni Koutsouri critically explores how systematic inequalities in HE access can be seen to undermine recognition, and points to some of the factors which underpin the lack of demographic diversity within the programme community. Finally, in 5c, we grapple with the role of learning and teaching in relation to the politics of difference, exploring in particular the nature of 'freedom of speech' in the classroom. Namely, section 5c is about exploring the question of which voices should be foregrounded and/or challenged in the classroom in the name of recognition. Various authors provide their own ethical response to this question. These are not set up as opposing viewpoints, but rather have contrasting emphases and priorities. We felt that this multivocality would not only do justice to the diversity of opinions indicated by our data but would also be in the spirit of criticality and academic freedom.

5a – Class, 'race' and critical consciousness

Samira Salam

People's experiences of Higher Education are deeply affected by their positionality and privilege. The politics of difference requires us to take note of this; assuming that all students bring the same lived experiences and perspectives into the classroom, and can therefore engage in learning and socialising in the same way, obscures the deep differences that are there in reality. There is a large amount of research, for instance, about students who are working-class and/or people of colour and their experiences of Higher Education; this research demonstrates the alienation, exclusion and misrecognition many experience by the institution, teachers and peers (e.g. Reay et al., 2010; Crozier et al., 2016).

Being a first-generation student and coming from a Muslim, Bengali household, I embody the very sense of feeling unacknowledged and out of place within an establishment in the prestigious Russell Group. I have experienced first-hand what is known as 'imposter syndrome' – a feeling of lack of belonging both within an academic context and socially. My previous educational experiences have been in contexts where people have had similar backgrounds to my own – i.e. being part of an ethnic minority, and working-class. Being surrounded now by people in university that are predominantly from privileged backgrounds is new to me, and it can feel quite isolating being in such an unfamiliar position and feeling the need to assimilate to differing social norms.

For instance, a great deal of students in the cohort have had parents who have attended university, with some of their parents even being lecturers themselves. Although my parents have always encouraged me and my siblings to recognise the importance and value of education, in being the first one in the family to attend university, there is a lingering feeling of lack of academic confidence in comparison to my peers. I do not have parents who can provide advice on my assignments or just general advice about university – in a way you sort of feel on your own.

Outside of the classroom there is a heavy emphasis on clubbing and drinking culture – an activity I cannot and do not wish to engage with due to my cultural and religious background. It is difficult to feel a part of a community within the course you study and arguably within the wider university, when it feels like you have to partake in such activities to 'get to know people better'. Within the classroom your voice can sometimes feel ignored or not recognised as much, even when you have lived experience of particular social issues. Being around a largely homogeneous group, you can feel like the outsider and that people don't know you very well or try to understand your positionality and outlook on the world.

As such, I was struck by the fact that our data contained very little emphasis by participants on the way that race and class affect people's lived experiences of the programme. Where issues around race and class *were* raised, it was generally by students who were working-class and/or people of colour themselves. In this section, I seek to lay out this contradiction in the data. I suggest that there is a lack of 'critical consciousness' in the community around intersectional inequality – namely in relation to race and class – that needs to be rectified if the programme is to realise a commitment to recognition.

Defining class

Class is a highly contested term that has been defined in many ways. Traditionally, class has been associated with economic position and income. Although this is still highly influential in the way class is conceptualised, class arguably goes well beyond economic factors. French sociologist Pierre Bourdieu (1984) argues class takes into consideration three key factors known as types of 'capital':

> 1) *Economic capital* – referring to material wealth such as assets and income.
> 2) *Cultural capital* – referring to the ability to appreciate and engage with whatever society deems to be "high-status culture" (Throsby, 1999:4). This might include modes of dress, demeanour and attitudes held (for instance, within educational institutions this could refer to familiarity with academic approaches – what Reay et al. describe as a "degree of confidence

and entitlement in relation to academic knowledge" (Reay et al., 2010:109).

3) *Social capital* – referring to the contacts and connections individuals have which allows them to draw on their social networks to achieve social mobility or preserve socioeconomic privilege.

Bourdieu's point is that although these three capitals may overlap, they are also subtly different, and that it is possible to draw fine-grained distinctions between people with different stocks of each of the three capitals, to provide a much more complex model of social class than is generally used. This recognition that social class is a multidimensional construct indicates that classes are not merely economic phenomena but are also profoundly concerned with forms of social reproduction and cultural distinction. Bourdieu's influential scheme has recently been incorporated into a new model of defining social class by Savage et al., which concludes that Great Britain has seven established classes. The 'Great British Class Survey' lays out that although certain occupations (a traditionally used class 'proxy') may predominate in each class, people with the same occupation can be assigned to different classes after factoring in their cultural and social capital (Savage et al., 2013).

Despite Savage et al.'s work going into a great level of depth to construct a more thorough definition of class, we cannot go into this level of detail within the scope of this work because we did not ask for descriptions from participants about how they understand their class identity. Participants tended to refer to themselves as either 'middle' or 'working' class. This could be described as a methodological shortcoming, but we believe this self-identification on the part of participants' class identity is of importance because of all the ways in which people have described the significance of their class identity in feeling included or excluded on the programme. Thus, while we understand and appreciate the work undertaken to produce the nuanced taxonomies of class outlined within 'The Great British Class Survey' conducted by Savage et al., we will be using the terms 'working-class' and 'middle-class' as rough indicators in talking about our participants identification of class positionality.

The concept of the varying types of capital offered by Bourdieu *is* of relevance here however, because of the descriptions offered by individuals and how their class status affects their lived experience of the programme. Although these descriptions often made reference to economic factors (such as not being able to afford certain social activities) they also referred to issues associated with cultural and social capital, such as feelings or experiences of class-based imposter syndrome and lack of belonging. I will refer to these different forms of capital at various points in my analysis.

Defining 'race'

'Race' has been historically associated with the ideology of racism: the belief (originating in the so-called 'race science' of the 17th century) that certain physical characteristics – including not only skin colour but a whole range of aesthetic characteristics presumed to indicate 'difference' – offer a marker of biological and evolutionary inferiority or even sub/non-humanness (Hill Collins and Solomos, 2010). Nowadays, there is scientific consensus that race has no biological or genetic basis (Gannon, 2016). Accordingly, the term 'ethnicity' has become popular as an alternative descriptor because (it is claimed) it is based on self-identification with social and cultural factors, rather than physical characteristics (Malešević, 2004). Yet Malešević has argued that focusing on self-identifying cultural groups risks turning a blind eye to the ongoing pervasiveness of race as a social reality (2004); that is, regardless of the scientific reality, people continue to be *racialised* – to have identities and characteristics forcibly ascribed to them on the basis of perceived physical characteristics (Solomos and Solomos, 2005) including, but not restricted to, the 'colour of their skin'. In this way, the distinction between 'race' and 'ethnicity' is actually highly blurred; both are socially constructed categories based on the racialisation of people's bodies (Solomos and Solomos, 2005). We will therefore be using the term 'race' and racialised terms like 'Black' and 'Brown' and 'people of colour' interchangeably with 'ethnicity'. Using both concepts also mirrors the range of language used by participants to identify their own positionalities.

It is worth noting that, although helpfully distinct (and mostly analysed separately in this chapter because of the focus of participant data), race and class are deeply intersectional categories. Just as one example: Black and ethnic minority groups are 'overrepresented' in lower socioeconomic groups (Office for National Statistics, 2018) and are significantly more likely than white people to live in poverty (Platt, 2007). Thus, it is helpful to bear in mind that lived experiences of either race *or* class positionality in HE mutually implicate one another.

Defining critical consciousness

Definitions of critical consciousness vary quite widely, but we have chosen to focus on a description by Hopper – drawing on the work of Paulo Freire – of critical consciousness as "learning to see [...] how history works, how received ways of thinking and feeling perpetuate existing structures of inequality" (1999:13). This is similar to hooks' definition of critical thinking as, "us[ing] our imagination [to] see [...] things from perspectives other than our own and envisioning the likely consequences of our position" (2010:10, citing Barnet and Bedau, 2005). Indeed, bell hooks has written that this empathic understanding is fundamental to criticality: "The heartbeat of critical thinking is the longing to know—to understand how life works" (hooks, 2010:7).

In this section, we will be exploring the role of critical consciousness in relation to class and race, as defined above. I argue that our data indicates a certain lack of critical consciousness about how race and class deeply affect and mediate people's lived experiences of the programme. As noted above, Taylor's notion of the politics of difference (1994) asks us to take note of the ways that intersectional inequality and marginalisation affects people's lives; it suggests that attempts at recognition which do *not* attend to these differences risk leaving them intact. In line with this, I believe that developing greater critical consciousness within our community – particularly around race and class – is integral to our attempts to foreground recognition.

What are participants' perceptions of the demographic?

When asked about the programme community's demographic, the vast majority of participants spoke primarily about gender and/or nationality.

For instance, many students described the programme as "diverse" because of its internationalism:

> Selena: The first thing I [thought] about when I heard your question was that we all come from different backgrounds, different countries, and it's amazing for me because that brings so much into the course and to our discussions and hearing people from all around the world sharing their experiences and opinions.

> Rachel: [Y]eah I think it's diverse because [...] we're such, like, a small cohort but then there's [...] people from so many different countries? So I think that's really special.

Many also lamented the cohort's lack of diversity in relation to gender, suggesting quite explicitly that they felt a perspective was missing from the classroom as a result of the lack of male students:

> Researcher: How does the demographic of students and staff influence how the course is experienced?
> Rachel: I think gender... like obviously, there's like five boys, and half of them don't even show up. [...] So there's not much gender dynamic on the course.
> Tia: I think gender, like, matters to some extent because like [laughs] we're only- like we're a lot of like... girls... which is, I don't know, a problem to some extent? Because I don't- you don't get the other... side, the other opinion about anything?

> Ryleigh: The demographic thing about guys and girls [...]. I think it [would] be really [...] interesting for this course to be [more] mixed... interesting debates, discussions, to see different points of view.

However, while gender and nationality are certainly significant features of the programme demographic, comparatively few people extended their analysis to discussions of race and class. Some participants did acknowledge that the demographic of the programme community is predominantly middle-class, with an even smaller number referring to the dominance of 'whiteness':

Selena: [...] [W]e all come from, well similar levels, in the sense that we all come from our middle-class families.

Tia: [...] [I]f we're in a seminar room and everyone [is] like middle-class, white, you know sort of the same age and like, kind of similar background and education [...] things like that. I feel like the conversation will be [laughs] trapped in the same [...] small circle, you know, and we go around, because [...] we all share similar experiences and it's hard to talk on behalf of someone else, you know? So yeah I feel like we could have more diversity...

Thus, it is clear that some participants had an awareness of a demographic imbalance along lines of class and race. What I will argue in the sections below, however, is that this differs from evidence of critical consciousness in two key ways. Firstly, very few participants, in discussing these demographic factors, acknowledged how minority groups on the programme might be impacted, nor how their own positionality might affect their perceptions. Indeed, the 'invisibilising' of experience outside a single demographic frame of reference is perhaps already implicated by the use in the extracts above of terms like "we all" or "everyone" to refer to middle-class and/or white positionality! Secondly, those who did directly acknowledge the lived experience of students in 'the minority' were, almost exclusively, students identifying as working-class and/or Black, Brown or a member of an ethnic minority group; many of these participants felt that there is insufficient consideration among the wider cohort of differences along lines of race and class, both in classroom discussions and other aspects of community life, like socialising.

Class and 'race': do they actually matter?

A lack of class consciousness is indicated in participants' suggestions that social class does not affect people's lived experiences of the programme:

Rachel: But we don't really talk about our social class that much. So I don't really feel that there's, like, a major gap there and I think what's really special as well is that we don't discriminate [against] people on our course? Like, we're all... like, really united, so even if there is, like, a difference, we tend to kind of look past that difference and just see those people as like people?

Susan: [The demographic] [...] would never be an obstacle for making friendships, or bonding together, or, so this would never be a problem in this sense, so I do feel like, yeah, obviously the majority of people, like, in Higher Education in general are one group of people, like mostly middle-class, but I do feel that in our course it's not- doesn't make any difference, if someone is not.

Marla: [...] [W]ith class I don't think I was aware of it [...] but then when we started talking about class privilege that's where people opened up and I realised that... people were very open, they were not judgmental about whether they came from different classes or not.

These participants seem to imply that the fact that most people don't talk about their class positionality means there is not "a major gap" or "difference" in terms of people's experiences of the programme, and that there is absence of "discriminat[ion]" and "judgement". In other words, because we don't talk about our own social class standing that much, it must mean that social class is not a barrier or factor affecting students on the course.

Meanwhile others seem to consider class positionality as affecting lived experience on the programme only after being asked a specific question around whether it does. Marla, for instance, acknowledged that they did not really think about it until curriculum content on class privilege was presented to them explicitly. They then echo Rachel by suggesting that when people *did* "ope[n] up" about their positionality they "were not judgmental" about whether other students came from different class backgrounds to themselves. This may well be the case in some instances, but it differs from accounts where students from under-represented groups have felt excluded from social events or classroom activities (explored more below). Such exclusion contrasts with claims that the demographic of the cohort "would never be an obstacle for making friendships, or bonding together" and that although most people in Higher Education are middle-class, that it "doesn't make any difference, if someone is not" (Susan). There is a sense among participants that, on the programme, "we tend to [...] look past that [...] difference and just see those people as [...] people?" (Rachel). This is in essence describing what Charles Taylor calls the 'politics of universalism' (as previously discussed) (1994). This idea of 'seeing people as people' however does not adequately address why minority groups for example may *still* feel marginalised and under-acknowledged within HE spaces (as we will explore further on). I would argue that this is precisely why a politics of difference – which attends more explicitly to people's lived experiences of marginalisation – is needed and why developing greater critical consciousness is a key step within that.

With regard to why students may not talk about their social class that much in general, it seems likely that this is grounded in the demographic that makes up the programme – the feeling that many students come from a middle-class background may lead working-class individuals to feel excluded in talking about their experiences (myself included) as it is difficult to feel "comfortable exercising [one's] right to 'free speech' [...] if it means [...] giv[ing] voice to thoughts, ideas, feelings that go against the grain" (hooks, 1994:179). As Reay et al. found in their research of working-class students in HE, when a small minority of working-class students were present amongst a predominantly large number of middle-class students, some would "approach [...] the subject of social class apologetically, as if it should no[t] [...] have any relevance for them" (Reay et al., 2010:113). This is perhaps also reflected within our project data – exemplified by the dominance of the belief that social class does not have that much bearing in shaping an individual's experience on the programme.

If we look towards the *race* consciousness of the cohort, we find a similar picture in that many participants do not appear actively aware of race/ethnicity affecting the course community. This is demonstrated in the extract below:

> Ali: I think [a major obstacle is] unconscious bias, but I don't know how you overcome that. I mean, we're all going to have certain biases I think, I think it's inevitable. But, I mean, I don't know how to put it into words, but we've got a range of nationalities which is a great

thing, but then, I would say that if you came into, say, the lecture you can kind of see the [demographic] breakdown if that makes sense... I don't know if it was just for me, but it was prevalent and I could see a split in the room.

Researcher: Did anyone else see a split like that?

Meira: Well, now that it's mentioned, I do feel like there's- but it- but I don't think that the community as a whole is in any way [...] 'less' because of this, or not as strong, or close-knit, or whatever. [...] I actually never thought about this, but I do think to some extent it's true, but I don't think that [...] it does anything to the quality of the community, like, as a whole. Because obviously [...] everyone will find one or two people that are really close [to them] because [...] [you] cannot be friends equally with everyone, but at the same time there is- on a whole community level I don't feel like [it] makes a difference, if that makes sense.

Ali is a student who identified in their interview as coming from an ethnic minority background and above notes seeing a "split in the room" when coming into lectures, referring to a divide in seating by nationality and ethnicity, as was observed by another participant (also part of an ethnic minority group):

Rachel: Some of the international students, like the Asians, still stick together, like the home students [...] and the Europeans... you kind of see it. Especially when we sit in [...] lecture[s], where there are tables, you kind of see the friend groups. We're still all friends with each other but we tend to stick to our own backgrounds.

Meira, however, is not as quick to see this 'divide' and only reflects on this after Ali has spoken about it. Moreover they reiterate their belief that they do not "think that the community as a whole is [...] less because of this, or not as strong, or close knit", seeming to deny that this "split" may be damaging community cohesion or affecting students' experiences. Had Ali not communicated the perception of a "breakdown", would the thought have crossed the other participant's mind? I pose that this would be unlikely as, by definition, to think critically and consciously is to (as referred to before), "envision [...] the likely consequences of our position" (hooks, 2010:10, citing Barnet and Bedau, 2005). Yet this participant did not anticipate the problem of division, denying that its existence is significant.

Our data indicates that there is a limit to the extent of critical consciousness around race and class on the programme. In the next section, we will explore descriptions of lived experience of marginalisation on the programme by working-class and/or Black, Brown and ethnic minority participants.

Case study: A lecture on class privilege

One rare occasion in the data where participants did problematise representations of class identity on the programme was in relation to representations of middle-class experience:

> Helena: [...] I recall [...] that we had a lecture on class, I think? Or, like, class upbringing?
> Sarah: Oh, is this the middle-class parenting?
> Helena: Yeah, yes! Where I felt like the lecturer in the way that they held the lecture, they were implying that one way of parenting – that I think a good part of the cohort actually experienced when they were younger [...] – was wrong? It was like they were [implying it was] somewhat controlling or limiting to [...] children and that was- not infuriating but it was definitely... confused me a bit because I don't think you can say it outright like that! I think it's a scale and it's also really specific to like individual parents and like there's so much more to it.

Helena and Sarah are referring to a lecture about Lareau's research on different parenting approaches in middle- and working-class families in the US. Lareau's work claims that, broadly speaking, middle-class families tended towards an approach they label "concerted cultivation", whereby parents have a more interventionist approach to parenting, organising children's free-time accordingly with activities such as piano lessons or football practice which allows them to "acquire skills that could be valuable in the future when they enter the world of work" (Lareau, 2003:4). By contrast, Lareau suggested that working-class families tended towards aiming for "the accomplishment of natural growth" for their children, whereby parenting style is less interventionist and more hands-off in comparison to middle-class parenting (ibid.); child-initiated play is emphasised, as opposed to organised leisure activities, most often due to financial constraints, meaning such children are unlikely to reap the benefits of "important institutional advantages" (ibid.).

It is important to question, as Helena does, whether Lareau's accounts are truly applicable to the range of parenting approaches in the world. However, the readiness to read any critical analysis of middle-class parenting as implying strongly negative judgement – e.g. "controlling or limiting" parenting – suggests a quite high level of sensitivity about class representation. Given that it is narratives of working-class parenting which are usually subject to such fierce criticism and homogenising or deficit narratives in politics and the press (De Benedictis, 2012), it's in some ways a shame that it's only representations of middle-class experience that are being questioned here. Particularly as Lareau's account explicitly avoids making normative judgement, but simply seeks to highlight the reproduction of privilege in a social system which more readily rewards particular forms of parenting. What we need is this degree of criticality in relation to representations of working-class experience. Yet this was less evident in the data; in fact, some participants suggested they had witnessed "deficit narratives" or damaging representations of working-class experience within the programme community, and suggested that this might be caused by a lack of awareness due to "positionality" and "privilege":

> <u>May</u>: Yeah, okay, so the demographic of the cohort, it's very interesting because a lot of the people seem to not care about the stuff we are talking about, which I don't know where that stems from- class privilege, maybe? And just not caring about stuff going on to poor people.

> Joe: I think the students bring into the room, as do we as staff, our- their own positionality in the world and, like, this can sometimes lead to people saying things that are based on a particular perspective that- they may not have witnessed other perspectives and therefore can [...] you know, inadvertently – not

> intentionally – kind of [be] reinforcing [of] stereotypes or using discourse that's actually quite, you know- for example, sort of, deficit language around working-class people.
>
> This case study suggests that the programme community needs to do more to extend its critical consciousness of experiences beyond those with a middle-class positionality, as well as to deconstruct deficit narratives and assumptions about working-class identities.

But what about people's lived experiences?

Our data demonstrate that, despite some participants' claims above, race and class *do* have a significant impact on people's lived experiences of the programme. This further underlines the importance of greater critical consciousness: we need to address the fact that not everyone experiences the same space in the same way As Young puts it, "social justice [...] requires not the melting away of differences, but institutions that promote reproduction of and respect for group differences without oppression" (Young, 1990:47). This is effectively echoing Taylor's argument that 'universalism' erases the realities of differential lived experience. That is, ignoring the fact that these differences *do* exist, can lead to forms of exclusion, as illustrated by the accounts below.

People feeling that they don't fit in

One way in which students may feel excluded within the programme is in feeling that they don't fit in or belong on the course, as one participant put it:

> <u>Ali</u>: So there are quite a few home students but, like, [laughs] sometimes I feel like I can't... even empathise with them, so sometimes in certain situations I feel like the only one... and I have to like look outside of the course to kind of find my people, if that makes sense. [...] So [...] sometimes [with where I come from]- like, people don't understand like the struggles? And, like, I find that I

have to go to like- for example- in- at King's we have 'First Generations', to find people like me, 'cos I- we don't have it on this course, I don't think so then that's kind of like a time where I live and like.... Like my class- like, I don't really think about class a lot, like, 'Oh I'm working-class' but it's just... yeah when you see like people with Macbooks for example [laughs] and, like, just other stuff and they're just talking about it like it's normal. It's not normal for me.

The language used by Ali here is particularly interesting and in a sense implies the student has feelings of imposter syndrome – of feeling like a "fish out of water" (Reay et al., 2009:1104), possibly also experiencing what could be called 'culture shock' (Bowl, 2003; Reay et al., 2009), exemplified by phrases such as, "I feel like the only one" and "people don't understand the struggles". Ali identifies as being a first-generation student – that is "students whose parents have not obtained a Higher Education qualification" (Spiegler and Bednarek, 2013:318). There is research evidence that first-generation students may be more susceptible to feelings of imposter syndrome and feeling out of place at university (Spiegler and Bednarek, 2013). As such, Ali expresses in their interview that they attend events hosted by the First Generation Network (a student network to support those who are the first in their families to go to university) at King's to "find people like me" and to "find my people". The use of the word "my" is telling of how the participant feels the need to find people that they can identify with and relate to, indicating that they do not resonate as much with the middle-class majority present in the cohort – they look elsewhere to share their "struggles".

Ali's experience as a working-class student also intersects with issues around race and ethnicity. A substantial body of research has shown that students from certain ethnic minorities are both *more* likely to be first-generation students and *less* likely to come from socioeconomically privileged backgrounds (e.g. Spiegler and Bednarek, 2013; Gibbons et al., 2011; Terenzini et al. 1996). They may feel the need to associate with other Black, Asian and Minority Ethnic students to find shared understanding and solace (Bhopal, 2010; Crozier et al., 2010). Ali's intersectional experience in being a first-generation student, coming from an ethnic minority background, *and* identifying as working-class can lead to particularly powerful forms of exclusion.

Bourdieu's concepts of capital – and their associated idea of 'habitus' – are useful here for understanding the "struggles" faced by such students. Bourdieu describes 'habitus' as "a power of adaptation [...] constantly perform[ing] an adaptation to the outside world which only occasionally takes the form of radical conversion" (Bourdieu, 1993:88). In other words, it is the way individuals perceive the social world around them and react to it; these predispositions are usually shared by people with similar backgrounds to one another and are rarely changed drastically. The availability of the three types of capital – (1) economic capital, (2) cultural capital and (3) social capital – impacts the nature of a person's 'habitus', as we delve into below.

We have mentioned the term 'culture shock' – an experience a person may have when they move to a cultural environment which is different to their own. Archer and Leathwood have argued that the assumption within HE institutions (that again are predominately made up of middle-class students) is that, "the working class individual [...] must adapt and change, in order to fit into, and participate in, the (unchanged) Higher Education institutional culture" (Archer and Leathwood, 2003:176). Thereby a power struggle persists within university as the 'dominant culture' endures in various ways – from what is offered in the curriculum to organisational practices – leading to marginalisation and exclusion of working-class and/or Black, Brown and Minority Ethnic students. This feeling of 'not belonging' is heightened even further if such students attend more 'prestigious' universities such as King's because, in general, first-generation students are, "more likely to study [...] at less prestigious universities" (Spiegler and Bednarek, 2013:324), meaning the proportion of students from disadvantaged backgrounds at an institution like King's would be far smaller. As noted in Eleni Koutsouri's upcoming section about broader inequalities in HE access, 'fitting in' is more likely to be a challenge if students feel part of the minority.

The issue of *economic* capital is also relevant in considering the extent to which students feel they fit in. To return once again to Ali's narrative above, their description of seeing individuals in the classroom with "Macbooks" and this not being "normal" for them, indicates a lack of access to material resources that others may take for granted. Economic capital evidently has practical implications (e.g. not all students can afford a laptop at all, let alone a Macbook!) but it can also have a *symbolic* impact on a student's sense of belonging. In Ali's case, the normalisation of highly expensive laptops as part of the 'student learning experience' is another way of implicitly reinforcing feelings that they 'don't belong' and that their individual habitus and the institutional habitus of the university do not match up.

People feeling excluded from social events

Another way students coming from ethnic minority backgrounds and/or identifying as working-class can feel excluded is due to the types of normalised social activities. This was noted by a staff member, Belle:

> Belle: [...] [F]or instance I [had] [...] a conversation with students, who said, you know, there were social activities that, like, social groups and they were mostly like going to a bar where there were expensive cocktails and mostly like white people. And in a sense that's kind of normal because like lots of the majority of students are also, like, white and coming from privileged backgrounds, right? So in a sense [...] that also means that some students might disengage, or they might feel 'well I'm not part of that'.

Although Belle seems to equate economic privilege here with 'whiteness' and that is not necessarily always the case, they are nonetheless highlighting an important point about the fact that, to their knowledge, some students have felt excluded from certain social activities which have been based on assumptions of privilege. Notably this also highlights the way that, in HE spaces, people tend to stick in clusters of people of a similar background to themselves (e.g. see Warikoo, 2016), thereby indicating that social class and background do have a bearing on the forming and maintaining of university relationships.

This is problematic to say the least. As Belle puts, "some students might disengage, or they might feel 'well I'm not part of that'" as, indeed, some students expressed in their interviews. I sympathise with this sentiment having felt these very feelings due to my own positionality. For instance, the activity of going to a bar with "expensive cocktails" excludes working-class students in the sense they are unlikely to afford the costs of such drinks and thereby may miss out on the opportunity to 'get to know' their peers better. Practising Muslims also won't be able to engage in such activity as they do not drink in accordance with their religion. This maintains the lack of social capital for groups disconnected from social events because in the long term these students are "less likely to be engaged in the academic and social experiences that foster success in college such as [...] interacting with [...] other students [and] participating in extracurricular activities" (Engle and Tinto, 2008:3). This continues the cycle of exclusion and marginalisation of minority groups.

It raises the question: how can we have a community feel within the programme if students are being excluded in this manner? We *all* need to be more conscious of our own actions and positionality in relation to others – the debate does go beyond class and race, we also need to consider factors such as religion, LGBTQ+, dis/ability[24], gender and so forth and really think about how to include everyone in the picture – creating a truly inclusive culture outside of the classroom too.

People feeling excluded in the classroom

Our data indicated that feelings of exclusion along lines of race and class are present within the classroom too:

> May: When talking about race, lots of voices in the classroom say very ignorant stuff such as, and I quote, 'there is no more racism in the UK'. [...]
> Rebecca: Yeah, I mean [...] saying something [like] [...] 'it doesn't exist anymore' is invalidating people's experiences in the room.

---

24 Language around disability is varied and contested, but our use of a forward slash here seeks "to highlight the constructed and interdependent nature of both ability and disability" and to challenge 'ableist' assumptions which centre "deficit meanings of disability" (Annamma et al., 2018:65).

> Maya: When I describe the dominant group I would say Western middle-class European. [...] When there's not as many people in the room who share my positionality, I feel less comfortable speaking out, [and] it typically tends to be those Western middle-class students speaking and when you're talking about class or say, even the environment for example, like their perspectives differ from like say mine coming from like an Asian country that – I dunno, is more impacted by the environment for example and I feel like environmental policies are say, like tailored- not in favour of, like, working-class people, 'cos I'm also working class. So, like, it can get a bit frustrating when, like, their voices are like – I feel like... the discussion's kind of dominated [by] their kind of policy ideas when... like- but then that's the reality in real life.

Maya notes that it can be "frustrating" when discussions are centred around mainstream policy ideas that traditionally aren't in favour of working-class groups, but that "that's the reality in real life". This implies that the course mirrors real-world inequalities in terms of who has more of a voice. It seems this student is fed up of discussions leaning a certain way – i.e. favouring policies and ideologies which relate to "Western, middle-class" perspectives; however they are uncomfortable speaking up, as they feel they are the only one in the room with a differing viewpoint.

An even more clear-cut example of marginalisation in the classroom is provided by May and Rebecca when discussing claims about the absence of racism, and how this "invalidates" the lived experiences of people in the room (this is explored further in section 5c where we discuss examples of classroom marginalisation in more depth as well as ways of tackling it).

Conclusions and ways forward

Our data indicates that there is a general lack of critical consciousness within our programme community of lived experiences of race and class. This is despite the fact that some participants described varying forms of class and race-based exclusion. This leads to the question: 'How can we rectify the situation?' In response, I suggest three 'calls to action' (these are not exhaustive but are drawn from the main issues highlighted in our data). Some of these are about tackling specific forms of exclusion, rather than strategies for building critical consciousness *per se*, but all have implications for the overall critical consciousness of our community:

a) Inclusion for all in social events and activities

We need to ensure that programme social and community events do not exclude people on the basis of their positionality. For instance, assumptions around what people can afford when going out together could lead to students without access to the level of disposable income being excluded. Events happening at particular times of day could exclude students who have to maintain employment (more likely in the case of working-class students – see Moreau and Leathwood, 2006), or have caring/family responsibilities (much more likely in the case of 'mature students' (Ross et al., 2002), a group which working-class students are also significantly more likely than their middle-class peers to fall into (Egerton, 2001)). Given the strong intersection of class and race noted earlier, these factors are likely to have connotations for Black, Brown and ethnic minority students also.

Separately, the strong emphasis on bars and clubs in student culture (as previously mentioned) could prevent particular cultural/religious groups like Muslims from mixing with other students, as these institutional arrangements can separate those who drink from those who do not, causing Muslim students to become socially excluded (Andersson et al., 2012). Although exclusion due to religion is different to exclusion on the basis of class or race, these factors can be *and* often are intersectional in nature. We need to consider how culturally exclusive events often have consequences for *racial/ethnic* exclusion. Therefore, a recommendation is that greater critical consciousness is applied to the planning of social events – e.g. arranging more non-alcoholic events and considering cost and time of day – so that as many students as possible will feel more comfortable in attending and 'recognised' as a result.

b) Greater levels of students from disadvantaged and/or ethnic minority backgrounds being able to access our programme

Students from more disadvantaged and/or ethnic minority backgrounds being able to access Russell Group institutions such as King's is of great importance – not only for tackling exclusion, but also for the critical consciousness of the community as a whole. This is due to the implication that our ability to develop critical consciousness is inevitably affected by *who is in the room*. Having an all-white staff team and not very diverse cohort will not progress our levels of critical consciousness to the level needed. Indeed, our data suggested that the people who have demonstrated a greater degree of critical consciousness tended, perhaps unsurprisingly, to be those with lived experience of marginalisation/non-recognition. We need to think deeply about how to ensure more people with said lived experiences actually get into HE so they are not in a minority all the time (this is explored more by Eleni Koutsouri in the next section).

That being said, it should also be noted that we need to attend to *intersectional diversity*. For instance, a fair amount of students on the course may fall under the commonly-used 'general category' of BAME (Black, Asian and Minority Ethnic). However many still come from highly economically privileged backgrounds, and don't necessarily bring the kinds of lived experiences of marginalisation into the room that people of colour from less wealthy backgrounds would bring, as one participant pointed out (albeit somewhat bluntly!):

> Rebecca: [...] [T]he majority of the students are from, yeah, from the West and the ones that aren't are incredibly rich and have very different experiences to maybe, like [...] the average experience of, like, a person of colour that isn't filthy rich.

Therefore, when it comes to developing critical consciousness through diversifying demographics, we need to be aware of the way that race and class intersect to produce *particular* lived experiences, which vary widely depending on people's specific positionalities. We cannot reduce our aims to a tick-box exercise in which we simply seek to increase HE access to people who fall within a single umbrella category such as BAME. This is important in terms of critical consciousness in general – not just in terms of admissions practice. We need to develop an understanding of how intersectionality produces widely different lived experiences along lines of race and class, as well as other axes of marginalisation; doing so will ensure we can separately identify the right support for each individual group's needs.

c) Creating a greater level of critical consciousness through our pedagogy

At the same time as recognising the unique value of people with lived experience, we need to avoid relying on those who are already facing intersectional marginalisation to 'educate' everyone else. We need to develop critical consciousness amongst *everybody*, regardless of who is actually in the room. We need to reflect more as a programme community about how to do this, but one obvious space is through our classroom practice. This is explored in some depth in section 5c, which explores addressing marginalisation through learning and teaching.

We *all* (students and staff alike) collectively need to understand that class and race *are* relevant and need to reflect more explicitly on how it can impact students' experience of the programme and Higher Education more widely. This critical consciousness around race, class and other intersectional forms of marginalisation is a core part of realising the programme's commitment to recognition. The above 'calls to action' are a non-exhaustive list of steps in the right direction towards the development of greater critical consciousness on the programme. They touch on a number of core themes which will be explored in greater depth in the remainder of this chapter.

5b – The effects of institutional and societal structures on access to HE

Eleni Koutsouri

As a white, straight woman from a middle-class background, I occupy a position of privilege which fits the 'traditional student identity' of an elite institution. That means that I have never experienced discrimination based on my class, race, or sexual orientation. My academic journey as a student will likely not be questioned but praised instead. However, completing all 12 years of education in Greece at a school where English was not taught, as well as being the first person in my family to attend university, has in some cases meant that I had to try twice as hard to reach the institution's academic level or adapt to the significantly different educational system in the UK. Sometimes, these challenges have been exacerbated by gendered expectations around women and academic success, as well as prejudiced political ideas; for instance, I have experienced people doubting my academic abilities and potential for the future based on my appearance or even my country's financial and political situation. Nevertheless, due to my privileged position in society I had the means to help me overcome these challenges. Writing this piece has helped me reflect on uncomfortable truths and has shifted my attention to the importance of listening. Listening to unheard and unrepresented voices, listening to the echoes of established inequalities, listening to ways of improvement. I am now on a journey of breaking patterns, knowledge and narratives in order to create space for new ones to be born, but that is only the beginning.

"By believing passionately in something that still does not exist, we create it. The non-existent is whatever we have not sufficiently desired." (Nikos Kazantzakis, 1961)

Creating the non-existent and the unconventional requires faith, passion, action. Some would even say that it requires 'trust in the process'. The nature of 'from scratch' creation is indeed complex and, in many cases, frightening. However, the change we are trying to achieve in the BASS programme lies on pre-existent territory. Higher Education in the UK has taken many forms and has grown with and adapted to societal development throughout the years, leaving behind a legacy of norms, patterns and ideals which comprise the foundation of the system to this day. When we live in a world where change is society's deepest need and desire, how easy is it to change the root complexity of an already grown tree? But while some patterns may seem invincible to change, even the tallest, strongest tree's roots meet and intermingle with the roots of surrounding trees. Thus, change is *not* a utopian concept; maybe the 'non-existent' is just something that we have not yet fought for hard enough?

Although our programme's ethos is strongly correlated with a desire for social change, we are facing challenges that derive from the wider institutional as well as societal context. If action is the ultimate form of theory, maybe we need to ask: what needs to change when *talking about* change? McArdle and Mansfield suggest we need to appreciate the importance of 'voice' in discourses of change:

> "Voice refers to a quality beyond practical language or choices. Voice in a context of the desire for change or transformation implies the need for a balanced understanding of self, expressing a personal discourse about important aspects of life. Voice is critical to those who seek change for themselves and those who seek change for others" (2007:490).

One way of understanding the voice of our programme is as its *demographic,* which the data of this project suggest is not as diverse as it seems on first glance and, moreover, reflective of wider inequalities in the HE sector:

Rebecca: I think our course, the makeup of our course reflects, wider, higher, problems within higher [education] institutions, Higher

Education problems, in that, you know, you're more likely to go to university if you're white middle-class, and that's reflected on our course in terms of the demographic in the room.

Why diversity in HE matters for recognition

'Who gets a voice' is a crucial concern of recognition theory which has been considered throughout this piece. At the start of this chapter, we explained how ideas of recognition based on the politics of difference problematise the idea that a simple commitment to giving everyone a voice is enough when it comes to tackling injustice and marginalisation (Taylor, 1994); if the voices which form the majority, or the voices which get the biggest platforms, are given equal weight to those which are silenced or oppressed, then isn't there a danger that 'universal' treatment ends up reproducing voicelessness (hooks, 1994)? If, by contrast, we believe that pursuing meaningful recognition requires us to focus on 'making space' for voices which are usually sidelined, this has significant connotations for education practice: it means we need to think about not only who gets a voice in the room and how, but *who gets into the room in the first place.*

"Valuing difference and [...] building democratic and organic practices that are responsive to and reflective of the voices of diverse constituents" (McLeod, 2011:181) is an important goal of Higher Education. This diversity is important for its own sake for enriching the pedagogical process: that is to say, that the more diverse the chorus of voices in the classroom, the more opportunity there is for learning to become more open-minded and understanding. As one participant puts it, "we have to have different opinions and to see different things to make our own opinion" (Erica). But diversity also has deep implications for tackling marginalisation. For instance, O'Donnell et al. (2009) describe the importance of 'the politics of listening' – an explicit commitment in educational spaces to shift the balance from speaking to listening, in an attempt to deconstruct the dominance of certain narratives. The right balance of *voicing* and *listening* can be an incredibly useful tool in acknowledging that there is no single truth and acknowledging that certain important voices may have actually been historically silenced.

Indeed, some students in our data pointed to how, when a certain demographic dominates the space, it can make it difficult for the minority to speak up. Maya, for instance, spoke about feeling that it can be hard to be 'heard', as an Asian working-class student, when "Western middle-class" experiences are the norm:

> Maya: When I describe the dominant group I would say Western middle-class European. [...] When there's not as many people in the room who share my positionality, I feel less comfortable speaking out, [and] it typically tends to be those Western middle-class students speaking [...].. So, like, it can get a bit frustrating when, like, their voices are like – I feel like... the discussion's kind of dominated [by] their kind of policy ideas when... like- but then that's the reality in real life.

If, as Maya puts it, these inequalities are "the reality in real life" and not just in the classroom, then failing to consider *who* gets listened to could end up reproducing misrecognition. We might therefore have to ask – not only who speaks for who, but *"whose voice speaks loudest"* too (McLeod, 2011:183, emphasis added). Evidently, this is not just about 'who gets in the room', but also about the dynamics of the space[25]. But, if there is such a demographic imbalance in the classroom in the first place, it is perhaps significantly more likely that people in the minority will feel sidelined. According to McLeod, voice is a "socially embedded practice, with institutional, collective and cultural histories that shape not only what is heard and recognized but also how difference and inequality are registered and negotiated" (2011:185-186). In other words, our own voices are always speaking from particular vantage points, conditioned and positioned by society. Indeed, participants themselves pointed to how people's positionality can sometimes lead them to reproduce problematic narratives:

> May: All these structures of oppression that we're talking about exists in the classroom too. It's not void [...] – the same stuff is going on. And yeah, I get that everyone can say what they want to say. But

---

[25] This is explored in greater depth in section 5c.

people talking about stuff they don't really know about, in a way that comes off as- not comes off as, *is* damaging.

Joe: I think the students bring into the room, as do we as staff, our-their own positionality in the world and, like, this can sometimes lead to people saying things that are based on a particular perspective that- they may not have witnessed other perspectives and therefore can [...] you know, inadvertently – not intentionally – kind of [be] reinforcing [of] stereotypes or using discourse that's actually quite, you know- for example, sort of, deficit language around working-class people.

Rebecca: I mean all the staff are white, to my knowledge? [...]. [And] the majority of the students are from the West and the ones that aren't are incredibly rich, and have very different experiences to maybe, yeah, the experiences are very different to the average experience of a person of colour. [...] I think, because a lot of people on the course haven't got these lived experiences and these topics are new to them, it does mean that the conversations we have are very entry-level [...]. Even if you haven't studied [...] race before, if you're a Black person in the UK, then you can offer something to that discussion that isn't, like, 'Is race a social construct?', if that makes sense? 'Cos you have your lived experiences and you can understand how society works and, and how being of a certain race impacts how you navigate through life.

Evidently, some of this could be solved by the forms of critical consciousness which Samira Salam called for in the previous section. Nonetheless, if students – and staff – come predominantly from similar backgrounds, however reflexive or critically conscious they may be, their voices can only ever capture part of the story; and the collective learning process will be necessarily restricted. Of course, it's important we don't end up arguing that it's the 'job' of marginalised groups to 'educate' people on their privilege, as Rebecca and May noted in their discussion of labour in the classroom:

Rebecca: So, do you think that if we're talking about the experiences of [people of colour], that the seminar tutor should allow you to lead the discussion? Or is that too much labour on you? How do we navigate that, when the demographics are so skewed in the classroom?

May: That's very interesting. [...] If it was a discussion on people of colour['s] experiences I would expect me to be given a chance to talk, of course. But, also, I don't think it should just be me talking the entire time.

Indeed, we are currently seeing widespread evidence of Black activists being bombarded by requests on social media to 'educate' people about white privilege and this simply reproduces inequalities in terms of intellectual labour! But what I am suggesting is that students and teachers – especially those in positions of privilege – have a responsibility, in the name of recognition, to both educate themselves in a general sense but also to *listen* to marginalised voices in the classroom, and to acknowledge our collective responsibility to make space for them. Thus, sociologist Les Back issues a call to action:

"Listen to your own voice and develop a mild aversion to it. Hearing yourself recorded on tape is a good way to achieve this. It may produce a situation where we become more judicious, careful and measured in what we say, and more able to stop talking and listen." (2010)

It is true that speaking holds a great sense of responsibility, but so does listening. In the context of conversations about injustice in the classroom, listening could be a useful mechanism in shifting the responsibility for recognition from the speaker to the listener (ibid.). A more diverse cohort could reduce the possibilities of some social groups talking on behalf of others as well as the dominance of certain voices. Expressing opinions or arguing for your own truth can be challenging within a primarily homogeneous space. And although some participants agree on freedom of speech being of great value for our conversations, others argue that the fear of provoking a debate or hurting someone by voicing their views results in a general homogeneity in opinions. Indeed, several participants suggested that conflict and debate are often avoided within our community. Would a more heterogeneous demographic allow more space for debate and conflicting opinions to co-exist in the same room? It is logical to think that it would. The homogeneity of the cohort and therefore of the cohort's voice risks the reproduction of silencing certain narratives as well as a detrimental effect on our efforts for a reflexive approach to learning. Thus, while our concern goes well beyond the diversity of the cohort, widened access to our course would be a small step towards tackling the reproduction of inequalities in Higher Education.

HE and its lack of diversity

All institutions around the country are required to follow the *National Strategy for Access and Student Success* policies regarding 'widening participation'. However, the universities have considerable autonomy in how they implement these policies in their institutional plan. An 'access agreement' is constructed and drafted by individual institutions and submitted to the Office for Fair Access (OFFA) which results in the adoption of different approaches to widened access by different institutions. As a result, Russell Group universities are provided with the freedom of doing justice to their selectivity and prestige ideals (Rainford, 2017). Indeed, one of the most marked differences between the older, prestigious Higher Education institutions and the post-1992, newer institutions is the "socioeconomic mix of their student bodies" (Boliver, 2015:614); in the former there is an over-representation of socially advantaged students and therefore an over-concentration of students who come from underrepresented social groups in the new, less 'successful' institutions (ibid.). The 'elite' university entry rate for students from 'lower socioeconomic backgrounds' in the UK is 3.3% compared to 20.7% for those who come from more privileged backgrounds (Rainford, 2016).

Similarly, the disparities in HE access between white and BAME applicants are still significant. The offer rates for applicants to Russell Group universities in 2015 differed significantly for white and BAME students with a 67% offer rate "for white applicants, [...] compared to 63% for applicants from 'mixed' ethnic backgrounds, 54% for Asian applicants, 49% for those from 'other' ethnic groups, and just 41% for Black applicants" (Boliver, 2018:72). The difference is particularly marked in the most 'elite' universities: for instance, in 2009 there were 475 Black applicants to Oxbridge and 292 Black students across the country achieved the requisite A level grades for Oxbridge entry (Lammy, 2010). Nevertheless, only a handful of those were accepted. The picture has not much improved since: in 2015, nearly one in three Oxford colleges failed to admit a single Black British A level student, leading David Lammy to conclude that diversity at the elite HE institutions – far from improving – was actually getting "worse" (Lammy, 2017). Though there is some indication that the diversity of this year's (2020-21) Oxbridge admissions are an improvement on the past (e.g. see Weale, 2020), the fact is that HE access remains starkly unequal along racial/ethnic lines; as Reay argues, "even very highly qualified ethnic minority applicants are substantially less likely to be offered places at some of the most competitive courses at Oxbridge" (2018:53).

These wider demographic trends seem to mirror our programme as well, as noted by one staff participant, Rosa:

> Rosa: I absolutely love our students, but I would suggest that there's a lot of fantastic students who cannot be on our course because of the way King's is seen and is, *is*, very kind of predominantly white, privileged, middle-class, and because of the AAB criteria – and then the inequalities in attainment in the wider world and who gets to do this kind of a course in this kind of a place. It's very different, so [...] I've been to sessions run by students in the Youth and Community Work course in Goldsmiths, and it's just very apparent that course is made up predominantly of people who've experienced structural oppression in terms of social class and race/ethnicity in particular and on many other dimensions.

Below, I analyse some of the reasons behind our demographic's homogeneity as well as the overall homogeneity of the Higher Education system, which is partly a result of wider power structures that dominate society.

The struggle of 'belonging'

Rosa raises concerns around "students who cannot be on our course because of the way King's is seen and [because it] is [...] predominantly kind of white, privileged, middle-class". It is important to acknowledge that regardless of the programme's ethos or how the admissions team handles the application process, there could be a significant number of students who refrain from applying in the first place, for fear of not belonging to our 'type' of institution. As explored in the previous section, Bourdieu's theory of habitus and field provides a good account of how a person's individual history – which consists of their economic, cultural and social capital – "determines the[ir] chances of success" within a specific social context (Reay et al., 2009:1104). Widespread evidence of working-class and/or ethnic minorities feeling like they don't 'fit in' (Read et al., 2003; Reay et al., 2009) indicates the significance of habitus for HE applications choices (Byrom and Lightfoot, 2012). As Reay writes, "when habitus encounters a field with which it is not familiar, the resulting disjuncture can generate not only change and transformation, but also disquiet, ambivalence, insecurity and uncertainty" (Reay et al., 2009:1105).

What could this mean for potential applicants of the BA Social Sciences programme? If students feel like their habitus does not belong to the 'field' of the King's College community, which some students on the course have admitted to be true, they may be more likely to choose a programme at an institution they perceive to be less elitist or exclusive[26]. The issue, however, is not so much that students would choose a less elitist institution over ours, and more that our institution does not provide enough space for diversity. It would seem in keeping with the social

---

[26] There is some interesting evidence of HE students resisting or strategically adapting to dominant institutional 'habitus' in ways which undermine a simple process of 'alienation' (e.g. see Read et al., 2003). Nonetheless, it is noted that such efforts are heavily "constrained" by the power of institutional norms and sometimes actually end up "complicit" in perpetuating elitist discourses (ibid.:274).

justice focus of our programme to try to create space for King's to place less emphasis on conforming perfectly to its -more or less- 'traditional' ideals and instead to allow for new community dynamics to emerge. Such changes could help break homogenous patterns in conversations about critical social issues, whilst ensuring that our demographic matches the priorities of our ethos and vice versa.

It could be argued that it is not only the student cohort's lack of diversity which highlights the wider issue of exclusion in Higher Education, but the homogeneity amongst the members of staff too. Applicants from marginalised and misrecognised groups who perceive King's as an elitist institution and acknowledge the dominance of white, middle-class students and members of staff might not be interested in interacting within a space where issues like structural oppression are taught by individuals who do not have lived experience of the issue. Consequently, they would not be able to deliver the purpose of an academic role model or simply a voice of representation in the classroom. Of course, BAME academics should not hold the responsibility of being role models and dealing with race issues just because of their ethnicity (Loke, 2018). The same goes for working-class academics. Nevertheless, these role models can be of great importance for students from marginalised groups – e.g. BAME and/or working-class students – to feel recognised and motivated to "navigate the barriers to progression" (ibid.:387). This issue was noted in our data by participants in reflecting on the demographic of the (all-white) staff team:

> May: I'm very aware of who is teaching. I really like these people, but then again, we do need a range of voices. I hope [in] second and third year we have more diversity of who's teaching us as well.

The lack of Black and ethnic minority staff, however, is a complicated matter which is to a large extent the result of the wider issue of institutional racism and classism in both Higher Education and wider society in the UK. "BME staff represent 8.6 per cent of Higher Education academic staff and 6.9 percent of professional and support staff" (Leathwood et al., 2009:1). BAME people's experiences in academia differ from those of their white counterparts; dealing with prejudice becomes part of their professional routine (Harlow, 2003). Scholars from BAME groups often describe racism, difficulties in achieving progression and promotions, cultural insensitivity, as well as social exclusion (UCU, 2016). Assumptions are often made about the legitimacy of their professional positions or even their presence, and progress in the academic sphere requires a certain network of support which will employ them with the 'right' social and cultural capitals (Bhopal et al., 2018). An Asian Indian female academic mentioned in a study by Bhopal et al. states that "it is a fact that as a black person, as a minority ethnic person you have got to be twice as good as your white counterparts" (2018:133) and that is because BAME groups have to 'shape' themselves in a way that 'fits' in the "White space of the academy" (ibid.:132). Evidently, academic professionals and students from BAME groups have very similar experiences within Higher Education and it is worth taking a moment to reflect on the continuity of the issue from the student experience to the professional reality. The students whose habitus survives in those homogenous, often alienating environments and choose a career path in academia, will become the scholars who then experience prejudice and inequalities in their professional environment (ibid.).

Wider educational inequalities

It would be naive to believe that inequality begins just at the late stage of Higher Education. Indeed, we live in a deeply unequal world, reproducing unequal realities and fulfilling unequal purposes and dreams. The issue isn't just who does and doesn't apply to King's. it's also who is *able* to apply – as Rosa noted earlier, getting AAB is the grade requirement for our programme, but not everyone is equally well positioned to achieve those grades. Grades are strongly affected by wider social inequalities, not least enduring economic inequality, as well as systemic discrimination such as classism and racism.

Elite classified universities like King's, "aim to admit 'the best' applicants as indicated by their formal academic achievements" (Boliver, 2017:425-26), namely their A level results. But entry requirements play a significant role in reproducing and maintaining demographics as unequal and homogenous. For instance, Dorling points out that privileged applicants (white and/or middle-class) are nine times more likely than their peers from certain ethnic minority groups and/or from lower socioeconomic status households to achieve three As by the age of 18 (Dorling, 2016). It seems that achieving the requisite 'academic excellence' for an elite university application is a much harder task for certain demographic groups. Indeed, "low income [...] has been shown to have a causal relationship with educational attainment" (Hirsch, 2007:9). It has been proven that children whose parents have more resources – or what we could also label *economic, social and cultural capital* – are better prepared for entering education and therefore have a higher chance of maintaining their 'success' until the end of their academic career and into their way to recruitment. Hirsch also writes that:

> "At the age of three, children from less advantaged backgrounds are already well behind their peers in identifying basic words and in other developmental milestones, such as counting, and recognising colours and shapes. Children in poverty are nine months behind the rest of the population in school readiness. Children whose parents lack educational qualifications are nine months behind the average, and 13 months behind the children of graduates. The risk of delayed development is also great if a child has a lone parent or is from a Black, Bangladeshi or Pakistani ethnic background." (ibid.:10)

Hirsch's findings suggest that the beginnings of people's lives are shaped according to structural flaws, resulting in them 'starting the race' numerous paces 'behind' more privileged groups. If the system recognizes the hardships of these students yet refuses to take context into account in their expectations of academic progress, the gap becomes bigger as the path becomes tougher. Yet there is also evidence that members of these groups go on to experience feelings of alienation and prejudice regardless of their rate of 'academic progress', suggesting forms of institutional discrimination may also be at play. For instance, if "a child in poverty has worse prospects at secondary school than a non-poor child with exactly the same results at primary school" (Hirsch, 2007:14), what does it imply for the wider school system and expectations?

Race and racism also have an impact on wider trends of educational attainment. Not only are ethnic minorities more likely to be from a lower socioeconomic background (Office for National Statistics, 2018; Platt, 2007) – which we saw above has a significant impact on attainment – but are subject to racism in the school system too (e.g. see Joseph-Salisbury, 2020) with direct consequences for attainment (Strand, 2012). And even if people do attain the necessary grades, trends of racism and classism are present at the point of university application. Bhopal argues that inequalities in admissions due to factors like unconscious bias are still a reality in elite universities which try to maintain their traditional identities (Bhopal, 2017). Access to "good schools and colleges" (ibid.:2299) is too often based on perceptions of whether the student is armed with the 'right' fit of social and cultural capital, which suggests the failure of the system to acknowledge and address issues around 'otherness' (Reay et al., 2009). These systematic norms which favour the traditional over the inclusive are also strongly related to the marketisation of Higher Education and specifically of the pre-1992 institutions.

For instance, King's College falls into the 'elite' category of the highly competitive Russell Group institutions (Rainford, 2017). The Russell Group consists of 24 "self-proclaimed leading universities" (Boliver, 2015:608). Their status distinction is formed by five factors, one of them being *academic selectivity* (ibid.). As Rainford argues, advantaged institutions act on a "survival mechanism" in order to survive competing in an elitist market (2017:48). Therefore, their primary consideration is maintaining their status and their students' 'success' according to certain criteria – so lowering their grade boundaries or expanding who has access is not always in their reputational (and connectedly, financial) interest. Creating ideals of the 'perfect' student, hence the 'perfect' graduate or professional partner, sabotages efforts to widen access but is key in the marketisation process (ibid.). These problem of these ideals in practice can also be related to graduate employment trends, and particularly the role of what are known as "Elite Professional Services (EPS) firms – prestigious legal, management consultancy and investment banking firms where salaries for newly graduated hires start in the high six figures" (Boliver, 2017:428). EPS companies fulfil the Russell Group institutions' goals and their students' expectations by creating a platform for graduates to identify the validity of their 'elite' degree in the recruitment world. EPS selectors organise social "lavish getting-to-know you events on campus and spend [...] considerable sums on prestigious venues for further courtship events and, eventually, job interviews for those shortlisted" (ibid.:428). However, even though candidates from BAME and/or working-class backgrounds are welcome, it is unlikely that they will be selected since they're outnumbered by their white/middle-class counterparts in the "elite institutions targeted" by EPS firms (ibid.:429). And even if they make the interview for the job they are less likely to get an offer "because they are less likely to score well on the subjectively measured criteria of 'polish' [...] and, crucially, of 'fit'" (ibid.).

Much more needs to be done to tackle these enduring inequalities. Yet HE institutions continue to claim that they are widening participation for disadvantaged groups. The irony is that this too often papers over the difference between accepting a greater number of students overall and accepting students who would *change the demographic balance* of the cohorts. The reality is that there is not just a rise in the number of applicants from poor backgrounds but in the number of those who come from privileged backgrounds *too* (Dorling, 2016). As Dorling points out, "the chances of admissions for students who come from poorer backgrounds rose by 0.3 per cent within a year, in contrast to the 1.1 per cent rise for students from the more advantaged families" (ibid.) Evidently, widening participation by increasing the number of admitted students is not enough to fight the wider structures and social divisions, so inequality keeps being reproduced. A relatively new – encouraged but not required – admissions policy which has been successfully used by universities for years (especially substantively in the United States), is the consideration of the applicants' contextual information (Boliver et al., 2015). In the UK, slightly more than a third of universities take socioeconomic context into consideration in deciding who gets admitted or rejected (ibid.). Taking contextual factors into account along with academic achievement is of great importance if we think of the differences in opportunities and educational backgrounds of the students. As Boliver et al. suggest, "the value of contextual admissions policies as widening participation tools is that, in theory at least, they can help universities identify a 'potential to succeed' in applicants whose formal attainment, relative to others, does not necessarily do justice to their true ability" (2015:307-8).

Conclusion

> May: I think, when picking the students, [...] [t]he ethos of the course needs to be kept in mind.
> Rebecca: I think that's more of an institutional barrier though, because I don't think the lecturers had any say on who is on the course.
> May: Who decided?
> Rebecca: So, the university admissions team decides, I think.
> May: Well that needs to change.

As May and Rebecca's exchange above notes, something "needs to change" with regards to HE access. In 2018, British rapper Stormzy announced plans to annually fund two Cambridge scholarships for Black students (e.g. BBC, 2018). While Stormzy's initiative is admirable, it is disappointing that some of the most direct initiatives for addressing enduring inequalities within HE are having to come from celebrity philanthropists, rather than proper transformation of the sector! When thinking about our programme's ethos and its commitment to social change it is an ethical necessity that our demographic reflects a diverse range of lived experiences — and avoids reproducing the hegemony of white middle-class voices. A greater diversity of voices being heard in the classroom would also enrich the conversation and strengthen the opportunity for greater recognition of uncomfortable social realities and inequalities.

The fact that the creators of the programme have little say in who 'deserves' a place on the BA, makes the idea of a more diverse community seem unattainable, since it is a concern which belongs almost entirely to and serves the purposes of the institution, not necessarily the programme itself. Since, however, the BA Social Sciences is a brand new course, there is hope that with time and as the programme evolves, our ethos could become the way out of the austere hierarchy which prioritizes the admissions team over the people who create, experience and teach the programme.

5c – The politics of difference in the classroom

One of the most interesting (and contested) themes in our data was around freedom of speech in education, and especially the extent to which teaching should take explicit ethical positions. This has deep significance for the politics of difference and how it can be realised in an educational context. Given that we live in a world in which certain voices are already given more airtime and vested with greater credibility, should those 'less heard' voices be foregrounded in the classroom in the name of recognition? Should practitioners adopt an overt ethical stance in favour of the marginalised? How does this relate to political bias, intellectual freedom, and multiculturalism in education? Because of the high level of contestation in our data around these questions, and the interest of multiple members of our team in responding to it, this section is structured a little differently to the rest of the book. Below is a shared data presentation section, in which we outline – as descriptively as possible – participants' perspectives on issues around freedom of speech and marginalisation in the classroom. Then, four authors offer their own ethical responses in short essay form, critically exploring challenges and implications for the programme's practice.

There was a perception among many participants (including staff) that the programme has a political orientation which leans towards the political 'Left':

> Bea: I think my whole impression is that our whole topics are quite Left. I mean the political Left, and we study homophobia and misogyny and these types of topics [...]. [T]he whole impression it gives me that it leans towards the Left.

> Neve: I'm not sure if the course has ever framed itself as, like, explicitly anti-capitalist but like, we seem to frame it in that way [...]. I think a lot of this I'm basing on like my personal conversations I've had with, like, the lecturers [...]. [B]ecause the academic staff have a

certain politics, and they are the ones that are writing the programme, that's gonna come through.

Belle: In a sense there is a lot of focus on [...] taking a very, I guess, Leftist and critical perspective about specific issues, right? About specific social issues, and so issues about inequality and power and poverty etc. etc. and so I guess taking a moral [position].

Some participants suggested that this had sometimes led to students feeling afraid to express their opinions, for fear of offending others or standing out from the dominant values of the space, and that this narrowing of the range of perspectives can lead to forms of exclusion:

Erica: Even if we have different opinions I'm not sure someone would actually dare say it because they know [...] [they] have, like, a divergent opinion and, you know, it's not the most inclusive one. For example, [...] if your opinion is homophobic, I'm not saying it's right but if that's your opinion you wouldn't really dare to say because you know that everyone around [you] thinks that being homophobic is really wrong [...] and you know you would be offending someone. So if I think you have different opinions we're not encouraged to state them.

Kima: [...] [F]or example when we're studying [...] Haiti, I think it was, and some of the opinions in a video we were shown were very... political? Like very, very skewed to one part of the political spectrum and some people in the seminar, as a result of watching that video [...] felt that if they felt opposed to that political stance that they were afraid to speak? [...] I remember an international student who was saying, like, to me afterwards 'I don't agree with the political stance in that video and that's why I didn't say anything', and then subsequently they didn't attend seminars for a couple of weeks after that so that's why I think it's a bit dangerous if things are presented in a way that students are made to feel that this is the only thing that's right? Because with politics it's not just one thing that's right, so I think people should be able to, like, decide for themselves.

Belle: [...] [S]ome of the students like told me about, you know, feeling a bit uncomfortable about expressing their opinions because they felt, like, different or [...] they don't feel like it's a safe space, right, to say that? [...] To say something different, that [is] different from the majority of the group. In particular related to, like, for instance [a] student saying, you know, 'I have more conservative views', right?

Interestingly, many explicitly located the problem in the belief that, ironically, the programme's emphasis on kindness had led to a kind of conflict averseness, where everyone "end[s] up agreeing with each other" (Tia) rather than engaging in frank deliberation:

Tia: I think it's really nice, like, being kind, I really- I need kindness in my life [laughs], like, kindness is a gift, you know, we should all be kind to each other, but at the same time we should all acknowledge that we are all, like, we all have [...] freedom of speech and we all are able to have our own opinion, and we should be able to have our own opinion, and like say it out loud, you know?

Erica: I think it's all also about this community that is so open-minded and inclusive that if you have a different point of view, well you would be excluded. I think that's also what people are scared of if they have different opinions.

As a solution to the problem of political exclusion, some participants emphasised the importance of neutrality and of valuing everyone's voices 'equally' without passing negative judgement:

Tia: I've never had an experience in class when, like, the seminar leader for instance has a certain opinion and they- they tell the person, 'Oh you're wrong' or anything like that. We never have like that 'right or wrong' thing in the classroom. In the classroom ever. Which is amazing [...] – I think that's how it should be.

Michelle: I feel like the ethos of the course is just, like, being inclusive to everything. [...] Whatever you are, whatever you feel it's like- yeah it's inclusive. Like, even if we have different opinions that, like, are not really normal, like for example if someone is racist or whatever obviously they're not gonna be like "It's fine that you're racist", but they're not gonna be like, "You're racist, go home", you know. They're gonna be respectful about it, like they're gonna try and help you to understand that, instead of just being rude about your different opinion.

Others suggested – both as a solution to political bias but also as a solution to the perceived homogeneity of the room that staff should manufacture "debate[s]" in class:

Michelle: [When] all of the group in the seminars has the same opinion on something, I feel like the seminar leader should like, make, like, not say that 'I'm against it', but just like, try to play it out as [if] 'I'm against it?' [...] [B]ecause, I feel like sometimes we're just agreeing [...] and not really, like, challenging our opinions. So, if that happens I think that the seminar leader should try to [put] the other point [of view] across, for a debate to happen.

Erica: I think that [the programme]'s so open that it becomes limited. I don't know how we could, like, challenge this, like, except actually organizing kind of a debate. Like, I remember when we were in English class [at school] last year, and like there was a whole debate on abortion in the United States and our English teacher forced, like, half the class to be pro-abortion and half the class to be against. [...] [The] fact is that it actually led to a natural debate and I think it could [...] challenge us to make our point[s] stronger [...]. But [at the moment] we're just scared to – if we have different opinions – to say them.

So far, we have focused on those participants who feel that the perceived Left bias of the programme, or an emphasis on kindness and inclusivity, can silence those whose opinions diverge from the majority. We have explored some participants' suggestions that 'neutrality' and 'manufacturing debates' might be important for creating a safe space for freedom of speech. Yet other student participants gave precisely the opposite perspective, suggesting that there is *insufficient* challenge of certain voices – particularly those on the conservative Right – in a way which ends up reproducing wider social inequalities. This concern is best captured by the discussion between May and Rebecca below:

> May: I think if [certain] comments like that do come up then the [...] seminar tutors do have to let it be known that this stuff is damaging [...].
> Rebecca: Yeah, I mean I think there's a difference between letting the conversation flow and, like, free speech [...] [and] someone saying something [like] [...] '[Racism] doesn't exist anymore', [which] is invalidating people's experiences in the room.
> May: Exactly, and that should have been like nipped in the bud. [...] All these structures of oppression that we're talking about exis[t] in the classroom too. It's not void [...] – the same stuff is going on. And yeah, I get that everyone can say what they want to say. But people talking about stuff they don't really know about, in a way that comes off as- not comes off as, *is* damaging.

May went on to raise concerns that the programme ethos of inclusivity is interpreted as an 'anything goes' iteration of freedom of speech, and that therefore an atmosphere of critically challenging exclusionary perspectives has not been sufficiently normalised:

> May: I can't imagine if we went up to students and said, 'Hey, you shouldn't say that', because they're going to act defensive. And I think it's the same thing with staff too. Because they know how the students react – they'll be like, 'Oh, they're not allowing, like free speech or whatever'. [...] I think the course, it tries to promote a community feel [...] [but] that's the one value: 'Community'. 'Openness'. Openness, like, in terms of people can say whatever they want.

It is worth noting that there was an element encouraging evidence in the data that some participants, at least, felt the programme had critically challenged them, and led them to question and deconstruct their preconceptions, particularly around forms of inequality and marginalisation:

Helena: Actually, like, [...] how we talked about racism with how we grow up, like before this course I never really thought about my upbringing. [...] So looking at it, like for example growing up and seeing people as equal, but now there's a difference, like, not everyone has equal opportunities, you know. Without this course I wouldn't have realised this because, like, we looked at racism with [a] historical view but I had never really done that to look at the root of it.

Marla: I was never aware for example [of] how the hierarchies of human beings began [...] in the Enlightenment. Even though I studied it in History [at school] [...] it was never mentioned that that's when also [certain] hierarchies began and seeing some humans as inferior [to] others. So, I would say that the course's values are teaching you also how to look at the world through different lenses [...]. [A]nother thing that I noticed is also about the way the course teaches me to question certain words that I never even thought that they could be questionable [...] for example women and the label 'women' and the impacts that has on society. I always thought of, like, for example gender and sex going together and being biologically determined and then the course showed me another perspective – another approach – and I think it's also teaching us how to make up our minds, so how to use our knowledge and engage with it critically, for example we're not learning facts, but rather we're learning how to think and how to make up our minds through what we read and learn.

The data above indicates an element of disagreement among participants about the role of the politics of difference in the classroom: some participants feel strongly that universalist principles of neutrality and equal esteem of perspectives should form the basis of pedagogical practice. Others feel that this can lead to the reproduction of mis- and non-recognition, allowing harmful and marginalising viewpoints to go unchallenged. These participants suggest that staff need to do more to step in and take an explicit ethical stance which foregrounds the lived experiences of the marginalised. In the upcoming three sections, different authors offer their own perspectives on the data above and the ethical implications for the programme.

Openness in the classroom: the key to recognition

Minkyung Kim

I am an international student from South Korea who studied secondary education in New Zealand. Although I come from a socioeconomically privileged background, growing up in a Western cultural context I have more often than not been one of the very few Asians in the classroom. Particularly in writing this piece, I recall the moments when I hesitated to speak up and was timid in discussion in spite of myself, which did affect my learning. That is, being often perceived as 'different' and 'other' led to moments when my voice was dismissed or inadequately valued. These experiences have not only eroded my confidence but also restricted my autonomy in education. For instance, there were many times when I felt pressured to behave in ways that complied with dominant culture and norms; to prove that I fitted into the community, I had to make efforts to speak with a corresponding regional accent and did not actively speak out when the class was covering certain topics like racism, which narrowed down the perspectives in discussion. Thus, my sense of identity as well as academic potential were negatively impacted. Having experienced first-hand the difficulty of raising one's voice against the dominant group, I hope this short piece of writing can contribute to improving educational environments for students so that all voices are heard and valued. Also, I hope those who are reading this recognise the significance of openness in the classroom along with the importance of the teacher's role in upholding it. In addition to the experiences highlighted above, coming from South Korea – a relatively new democracy which has had periods of autocratic rule, and is juxtaposed geographically with the dictatorship of North Korea – has strengthened my own belief in the critical importance of openness in education for democracy.

"We all speak with different voices, all of which can be heard." (Netting and Rodwell, 1998:309)

203

When discussing complex social problems or topics in the classroom, should students feel pressured to take a particular stance, or should they fearlessly express their opinions and raise concerns? Throughout our participant data, a tension around issues of possible political bias and different understandings of 'inclusivity in the classroom' was identified. There were instances when students said they found the programme relatively 'open', while others described experiencing inadvertent exclusion, either because of perceived political bias or because of concerns about offending one another. Hence, despite the fact that spaces like CCMs and seminars have encouraged an inclusive environment for students to share knowledge and concerns, not all individuals felt comfortable enough to be actively involved in the classroom. This is perhaps compounded by the degree of cultural diversity within the cohort, and attendant concerns around inadvertently causing offence, as one participant explained:

> Connie: [B]ecause we're from different countries we have different cultures/backgrounds. So for example we need to share our own experiences but it may cause a controversial thing to other people with other social background[s].

To ease this anxiety and suggest a solution to this matter, I intend to articulate the idea of 'openness' and its purposes in learning spaces, particularly in Higher Education. I define openness in the classroom as 'all voices being heard and valued' and believe that this 'universal' principle is actually the best avenue for recognition in education. Otherwise, there is a danger of reinforcing narrowness in the classroom. For instance, in her text *Teaching Critical Thinking*, bell hooks shares their journey in coming to recognise the importance of valuing a plurality of perspectives in the classroom:

> "I often talk about radical openness because it became clear to me, after years in academic settings, that it was far too easy to become attached to and protective of one's viewpoint, and to rule out other perspectives." (hooks, 2010:10)

Kindness in the classroom: closing down debate?

Our data suggest that people's interpretations of the programme's commitment to 'kindness' may have led to students being disingenuous with one another about their views and perspectives, subsequently damaging the capacity for open, critical discussion. Teaching difficult and complex subjects like race, culture, gender and sexual orientation is an inherent part of the programme. The programme aims to question and understand the current social system and support "creativity, risk-taking and social action" of students through its teaching of knowledge and skills (KCL website, 2020). To do this, the programme provides space like CCMs and small-group discussion-based seminars for students to reflect and exchange concerns in a way that builds mutual understanding and healthy educational relationships based on trust and honesty. However, as stated above, despite such efforts, the dataset shows that a number of students are not yet confident about raising their voice in the classroom. They explicitly state that they fear alienating fellow students with contrasting opinions or personal experiences. Interestingly, while some located the problem in issues of perceived liberal/Left political bias, many explicitly located it in the programme's emphasis on kindness – and attendant ideas such as 'inclusivity'. Participants felt that, ironically, this had led to a kind of conflict averseness, where everyone "end[s] up agreeing with each other" (Tia) rather than engaging in frank deliberation. It seems that *perceptions* of what kindness means in the classroom are having a great influence on students feeling comfortable expressing themselves honestly.

This raises important questions about our definition of kindness in education. Clegg and Rowland claim that kindness should be about recognising and respecting 'difference'. They write "kindness is not simply the projection of one's own needs and desires" onto other people but about recognising that others may have different positions, needs and priorities (2010:724). Sometimes, that means there may be conflict between people; kindness – far from avoiding this conflict – should be about positively "embrac[ing] critique", but in an empathic way (ibid.:723).

Through recognising difference, kindness can also support what McAvoy and Hess call a "democracy sustaining" approach in the classroom (2013:17); they state that learning to deal with difference constructively "is the cornerstone of a healthy and well-functioning democracy" (ibid.). That is, kindness can not only promote the necessary sociopsychological understanding between individuals but also allow students to reflect on the ways of integrating contrasting beliefs in a multicultural or pluralistic democratic community.

Yet, despite the fact that kindness is theorised as facilitating constructive conflict and expressions of difference, our data suggest that it can actually lead to inactive participation of students in the space, primarily due to concerns about "offend[ing]" and "excluding" (Erica) people, or causing "controvers[y]" (Connie).

Why 'openness' is important in addition to kindness

Even if (as above) we theorise kindness as including a commitment to criticality and constructive conflict, if people do not *perceive* kindness in this way then maybe we need to couple it with another pedagogical commitment – one which ensures frank, honest debate. I have termed this 'openness'. Especially in the classroom, each individual's voice should be clearly heard and appreciated. While the politics of difference suggests that recognition requires us to attend to structural inequality, there is a danger that, if that means explicitly prioritising certain voices and silencing others, we could end up with a culture of fear around conflict; this may actually diminish the chance of crucial issues of inequality being addressed and understood, as Les Back argues:

> "Dismissing racist views [...] as drivel does nothing to evaluate and understand their resonance or reach. It is for this reason that, though I've spent much of my adult life fighting against racism, I no longer subscribe to the 'no platform' argument with regard to racists. We need to know what a racist argument sounds like. This is not the same as saying that organisations like the British National Party or the Danish People's Party or JOBBIK in Hungary should be given a comfortable seat at the debate table.

Rather, it means paying close attention to what they say and subjecting these sentiments to critical judgment." (Back, 2010:26-27)

In other words, suppressing prejudiced viewpoints restricts opportunities for individuals to learn how to effectively deconstruct and challenge them. This could actually perpetuate forms of harm and misrecognition.

Beyond helping us learn how to deconstruct prejudice, openness is also about students learning how to become competent in respecting the differences of others – a crucial part of multicultural, democratic society. This is closely connected to Mcavoy and Hess' idea of the 'political classroom' (2014). According to Mcavoy and Hess, political teaching is essential as we are living through the time of great political polarization (ibid.). In such a climate, we need to create a 'deliberative classroom' where students are encouraged to openly share different opinions and to disagree respectfully with their fellow students and teachers (ibid.). Thus, promoting a political classroom corresponds with promoting an open classroom since it provides students with a safe, risk-free space to practise democracy and the chance to acquire skills for critical thinking and constructive conversations. In other words, by increasing the effectiveness of communication of students in the classroom, openness supports a wider aim of improving communication throughout society. Although a full discussion of the importance of democracy is not within the scope of this chapter, according to Dewey, communication establishes a democratic public and democratic education creates a democratic society:

"What nutrition and reproduction are to physiological life, education is to social life. This education consists primarily in transmission through communication. [...]. Communication is a process of sharing experience till it becomes a common possession. It modifies the disposition of both the parties who partake in it." (Dewey, 1916:13-14)

Dewey regards learning space to be a miniature of society and active communication and participation of individuals (the core features of the openness) to be powerful tools for upholding principles of democratic life at school. Therefore, through the experience of an open classroom, individuals progress to become democratic people.

In addition to supporting the development of democratic skills through a political classroom, openness can also act as emotional support. What I mean by this is that openness encourages effective recognition of all individuals and trust and respect between one other. Hence, the fact that a student's opinion is engaged through mutual partnership with peers and teachers (discussed more below) and in a way rooted in care, promotes psychological comfort, especially to those who hold minority viewpoints. This brings us full circle to the concept of kindness explored above and underlines the interrelationship between these concepts.

How to embed openness in the classroom: the significance of staff roles

Teachers are inevitably in a powerful position when it comes to creating a certain class environment. This implies that ensuring openness in the classroom will be to some extent dependent upon the roles that teachers play. To effectively promote openness in the classroom, teachers should remain impartial towards the issues under discussion. The reason is that I believe their roles in the learning environment is that of 'facilitators' of debate and 'guides' for students. That is, although teachers are more educated learners, when promoting an effective learning environment, they are aiming to work in an as equal a partnership with students as possible when working together in the space. This I would like to call a 'friendship through education'. Thus, teachers should make certain efforts to provide a wider knowledge of the issue so that students then can thoroughly educate *themselves* (rather than being pushed in a particular direction by the teacher) and actively seek their positions with reference to a wider range of contrasting viewpoints.

Students in the data explicitly point out the problems that can occur when teachers take an overtly political or ethical stance. For instance, some participants shared difficult moments when the teacher frankly informed the class of their view. The participants added that such actions should be restricted in the learning space:

Erica: I think I do prefer [staff to try to be neutral] 'cos then teachers are really careful about what they say and how they say it, you know. Like my previous teacher [at school] they would just say their opinion and, like, they could say 'Yeah I don't think colonialism was a bad thing'. Stuff like that and we were like 'Wait what the-', 'cos they're teachers and we're supposed to learn from them and they're not supposed to just give their opinions like that. So, respecting ethics, it's like- in that sense it's a good thing because you try to stay objective. [O]bviously it's not good to just state your opinion to your students that think that your words are like God's words. Then they will just repeat 'Oh yeah colonialism is a good thing', you know.

Sarah: [There] was a situation where a staff member directly disagreed with a student's opinion. But that was the only time when I felt very uncomfortable. Because it was like a student's specific, like, family perspective and, like, a piece of information that they felt open enough to share. Then to have a staff member turn around and be like 'I don't agree with that' and imply that they were kind of, like... wrong in their sort of experience... that was, like, really uncomfortable. But that's really been the only time when I thought we're reproducing these toxic power traits where, like, staff are 'above' teachers [students].

It is noteworthy that Sarah felt a degree of power difference and hierarchy when the staff explicitly took a political stance in the classroom. Despite the programme staff's commitment to egalitarianism on the programme, the impact of this moment was strong enough to recall the traditional power relationships between teachers and students.

The neutrality of teachers that I argue for here can be understood as what Bomstad calls "procedural neutrality" (1995:199). According to Bomstad, there are two core versions of neutrality in the classroom (1995). The first is 'classic neutrality', according to which a teacher presents the "same amount of evidence for all sides of an issue" and "remains impartial by presenting the strongest version of each position [without] [...] letting it be known which view she herself holds" (Bailey, 2011:9). In other words, teachers hide their own stance and seek to present the strongest version of alternative viewpoints – which Bomstad calls generating a "fair hearing":

> "Fair hearing is achieved when a teacher plays the role of serious devil's advocate for a full range of views, rendering for balanced examination and critique the strongest and most charitable version of each viewpoint and its supporting arguments." (Bomstad, 1995:198)

The second form of neutrality is what Bomstad calls 'procedural neutrality'. According to Bomstad, this involves active "disclosure" (Bailey, 2011:11) by the teacher to present their own viewpoint *as well as* those contrasting to it; that is, teachers are honest about their beliefs, but open up debate through actively sharing other viewpoints and explaining the justifications behind them (1995). Bomstad believes that this addresses some of the core criticisms of 'classic neutrality', including that it "promotes dishonesty, moral relativism and a lack of commitment to values" (1995:199). In other words, that teachers hiding their own positions is a neglect of moral duty because it implies all sides of an argument are always morally equivalent, and could damage students' trust in a teacher's integrity by implying that a teacher defends a viewpoint they may in fact find deeply problematic (Bailey, 2011). Nonetheless, by sharing their own view as just part of the picture, teachers can to some extent overcome the risk of unduly coercing students into accepting their views as the only acceptable ones (Bailey, 2011).

Although the dataset shows that students felt uncomfortable when staff explicitly stated their opinion, I believe this can be mitigated through openness based on 'procedural neutrality'. Openness promotes more equal relationships in learning by valuing *everybody's* viewpoint; thus, even if a staff member states their own opinion, the fact that they are doing so alongside presenting other perspectives, and seeking to value a wide range of voices in the room, means students come to realise the teacher can be a partner or even a 'friend' in the space. For example, teachers can provide explanations of, and the reasons behind, their stances as well as encourage students to provide comments, which may involve critiques. Thus, students can deliberate their positions while subjecting each point to discussion. Teachers' words are no longer assumed to be, as one participant put it, "God's words" (Erica). Rather, their view is understood to be merely one view in the debate, which can be freely critiqued by anyone.

Therefore, the difficulty of separating viewpoints from teachers who are in authority positions – and therefore might have powerful sway over student perceptions – can be effectively resolved. Interestingly, the need for such 'neutrality' of teachers to the space was echoed by participants, who suggested that staff should organise 'debate' style situations in the classroom in which some people are positioned as 'for' a particular position and some as 'against':

> Michelle: [When] all of the group in the seminars has the same opinion on something, I feel like the seminar leader should like, make, like, not say that 'I'm against it', but just like, try to play it out as [if] 'I'm against it?' [...] [B]ecause, I feel like sometimes we're just agreeing [...] and not really, like, challenging our opinions. So, if that happens I think that the seminar leader should try to [put] the other point [of view] across, for a debate to happen.

The power of the teacher in the classroom is such that, when they present a viewpoint, it may disturb the student's commitment or as the data shows, lead to them feeling 'uncomfortable' throughout the discussion. By contrast, when teachers adopt procedural neutrality, this promotes openness by leaving space for students to determine the most acceptable case and adopt it for themselves.

The limitations of open classroom

As mentioned above, performing openness in the classroom is heavily affected by teachers' contribution and behaviours. Their roles become even more important when it comes to overcoming the limitations and weaknesses of openness in the classroom. To give an example, while openness provides equal opportunities for students to raise their voices, if certain viewpoints are more commonly raised or dominant, then traditionally marginalized opinions can be underrepresented. This is the concern raised by Taylor's articulation of the politics of difference. Although this problem is to some extent inevitable if we are committed to the definition of openness defended thus far – which opposes manipulating the balance of voices in the classroom – teachers can nonetheless prevent minorities' voices from being forgotten and try to help illuminate dynamics in the space that people may be oblivious to.

This matter can be mediated by a slightly different version of procedural neutrality by teachers. For instance, although Bomstad's definition focuses on teachers frankly sharing their views and maintaining neutrality by presenting a wide range of competing views, in such a case, teachers could purposefully seek to bolster the most underrepresented voices in the space. In doing so, we can ensure marginalised views are subjected to discussion and the focus can be broadened by teachers' contribution of competing arguments and students' active responses. Thus, it conveys to the class that just because a voice is in a minority does not mean it cannot be platformed with equally strong conviction. I am not arguing that all the voices of minorities should be highlighted by teachers but there are perspectives that must be acknowledged and should receive additional platforming to facilitate effective learning of students. Hence, it is important for teachers to rigorously identify the dynamics of voices in the space and to consider what kind of procedural neutrality to uphold in class in light of this.

Another limitation of the open classroom is that it can only go so far in addressing systematic patterns of exclusion because these are often caused by wider problems outside of the classroom. Teachers can transform the classroom into an open space through education, but they cannot stretch their influence to the whole of society. For instance, the power of external influences on students' perspectives – including prejudice – may mean that, despite teachers' efforts, some viewpoints are still denigrated and disregarded. Conflict – and in extreme cases forms of bullying and discrimination – can be identified between students inside and outside of the space which can interrupt learning and cause serious harm. Students should not be left alone to explore ways to cope with these emotions. As 'more experienced learners', teachers should enforce and inform appropriate behaviours by designing working agreements to guide pedagogical practice. Thoroughly conferring and negotiating the working agreement with all teachers and students in the class is essential. Because everyone is involved in the process, it generates a greater collective understanding of its implications, as well as indicates that teachers and students are *partners* in upholding a conflict-free classroom environment. Though I argued before that teachers should *generally* not interfere with students' discussions, I view teachers' intervention to uphold the principles of a working agreement as an ethical act – not an act of political bias – and one which takes place only on occasions where the working agreement is clearly being breached.

Furthermore, despite teachers' efforts to form an open environment, if there is a lack of awareness towards the issue, effective open classrooms cannot be formed. For example, critical consciousness and reflexivity are essential around issues such as racism, as free speech contains the risk of reproducing another form of harm. Indeed, some participants highlighted potential drawbacks to openness of debate because of dangers around students with a lack of awareness reproducing marginalisation in the context of open discussion:

> May: I mean with academic staff, it's cool because they have a degree, they understand how to talk about race [...], but I guess letting students carry these topics without giving them sensitivity talks as well, it's leading to disaster. If you're not giving people like anti-racism training, or training on how to facilitate discussion.

Interestingly, the participant points out the importance of staff's role when facilitating debates around "sensitive topics" as it may lead to "disaster" with only students involved. On that account, before achieving openness in discussion, teachers should deliver sufficient knowledge of the issue and seek to inculcate skills – like 'critical consciousness' and 'reflexivity' – which enable students to reflect on how their perspectives may affect and implicate others. The teacher's role is significant in students' development of such skills. For instance, reflexivity cannot be easily practised through 'passive learning'. Rather it involves active engagement by students in critically evaluating their experiences, attitudes and responsibilities "within the classroom, Higher Education and other nonacademic contexts" (Grenier, 2016:168). In other words, teachers must present students with significantly more questions than just 'How much do you know in regard to the content?' Rather, teachers must help students to engage in a "complex process of knowledge (re)production" and support them in reflecting on the past and engaging with their potential actions in the future (Grenier, 2016:155).

Thus, it is the teacher's role to identify whether students are ready to face such questions and, if so, to help them develop skills and mark out any concerns to reflect on. Teachers are also essential for this because they can draw on their own learning to ground students' perspectives in "diverse structural, cultural and personal" analyses and thus provide the scaffolding for reflexivity in the classroom (Feucht et al., 2017:235). Therefore, the risks of openness in the classroom can be ameliorated by the active involvement of teachers to embed reflexivity in the classroom.

Conclusion

In conclusion, openness in the classroom promotes students feeling recognised and valued as well as preparing them to become democratic members of society. While kindness can be misconceived as conflict averseness, openness promotes the full engagement of students as it secures *all* voices being heard and valued. Especially in a multicultural space, students learn to become proficient in respecting the differences of others which prepares them to become democratic people in the future. In addition, the fact that all student voices are appreciated and paid attention to can offer psychological support to students. Thus, openness actually *facilitates* forms of kindness in the classroom.

Teachers' roles are integral to successfully implementing openness in the classroom. By acting as facilitators of debate and guides for students, they need to maintain an equal partnership with students and impartial attitudes through the learning process. I suggest that teachers taking particular value-laden stances in the classroom risks the resurgence of traditional power differences between teachers and students. By contrast, I suggest teachers take a procedural neutrality approach in the classroom as it helps to embrace diverse voices into the community as well as resolve the difficulty of separating the teacher's viewpoint of the issue.

Though some limitations and weaknesses of the idea of openness were identified, through appropriate roles of teachers, those can be overcome. For instance, traditionally marginalised voices can be presented with equally strong conviction by teachers, and acts of exclusion can be mitigated by teachers' effort in implementing and conferring a working agreement with students. Lastly, teachers' roles are significant for inculcating skills like reflexivity, which can prevent or ameliorate difficult consequences during sensitive discussions. Accordingly, openness in the classroom can be achieved through teachers' particular contributions to the learning process.

When love entered the classroom

by Eleni Koutsouri

And there it was.
A silence that echoed fear.
A silence that was blue.
The gazes uncomfortable.
Palms sweaty and cold.
Too many questions to ask,
Too many truths untold.
Vulnerable,
Honest,
Raw.
Unexpected in the pages and screens.
Unexpected on the competitive way to your dreams.
Exposing yet kind,
It felt unreal but was bright.
There was a touch,
There was a smile,
There was a look,
There was one time,
When love entered the classroom and it was finally alright.

Diversity and the challenges of recognition

Being brought up in a multicultural environment, I never identified as belonging to a specific home country. Although I am Korean by birth and a Korean national, my education experience has definitely not corresponded with the Korean education system. Despite spending eighteen years of my life in South East Asia and East Asia, I've been exposed to a predominantly Western curriculum, attending a British international school since I was young. This has not only heavily influenced my perspective on and understanding of certain social and political issues but also given me the immense privilege and opportunities that come with being able to attend international schools. Furthermore, the relative homogeneity of the demographic at my selective international school meant issues of exclusion were rarely in the foreground. Only in adulthood did I develop an awareness of the persistent inequalities within the education system. I began to confront questions of 'Who had access'? 'Who was excluded or marginalised from access'? 'What does it mean to have access'? Reflecting from my positionality where I haven't felt excluded or not given the opportunity to access education, I realised the importance of understanding that this wasn't necessarily true for everyone; the question of 'Why?' emerged for me. This has influenced my understanding of marginalisation and what it means to be marginalised, it has shown me that understanding and listening is key to shedding light to those who don't necessarily have the opportunities due to the persisting inequalities that continue to define our society. Being a writer for this research project has been a learning opportunity, involving educating and reflecting on myself as a writer and recognising the power of words. I hope this research paper can do the same for those reading it.

"In the midst of the conflicts and inequalities that now characterize so many nations, can [educational institutions] be part of the process in which a society becomes more democratic, more respectful of its people, more responsive, and more committed to equality?" (Hess and McAvoy, 2014:xiii)

The debate surrounding the purpose, structure and goals of Higher Education (HE) in its many forms is a source of contention. One significant question we can ask is whether HE can change the fabric of society and instil modes of knowledge which help to address current social and political issues – not least issues around inequality, exclusion and marginalisation. As I will argue below, HE has continued to work within a framework born from the colonial past, which perpetuates microaggressions towards those who do not 'fit' within it. HE institutions need to consider how power relations and power struggles directly impact education and its curriculum as well as the individuals involved – especially in regard to those who have been marginalised through consequences of our colonial past – to avoid perpetuating prejudice and ostracisation. The politics of difference asks us to recognise this and raises questions around how to eliminate marginalisation in the classroom – e.g. regarding the extent to which teaching should take explicit ethical stances, or whose voices get recognised.

In response, I emphasise that HE institutions need to not only promote openness but also acknowledge and understand the pervasiveness of institutionalised oppressive practices and the need to recognise marginalised students (Kose, 2009). Rather than changing students to fit in the existing framework which revolves around the dominant culture and norms, the framework itself needs to change. This matters not only within the educational context; it is a matter concerning social justice more broadly. By introducing forms of dialogue and openness which recognise structural marginalisation, students are encouraged to diverge from the self-interested questions of 'I' (i.e. What's best for me?) to deliberative questions concerning wider society. Green (1998), similarly, is described by Simone (2012) as "posit[ing] the notion of an egalitarian society" in which binary thinking of 'us' and 'them' is eliminated, and in which educators move beyond emphasising students' differences and instead focus on "commonalities", in the interests of "fostering a 'we' mentality" (2012:42).

Our programme ethos strives to reject existing practices within education and emphasises a similar idea of 'we' by fostering a sense of collectivity and inclusivity through reflexive consideration and awareness of our own agency and positionality, and the acknowledgement of our contextual influences and backgrounds. By doing so we hope to create an education system that recognises everyone within the community. Creating a collective 'safe space' for realising these recognition aims is important, not only because it allows both students and staff to have rich and multi-voiced political discussions in the classroom, but also because it fosters practices that enable people to experience the world through the eyes of others – most crucially the marginalised.

Diversity and the Classroom

Diversity and multiculturalism in education can be a deliberative strength in HE as well as a pedagogical challenge. Diversity can provide and stimulate rich discussions and deliberations that enable people to mutually engage with one another to seek solutions that promote the common good (Mansbridge et al., 2010). Simone (2012) suggests diversity can be a valuable tool for tackling exclusion, highlighting how it can catalyse transformative conversations which are paramount in creating new structures and ways of thinking.

However, dealing with diversity in education can also be challenging. Where student demographics are diverse in terms of race, class, culture, power and privilege, there is the potential for marginalisation to actually be reproduced. Our data suggest that this may be due to two factors: Firstly, in a space enriched with differing opinions, marginalisation may occur if students are unable to express their views for fear of judgement – especially if their opinion doesn't fit in with the majority. For instance, it is evident in our data that some students were subjected to not being heard or did not necessarily want to engage in discussions where their opinions differed and deviated from a perceived Left/liberal consensus. This will be explored in greater depth below. Secondly, the wider inequalities of society can be reproduced, in which students feel marginalised and excluded in conversations due to the pervasive impact of forces such as systemic racism, classism and sexism. Spaces which claim to be diverse may still reflect these wider structural inequalities. As I will explore more below, deep roots of coloniality and white supremacy persist in systems of HE which serve to reproduce this form of marginalisation.

Dealing with fear of judgement

While some may see the value of practitioners disclosing their personal political views in the classroom, others may argue that practitioners should avoid this, because of concerns about either unduly influencing students' perspectives or suppressing students' participation and engagement. The ethics of disclosing or withholding political views in the classroom proved to be a contested and sensitive issue reflected in our data presentation earlier. Some participants expressed that teaching on the programme leaned towards a Left/liberal consensus and suggested it didn't feel 'safe' to go against this. As a solution to the problem of political bias and disclosing certain ethical stances, some participants emphasised the importance of neutrality and equal esteem of perspectives:

> Kima: [S]ome people have [...] felt that if things got perhaps a bit too political than they should have – because as a member of staff you're not usually supposed to impose a political opinion upon students in these kinds of courses, but when that does happen, students have had occasions of feeling intimidated by that so… that also has prevented a couple of people from coming [to class] that I've known.

Calls for neutrality could be understood as a version of what Taylor calls the politics of universalism (1994), whereby practitioners attempt to treat all viewpoints with equal recognition. However, I argue that neutrality in the academic classroom may be detrimental, not only to the individual but also by unconsciously contributing to problems faced by the wider collective community. Whilst the innocent and unprejudiced nature of the term neutrality may seem quintessential good classroom practice, it can actually reinforce prejudice, through one of the most ethically problematic acts: silence. As Holocaust survivor Elie Wiesel once said, "neutrality helps the oppressor, never the victim. Silence encourages the tormentor, never the tormented" (1986). Thus, lived experiences of marginalised students must be considered and materials taught in the classroom which account for this. There are no simple ways of achieving this while still committing to openness and dialogue. Indeed, our data reflects the challenges faced by practitioners in balancing what they feel is right in the name of recognitional justice, against concerns about upsetting or silencing students by challenging them:

> Marnie: [I]f you call people out too much or create a space where you are constantly challenging people [...] my concern is that the less confident students end up feeling kind of [...] ostracised. It's not okay to allow prejudice to go unchallenged either but there are quite a few students who I think need to build their self-confidence before they can really start to openly engage in challenging their own, or other people's mindsets. For example, I've had students speak to me outside of teaching time and say stuff about starting to question their own political ideas, partly because of the course, and the people they've met here, and I just feel like, maybe if we created a space that was more kind of blunt [...] or put people on the spot more [...] then maybe those students wouldn't have been able to do that- that kind of challenging of themselves- in their own time? So there's a really, really difficult balance to strike here and it's not at all easy, there's no rulebook.

> Hester: I feel like it's very difficult because [...] there's a very, like, huge grey area between what I think is right, and what is acceptable, you know? [laughs] There's a few things obviously you can't tolerate [...] [and] you should definitely stop this, like a case of racism [or] sexism, [...] but then there's like 'soft' opinions – that I completely disagree [with] [but] it's really hard to work- like for example [sighs] [I might] see how someone's opinion [on gender roles] as problematic, but it's not as easy as saying 'Well that's problematic', you know? Like, it's [got to be] 'Why do you think that way, do you think that's influenced by stereotypes', you know what I mean? Like it's really difficult to negotiate, like, not to make someone feel bad about an opinion that [they] probably heard all their life. [...] I think it's definitely difficult for me to determine, like, when it's something I

should stop, and when it's something that I should like try to [initiate] dialogue [about].

As Simone argues, "changing a seasoned educator's thought process is daunting, but it is necessary. Such a daunting task can result in meaningful pedagogical change" (2012:51). Whether it puts practitioners in an uncomfortable state or not, we need to ask critical questions and expose students to 'uncomfortable' issues, not just perpetuate an existing curriculum which is characterised by dominant norms. Navigating diversity in the classroom in a way that tackles marginalisation may necessitate practitioners taking certain ethical stances and political positions through teaching or learning. Education practitioners not only need to consider what they bring into the classroom but must anticipate how dominant group practices impact learning and the curriculum. In particular, they must acknowledge and critically reflect on their *own* positionality in terms of their power and privilege and how this affects their interactions and relationships with students who are marginalised (Shields, 2003).

Marginalisation and coloniality

In the previous section, I mentioned marginalisation persisting in diverse classrooms in two ways and briefly explored the first: the issue of people feeling excluded for their conservatism. This section will concern the second: how diversity often co-exists with marginalisation in classrooms due to wider threads of coloniality and white supremacy. I will offer some solutions to how this form of exclusion can be resisted in ways that move towards a learning experience based on recognition for all. This leads us on to questioning the *definition* of marginalisation, which has so far been implicitly based on simply 'feeling excluded'. Yet Freire and Macedo (1995) define marginalisation as when minority groups are divided from dominant groups and structures along lines such as race, class, gender and language. This is quite a different form of marginalisation to someone simply feeling that their conservatism is not valued by a liberal/Left consensus, because it is based on wider structural currents of oppression, rather than merely having marginal political views.

Freire and Macedo's form of marginalisation may occur in education through people feeling that they are 'not heard' because of discriminatory or silencing classroom contexts. Freire (1998) calls this the 'culture of silence', highlighting how agents become powerless to the extent that they are unable to express their lived experience of marginalisation whether within or outside of the educational context. Creating a classroom space in which openness, transparency, accountability and kindness underpin dialogue and discussion may be the answer to these silences. Our programme does seek to implement such values by deconstructing traditional hierarchical structures that presently dominate current institutions, moving from centralised decision-making to decision-making that is more transparent and involves everyone in the community. This has been mainly reflected in our quasi-democratic meetings referred to as the CCMs, which encourage free sharing of ideas and allow relevant agents such as students and staff to be involved in the decision-making process and perpetuating the ideas of inclusivity and transparency – all crucial steps towards the development of openness in HE. The fact that we have small-group learning spaces in which students are encouraged to be 'engaged' rather than 'spoken at' by a teacher is also an attempt to break down these traditional forms of domination.

However, enduring forms of marginalisation are very deep-rooted and there is always more work to do, as evidenced by our data. For instance, it is undeniable that coloniality is with us to the present day (Puwar, 2004), including in HE. The historical subjugation and domination over colonised lands was justified using discourses of race. These discourses portrayed non-white populations as primitive, infantile and incompetent in achieving modernity – they were rooted in concepts of white supremacy. The legacy of colonialism perpetuates unequal systems of power and is routinely reflected not only in the narrative of wider society but also in educational institutions. Edward Said (1978), for instance, famously highlights how knowledge as an instrument of power gives authority to whoever possesses it. This perpetuates inequalities and marginalisation by producing modes of knowledge and thinking which work to maintain and legitimise control over those who don't fit the dominant narratives.

It is perhaps therefore unsurprising that spaces which both produce and reproduce knowledge, such as universities, are so often guided, as Puwar argues, by ideologies of 'whiteness' (2004). Puwar points to the ways that intellect in universities is always *already codified* as white (2004). Ideologically then, the university is not just an intellectual space, but a white space (2004). Puwar goes further to argue how marginalised students are seen as "invaders" in a white space and how 'webs of whiteness' have continued to define spaces in education (2004:8). We see how these 'webs' are perpetuated in current affairs. The social media hashtag #blackintheivory (initiated by Shardé Davis and Joy Melody Woods) has recently illuminated incidences of prejudice, personal experience of discrimination and racial inequality in Higher Education.

While not all educational institutions reproduce these practices to the same extent or in the same ways, threads of colonial history are inevitably widely present. Marginalised people who don't fit in with the dominant discourse of 'learner' are deterred from receiving an equal and equitable education, being excluded from opportunities of dialogue and discussion that their privileged peers are afforded (Simone, 2012). The notion of a "thousand tiny cuts" (Ladson-Billings, 2006:586) emphasises the microaggressions experienced by people both inside the classroom and out, something strongly evidenced by research literature in HE (e.g. Arday, 2018; Harris, 2017; Johnson and Joseph-Salisbury, 2018; Rollock, 2011). Racial microaggressions still persist to define our educational environment in ways which must lead us to reject claims of a 'post-racial society' (the idea that racial prejudice and acts of racial discrimination no longer exist).

Ongoing campaigns based on personal experience, coupled with a wide range of academic research literature, such as those referred to above reinforce the notion that inequalities in education such as structural racism are not isolated incidents of the past but contemporary phenomena that need addressing. The empirical study of microaggression illuminates the lived experiences of students of colour at university, but more importantly has supported students, practitioners and other professionals to strive for change to the wider institutions and their practices which perpetuate fertile conditions for racism to manifest (Puwar, 2004) (e.g. the Why is My Curriculum White? campaign (see Peters, 2018), the 'Decolonise the

University' movement (see Bhambra et al., 2018) and the pivotal 2014 panel event at UCL 'Why Isn't My Professor Black?' (see Black, 2014)).

Thus, despite widespread claims that HE spaces are neutral and uniform, education practices still seem to be deeply racialised (Puwar, 2004). Despite the many efforts and campaigns within the field of education (see for example Brait, 2015; Cullen, 2016; Gebrial, 2018; Nylander, 2017) to dismantle structures within HE that reproduce marginalisation, the hegemony of the 'post-racial society' claim seems to preserve the conditions of inequality.

Moving forward

To move towards resolving marginalisation in the classroom, we must deviate from simply upholding dominant discourses and instead focus on decolonising existing structural systems of HE. Establishing a space in the classroom that ensures the lived experiences and the voices of the marginalised are heard is key to resisting dominant trends and endorsing truly democratic education (Pearl, 1997). This is essentially what the politics of difference calls for: engagement with deliberate conversations which foster social consciousness and enable individuals to begin to confront and address the structural inequalities around them.

I call for dialogue as a way to make space for the voices of those who have been marginalised and excluded. As discussed above, traditional education spaces have not provided certain students with opportunities to participate in dialogue and thus their perspectives have been overlooked. Dialogue and discussion allow these marginalised voices to be foregrounded in the classroom, and also enable us to understand and connect with those whose life experiences may be different from our own. Deliberate dialogue is about more than just communication – it is something that we owe to those who have been silenced. Dialogue, which is surely the main purpose of freedom of speech, enables students to work to deconstruct preconceptions and recognise that dialogue as a practice has not always been afforded to everyone (Simone, 2012). Freedom of speech, when framed in this way, facilitates a truer sense of community and of recognition by allowing silenced voices to be included in the classroom.

Dialogue also perpetuates reflexivity, creating space for systems of power and inequality to be questioned, and for people to consider their own actions in relation to those systems. There is some evidence we are already partway to achieving these aims on the programme. Although some participants went on to raise concerns that the iteration of freedom of speech and the atmosphere of critically challenging exclusionary perspectives has not been sufficiently normalised, other data from participants showed that discussions and dialogue within the programme have critically challenged them, leading them to question and deconstruct their preconceptions on inequality and marginalisation.

Education practitioners may also consciously or unconsciously cultivate prejudices affecting those who are marginalised. For instance, there is evidence in education literature of practitioners reinforcing assumptions that certain groups are unable to function at a level equivalent to their peers (Bereiter and Engelman, 1966). Freire and Macedo (1995) share an insightful outlook regarding the importance of staff considering their own privilege and positionality in understanding their power relationships with students. As Simone argues, this "require[s] those with power to reposition the self" (2012:34); by recognising and identifying their own roles, educators can shift the imbalances of power in the classroom, fostering systemic change. Questioning this dominant mode of thought in the classroom is never easy and there are no simple and definite solutions, but it is urgently needed.

Resolving conflict: love, kindness and reflexivity

Dialogue, as discussed above, is key for ensuring a commitment to tackling marginalisation in the classroom. However, particularly when it comes to conflict, I believe other factors – namely, love, kindness and reflexivity – are also key. This is because dialogue in the classroom needs to allow for inquisitive discussion, but without being harmful.

Kindness is crucial for the recognition of difference; we can't have constructive disagreement and we can't challenge each other and we can't be open to changing our minds or thinking from other perspectives if our intentions and interactions are not rooted in kindness, care and respect (Clegg and Rowland, 2010). Kindness is not just 'niceness': it involves critical reflection and considering things from others' perspectives, including how our knowledge of the world impacts those who are different from ourselves. In this way, kindness builds relationships of recognition by helping us to respect differential power and positionality and recognise others' lives and projects, which may be very different from our own. Clegg and Rowland argue that kindness has always been a core quality in 'good' teaching but not always a prominent or valued quality; this section is thus not offering a new way of theorising teaching but elucidating often 'forgotten' qualities in HE.

Love is a concept that I explore as another crucial factor in resolving conflict in the classroom without diminishing anyone's spirits. hooks (2010) calls for greater appreciation of the concept of 'love' in education, as it provides optimal learning conditions by ensuring conflict is addressed through principles of mutual understanding and respect. hooks rejects the posit that love in education can become "too enmeshed in a student's dilemmas" (2010:161) or lead to worry of favouritism or competition in the classroom. Rather, she puts forward the idea that love possesses transformative power in which mutual practice of partnership is enhanced, thus establishing appropriate and healthy boundaries between student and staff. Only then is recognition possible. As mentioned previously in this section, one of the ethical dilemmas of freedom of speech lies in the fact that diversity can lead to worry/fear of judgement, and threaten the existence of honest, critical exchange between teachers and students. Love and kindness in the classroom may help resolve such fears of conflict. The relationship between love and education may not be the most obvious, but is necessary on the justification that it embraces and empowers everyone, the foundation of an equitable and equal education that HE should strive to become:

"Love will always move us away from domination in all its forms. Love will always challenge and change us." (hooks, 2010:163)

In addition to the concepts of kindness and love, reflexivity is also part of ensuring classroom practices support inclusivity. Community is not possible without resolving conflicts constructively and making sure that all voices are heard. Our programme ethos works to promote an atmosphere where the community operates on the basis of openness and transparency. However, we must make sure responsibility and accountability are at play among everyone in the community, so that the safety net of 'teacher dependency' can be gradually diminished. Reflexivity is key for ensuring those responsibilities are in the foreground. Reflexive consideration starts with recognising one's positionality and privilege and thus how this integrates into dialogue. Here the idea of critical consciousness comes into play also (as mentioned in Samira Salam's chapter earlier) where consciousness around students' lived experiences of race and class helps ensure recognition in the classroom.

To be reflexive also involves listening; sociologist Les Back posits the importance of the art of listening and how it is collective, social and ethical. Back accentuates the values of listening as it connects and blurs the lines along the past, present and future. The listener seeks to give voice to those who are excluded from the public sphere and should always be reflexive of the knowledge they possess. Les Back explores how political opinions suffer from too much certainty, which may produce veils of ignorance. "The task of thinking is to live with doubt in the service of understanding"; freedom of speech in the classroom doesn't entail dismissing an unpopular belief or view but instead challenging these sentiments through criticality and a reflexive lens. We must teach students and teachers to 'tune their ears differently' and listen to their own voice in an analytical and open manner; only then can we entrust individuals to take responsibility and accountability for their words and actions.

Conclusion

Diversity in the classroom yields strength through enriching questions and dialogue; this is necessary in a world undergoing dramatic social and political change. However, diversity does not necessarily lead to the deconstruction of marginalisation. The roots of marginalisation are deep – stemming from collective histories to the present day. The multiple threads of marginalisation are reproduced in a plethora of ways in HE. I have mentioned two ways in which our data suggests marginalisation is present. The first is exclusion in the form of feeling left out from the perspective of a perceived Left/liberal political consensus. I have argued that neutrality may perpetuate existing problems of marginalisation, rather than solve them, especially in terms of reproducing prejudices by leaving certain assumptions unchallenged. The second form of exclusion is marginalisation stemming from wider structural inequalities. I suggest dialogue offers a possible solution, but emphasise that it must be pursued hand in hand with kindness, love and reflexivity.

Social justice is not just a priority for wider society or something for people to learn about in books; its realisation starts in the classroom. We need to deconstruct preconceptions and engage all relevant agents in decision-making and dialogue, deviating from a culture of deficit thinking to one that embraces the lived experiences of those who are silenced. Establishing a space in the classroom in which we seek to tackle the institutional and structural systems of HE which enforce dominant discourses is difficult but not impossible. I hope to witness the fostering of values of a collective community in which conflicts are resolved constructively and critically without silencing or diminishing anyone's spirit.

Ultimately, dismantling long-standing structures of inequality and marginalisation is in everyone's interests – it is a step towards truly 'universal' recognition. But to instigate these changes, we must first confront our past and critically reflect on how multiple threads of histories and our colonial past have come to define the purpose of HE. This does mean emphasising particular narratives, particular stories. But by confronting the microaggressions and prejudices which define our education system, I hope to see HE in its many progressive forms to foster inclusivity and equitability. I hope that HE and those who teach and learn within it to view the world through the eyes of those who are presently neglected, and to consider their lived realities. I repeat the word 'hope' in recognition of the optimism and prospect that HE can change; I hope through this as well as our programme's collective endeavours, we can take a step towards a blueprint of justice and recognition.

I don't think cis white people
Should be deciding whether we show
Videos of violence against Black trans women.

I don't think people should have to watch it
        to feel sad or closer to the subject.

I don't think that if somebody's racist
We should be 'respectful' about it.

For me there are some things we don't sit around and debate.

Particularly when it's clear
that nobody here
        in the room
has that lived experience.
For instance,
            Why can we see
            the humanity of someone that's lost their life
                from suicide
            But not of a Black trans woman that was violently attacked
                by the roadside?

Because all these structures of oppression exist in the classroom too.
            It's not a void.

There's a demographic imbalance
So there's a power imbalance
And it unintentionally reproduces patterns of violence

How do we navigate that?
When it demands a self-awareness
        and accountability
That we cannot assume exist
                Universally

What's the distinction between
letting the course be studentled,
and also enforcing the ethos of justice?
Maybe staff sometimes need to say: 'There's a line,
and *we* decide on stuff like this'.

Because I know that we love this space and I know that we're proud
But is freedom of speech about people saying whatever they want
    Out loud?

Regardless of whether that creates further exclusion?
Is that the definition
    Of 'open education'?

I don't think just being in a room together makes us a family
or a community.

I don't think it's enough to just emphasise inclusivity.

    There's more to it than being nice to each other–
    There's more than that to love and care.

    It's also about the values we share.

In defence of the politics of difference

Tope Mayomi and Freya Aquarone

Tope: As one of the few Black and openly queer students on the BA course I occupy a difficult position, often feeling as though I have to speak on behalf of both Black and queer communities, despite the fact that my lived experience as a cis woman means I will never experience oppression for my gender identity and cannot adequately speak to the trans experience. The reality of being a Black queer student in Higher Education today is being both hyper visible and invisible; our lives are constantly up for debate yet our needs are ignored. Writing this piece has highlighted for me the tension between my position as a student who is trying to learn whilst feeling obligated, particularly as an organiser, to educate others.

Freya: I am a PhD student and member of staff. As a white person from a middle-class background, I occupy a position of particular privilege when it comes to teaching: I will never experience institutional race- or class-based discrimination which place my job at risk or hinder my career progression. I am unlikely to be accused of having a personal 'race- or class-based agenda' for making claims or critically questioning people's views in my teaching. Being LGBTQ+ gives me some personal insight into the workings of non-recognition in education contexts: in particular, how easily identity and being can be intellectualised in classroom discussion, with little consideration for how they are lived and experienced by real people. And yet, writing this piece has involved many moments of uncomfortable reflection on the times when I did *not* speak out – when my silence as a practitioner allowed marginalising narratives in the classroom to go unchallenged. Allyship in education – not just in the face of racism and classism but all forms of structural marginalisation – is rarely straightforward; it's an ongoing journey, and I've got a lot to both learn and unlearn. Writing this piece is part of that journey.

We both hope this piece offers something useful to the ongoing conversations around how we can – as both students and practitioners – generate shared understandings of recognition which can work to resist systemic injustice in education.

Our data contain many contrasting perspectives on questions such as who should 'be heard' in the classroom and what freedom of speech really looks like. It strikes us that at the heart of these questions lies another, more basic, one: *what are our priorities in terms of recognition in education?* Are we so committed to a form of 'universalism' that all voices are prioritised equally, regardless of what those voices say, or how they affect others? Or do we believe that a commitment to recognition entails a duty to attend to broader inequalities of society, which often means explicitly foregrounding perspectives and lived experiences of and about marginalisation – even if this leads to perceptions of 'political bias'?

The latter articulation can be framed as a version of the politics of difference in the classroom: of seeing recognition *not* as identical treatment of all voices, at all times, but as the duty to challenge perspectives which contribute to reproducing harm. To explain how this might manifest, we first explore how pedagogical practices based on alternatives – such as 'neutrality' or 'devil's advocacy' – can reproduce harm and non-recognition. We then outline an alternative approach – drawn from principles of transformative justice – which is based on developing collective trust and accountability, grounded in overt ethical principles.

The trouble with 'neutrality'

> "If you are neutral in situations of injustice, you have chosen the side of the oppressor." – Desmond Tutu (1984)

Neutrality sounds like such a reasonable position. As one participant asked: isn't there a danger, if we allow values to shape classroom debate, that students will take staff words 'as gospel', and fail to develop the capacity for reflection and argumentation? In such a context, students –

far from building partnerships with staff, or building critical consciousness and reflexivity – could just end up as sheep, or parrots, or whatever animal you want to use for invoking docility. These are legitimate concerns. The trouble is neutrality *itself* is rarely neutral. It's a beautiful irony. Rather, neutrality can often be, quite simply, a lack of due care to ask critical questions about the status quo. And if the status quo is already unequal or violent then 'leaving it be' is not neutral: it's complicit.

For instance, it was implied by some participants that neutrality in the classroom means giving every opinion and voice the same bandwidth, and that teachers should avoid taking 'positions', in case they put people off expressing themselves:

> Michelle: At the end of the day the course is all about, like, saying your opinion and [...] if you feel that you can't say something because you think that the course has these values that [are] [...] not the same as your values, then you're not gonna feel represented in the course.

Yet the implication of this pedagogical 'neutrality' is that the programme has an unqualified commitment to "represent[ing]" – or, we might say, 'recognising' – all "opinions" *regardless* of what they confer. This is a rather extreme manifestation of Taylor's 'politics of universalism'. It suggests that however damaging or violent a perspective is, it deserves an equal platform with all others. The problem with this becomes particularly apparent in a space already marred by deep inequalities in the representation of voice. If a large number of people hold a particular viewpoint, a commitment to neutrality suggests they must be given equal airtime even if a minority view might actually need or deserve prioritised recognition. A valuable example of this is provided by the case study of the CCM concerning the video of the Muhlaysia Booker attack, outlined in chapter 3a. At the CCM, the core voice (Neve) speaking out against the majority view that the video was a useful learning tool, was defending what they perceived as the basic rights of a marginalised community. As the extract from Neve below implies, when certain voices are not present in a community space, it can too easily lead to a 'tyranny of the majority' in which particular needs are disregarded by virtue of demographic:

> Neve: [F]or me there are some things that we don't even sit around and debate, particularly when it's very clear that there's nobody in that room that has that particular experience. [...] I hate being in situations where it's just like... six cis people in a room talking about trans people, and there's no acknowledgement of the fact that none of us are trans [...]. Because even like, you know, [in the CCM] I was sort of [...] like speaking for a certain community, but I don't really have the right to do that either – I don't wanna do that, I don't feel comfortable doing that... but [...] I did that because I didn't want to see that video to be honest and, like, yeah I have Black trans friends that wouldn't want to see that video either.

Though we need to be careful about homogenising or essentialising, people's positionalities and lived experiences strongly inform their worldview. In a context as unequal and non-diverse as Higher Education (as demonstrated throughout this chapter), the idea that this is in any way representative or democratic is evidently incoherent. No wonder then, as bell hooks observes, "many students, especially students of color, may not feel at all 'safe' in what appears to be a neutral setting" (1994:39). Enduring inequalities demand much more of practitioners than the treating of all voices with identical esteem. Indeed, most democracies are underpinned by specific deontological values, to avoid the violation of basic rights in the name of the 'will of the people'.

With all this in mind, it seems reasonable, as Neve puts it, that there are "some things that we don't even sit around and debate" – some basic ethical limits to deliberation. Such premises have sometimes led to accusations in the media of Higher Education becoming characterised by censorship or 'cancel culture'- especially in relation to votes by student unions to 'no-platform' speakers whose views they believe violate fundamental principles (e.g. Turner, 2018; Roberts, 2017). Evidently, drawing such 'lines in the sand' is no easy task, and there are concerning implications for academic freedom which need to be faced head on. But the idea that there is ever a total lack of principles underpinning free speech is a misnomer: freedom of speech is not the right to say whatever you want without consideration for the consequences. Rights come with attendant responsibilities. Otherwise, a 'free' classroom is one where we would have to give equal credence to 'debating' whether women are less intelligent than men, or whether the Holocaust 'happened'. Quite apart from it being a shame to spend what limited time we have on such patently ridiculous (and, frankly, intellectually boring) questions, this strategy is in direct conflict with a commitment to recognition. Because this kind of limitless opinion-sharing too often means reproducing discourses which deny the humanity of the marginalised. Thus, Leonardo and Porter – in analysing definitions of 'safe spaces' as "environment[s] where fundamental issues can be broached and no one will be offended" (2010:147) – suggest we must always ask: "safe for whom?" (ibid.:139)

The trouble with manufacturing debates

> May: I think there needs to be an understanding that this stuff is real and people are actually experiencing this stuff and it's not just something that we need to learn and then be assessed on and move on.

The importance of Leonardo and Porter's question – 'safe for whom?' – is well exemplified by the idea that staff should 'manufacture debates' in the classroom. This was suggested by a number of participants as a means of stimulating more diverse discussion on the programme. It was suggested staff should adopt positions for or against specific issues, and either play – or encourage others to play – 'devil's advocate' for a range of perspectives. Once again, this may sound appealing at first glance, but it raises problems for recognition, not least in terms of concern for wellbeing. Privilege affords the luxury of seeing discussion of injustice as a purely intellectual exercise (Leonardo and Porter, 2010); as hooks writes, "the person who is most powerful has the privilege of denying their body" (1994:137). For someone with lived experience of injustice, however, the process can never be purely intellectual; others parading pretend opinions about racism or homophobia or sexism could just be yet another reliving of prejudiced discourse (Leonardo and Porter, 2010:151). This was well highlighted by an exchange between participants on how debates could be manufactured in the classroom in relation to sexual assault:

Michelle: Yeah, like, I feel for example we're talking about, like, sexism and [...] we're all girls, everyone's like "yeah, yeah, yeah, yeah, yeah", like...

Erica: And if there is one boy who would think differently, he would never say 'Hmm, I think it's okay to get raped', you know?

Michelle: [...] And I think [the seminar tutor should] [...] just, like, say the other point like 'Imagine I'm a boy, I think that like, rape is blah, blah, blah or, like, sexism doesn't really exist', things like that to trigger us to like respond to her, so like [the tutor] could play out as an actor just to say that they have an another point? Make clear that that's not her [own opinion], but just try to make the other point because the other point is not [represented] in the class. You know what I mean?

Researcher: Yes. Isn't it dangerous though, putting out there some very controversial point, even as acting?

Michelle: But not really controversial, not like, saying like, 'Rape is fine' or saying things like that. [...] Just saying, like, things that we hear all the time, like, 'I think it was [...] the girl's fault', [...] things like that.

It is interesting that the word "trigger" is used above to refer to generating *debate* when the subject matter under discussion is also a clear example of that which could trigger a trauma response from survivors of sexual violence. We cannot know what lived experience people bring into the room with them, but 'debating' a subject like this is clearly problematic if we want the classroom to be a space which prioritises love and care. Returning once again to the CCM about Muhlaysia Booker, we face the same problem of differential lived experience. Some participants were clear (as were the majority of people who spoke in the CCM) that the video was educationally important because it helped them to understand the issue of violence against Black trans women and to "feel closer to the subject" (Michelle). As one participant put it: "we have to face it to learn it" (Erica).

But this is questionable. The idea that classrooms should be places in which tough issues are treated 'on the nose' and people are made to confront the discomfiting realities of the world and its injustices is not incompatible with rejecting the idea that issues should be debated without restraint or consideration of their emotional impact. Proximity may facilitate empathy, as argued in chapter 4, but there are ways of achieving proximity which do not involve giving a platform to violent video footage or engaging in polarised 'debate'. Much of this is about the extent to which our intellectual discussions are grounded in a context of collective trust and accountability, which enables us to hear one another, and to encounter difference, without reproducing harm and misrecognition. We explore this more in due course.

Which voices to prioritise

In light of the above concerns, we echo bell hooks' suggestion that, while a commitment to engaged pedagogy "assumes that every student has a valuable contribution to make to the learning process", it does "*not* assume that all voices should be heard all the time or that all voices should occupy the same amount of time" (hooks, 2010:21, emphasis added). In other words, redressing systemic inequality in education may mean making explicit ethical choices to foreground certain voices, and to challenge others.

We have taken it somewhat for granted so far which voices should be challenged and which should be foregrounded. It is perhaps worth addressing this, because there is a danger of inadvertently suggesting that being a "minority" view *per se* is enough to justify special treatment in the name of counter-hegemony. This would mean that the white supremacy of the *English Defence League* would have to be classified as some kind of 'marginalised perspective'. Luckily, there are ways to escape this paradox. Social justice theorist Nancy Fraser, for instance, argues that true recognition is about ensuring "parity of participation" in society – about deconstructing social and institutional patterns of exclusion and prejudice which would prevent certain groups from being recognised as "full partner[s] in social interaction" (2008:58). If parity overall is our aim, then it seems clear that our recognition of a particular group is always subject to a caveat: a demand for recognition cannot itself be predicated on the non-recognition of others[27].

In other words, the EDL's demand that whiteness be the basis of English nationality, because it is *predicated* on racism, voids its own legitimacy. Similarly, viewpoints in the classroom based on non- or mis-recognition ('racism doesn't exist', 'women are inferior to men', 'being gay is a sin') do not ethically warrant recognition in the same way as do opinions which merely *differ* from one another, but without being predicated on overt exclusion. There is so much interesting diversity in opinion on how to solve social problems – why must we limit ourselves intellectually to baseline prejudice rather than more nuanced, urgent debates? Let's take the example of trans rights (crossly described by anonymous academics at our own College last month as a "fashionable orthodoxy" used to justify "censorship" and "cancel culture" (Less and Coutts, 2020)). There is so much of interest to discuss in relation to gender identity without giving time to tired essentialist tropes such as 'trans women are not women'. Questions like 'How would the sporting industry adapt to a world in which people self-ID gender?', or 'Where do non-binary people fit into discussions around trans identities?'. These are the kinds of genuinely interesting questions which emerge when we move from polarised opining to real-world experiences and solutions, and they deserve our intellectual energy.

---

[27] This dilemma and its proposed resolution are connected to debates around what Karl Popper (1945) calls the 'paradox of tolerance': the problem that if we decide, in the name of tolerance/inclusion, that all values/beliefs/practices should be tolerated or included in society, then this principle will eventually be undermined by the inclusion and tolerance of values/beliefs/practices that are themselves *in*tolerant and *ex*clusive. Numerous commentators (e.g. Popper, 1945; Cohen-Almagor, 1991) have offered solutions to the paradox which, though contrasting in their terms and application, are along the lines that, to be granted tolerance, a value/belief/practice must not *itself* be explicitly intolerant of others/particular groups. Evidently, this principle is more clear-cut in some instances than others, but it is embedded in part in the Universal Declaration of Human Rights - in its refusal to grant legal protection to extremist speech - and is at the root of a number of more specific national legal framings of free speech (a common example being the belief that Holocaust denial is such an obvious breach of recognition of a violent historical event entailing the death and suffering of millions that some countries - such as Germany - legally restrict dissemination of materials and resources promoting it). A similar principle is being increasingly firmly applied in social media platforms' policies on 'hateful conduct'.

In case it seems that we are setting up a straw person in this discussion, and you are starting to wonder whether such dilemmas ever actually occur in real-life classrooms, here is a semi-fictionalised[28] scenario based on our classroom experience:

In a seminar we are discussing the gender pay gap and various theories about its cause. One student says that they think we need to discuss the idea that maybe women are just 'different' to men. There is a difficult pause in the room because no one is quite sure of the implications of what is being suggested. The seminar tutor asks the student to elaborate and the student puts forward a position which suggests that women might just be less capable than men because of innately 'different strengths', and that they may be particularly ill-suited to high level management or 'leadership' roles. Some students in the room respond very strongly that this position is harmful and flawed. The seminar tutor steps in and explains how a perspective like this could reinforce both essentialist narratives of gender and also ideas of women as 'inferior'. They explain that – to their knowledge – there is no evidence that women are innately incapable of management and leadership. However, the seminar tutor also attempts to reframe the student's perspective in a different light, suggesting that the idea that social assumptions around gender may condition some women into feeling they are not 'right' for certain jobs could add an interesting dimension to the debate, and that there is plenty of useful and contested literature about the impact of gender conditioning in the field of employment. The student rejects this rearticulating of their position and restates their original claim about innate differences and the consequences for professional 'leadership'. The seminar tutor says that they would be happy to talk more with the student about this if they can find any relevant literature, and swiftly moves the discussion back to the rest of the group's ideas and questions around the gender pay gap. The student looks frustrated and says little else for the remainder of the seminar.

---

[28] This semi-fictionalisation is to protect the identity of those who may be implicated.

In this example, the teacher faces a choice. The seminars only last an hour. They can pause the rest of the group's discussion to attend in depth to the claim that being a woman makes someone innately less capable of leadership. This would effectively mean redirecting time and attention to this student's gender essentialism, and away from the nuanced and complex debate around the various possible causes of the gender pay gap. They could take the student aside and talk to them one-to-one, but this would mean directing their energy away from the rest of the group. Or they could – as they did in this instance – draw a line under the discussion, and decide to deprioritise this student's perspective, even if it risks them feeling silenced. Is this censorship, or ethics? While we appreciate Les Back's claim – cited in an earlier section – that "we need to know what racist arguments sound like" (2010), there is an equally powerful argument in Toni Morrison's position that constantly attempting to counter clear-cut articulations of prejudice is a "distraction" which keeps us from the more important tasks of social change[29]:

"The function, the very serious function of racism is distraction. It keeps you from doing your work. It keeps you explaining, over and over again, your reason for being. Somebody says you have no language and you spend twenty years proving that you do. Somebody says your head isn't shaped properly so you have scientists working on the fact that it is. Somebody says you have no art, so you dredge that up. Somebody says you have no kingdoms, so you dredge that up. None of this is necessary. There will always be one more thing" (Morrison, 1975).

This is why Black Lives Matter campaigners have been calling on people to stop arguing with overtly racist family members, and instead spend their energy on the people who can be meaningfully engaged with, and on

---

[29] Not least because, arguably, we already know what racist arguments sound like. People are constantly bombarded by such viewpoints, not least if they are themselves Black, Brown or a 'person of colour'; the dangers of the 'echo chamber' – so often invoked by the political Right – are only a reality for those not forced to grapple, daily, with other people's prejudice.

genuinely unresolved, urgent questions around how to commit to anti-racism.

To some extent, these decisions are determined by context. There is evidently no cut and dry rulebook for when to engage and when to move on – for what is useful and what is distraction. Sometimes it is necessary to move on because dialogue isn't working (as in the case study above) or because serious harm is being caused, and sometimes it's necessary to open up a conversation about *why* a particular viewpoint is problematic[30]. Sometimes people in the room need to respond to what has been said in more depth than can be achieved in a couple of sentences. And sometimes someone expresses a perspective which, though reductive, may provide an important springboard for exploration (e.g. 'poverty is mostly caused by people's choices', 'violence is the only way to achieve change', 'capitalism/communism don't work'). Choosing to spend time delving in further in these instances can be both emotionally and analytically healing and/or constructive. The process of making these decisions demands the constant critical reflexivity of those who wish to educate in the name of justice, as well as of the communities of learners in which they live and work.

Some people may still perceive the decision to delineate certain views as beyond ethical, legitimate debate – or to expose particular viewpoints to a greater degree of challenge and critique – as bias or as narrowing the debate. There are echoes of this in the debates around 'decolonising the university'; opponents often suggest the movement seeks to 'erase' content from curriculum and practice, and narrow intellectual enquiry. Yet it can actually be framed as a matter of ethical integrity – of allowing space for new and often silenced voices to come to the table. When the world has removed the history of certain peoples from our dominant consciousness, the decision, as learners and educators, to re-centre it – to "exhum[e] it from the past" (Fanon, 1952:99) – is surely less a terrifying act of censorship and more an act of illumination: of widening our cognitive horizons.

---

[30] This is the essence of the 'calling in/calling out' distinction, explored below.

Building trust and accountability: the importance of shared values

Above we established some ethical priorities in terms of 'voice' in the classroom. We argued that neutrality isn't helpful – that a commitment to recognition means asking questions about "Who speaks? Who listens? And why?" (hooks, 1994:40) – and that manufacturing debate can often be a harmful way of trying to highlight difference. Of course, there will always be difference in the classroom – even conflict – and this need not be about causing harm. On the contrary, when conflict is constructive, it is a healthy part of any human community. That is precisely why a commitment to 'freedom of speech' – so long as it goes hand in hand with responsibility to consider others – is fundamental to democratic, inclusive pedagogy.

The crux of the question lies, then, in how we can create an environment where conflict and difference can manifest *without* the reproduction of harm – where people can feel heard, whilst also upholding a shared commitment to accountability. If everyone is too concerned about people's feelings to speak out openly, then that needs to be addressed through building a space of trust and comfort with opposition and with challenge. Part of that is involves setting expectations collectively about the way a space works. About what is and isn't okay to share and to show. About how to take others into consideration when we explain our perceptions of the world.

bell hooks (2010) describes this in relation to the context of a loving relationship – no one thinks that the absence of conflict in this relationship would be healthy, and yet in genuinely loving relationships we know that when we raise our voice or get upset, it is okay, it is safe to do so. That it's also okay to get it wrong sometimes – and that doesn't mean we'll be shamed or humiliated. Because we trust and care about one another. In other words, the shared values and responsibilities that underpin loving relationships mean we can enter into conflict, safe in the knowledge that it will either be constructive, or that harm caused will be meaningfully addressed. hooks suggests that, similarly, love and trust are integral to education: both for holding ourselves accountable when harm is caused and – ideally – protecting the possibility for open, non-harmful, constructive conflict. She writes:

"It is helpful to explain to students from the start of a new class the importance of trust and the ways we link it to accountability. To trust means having confidence in one's own and another person's ability to take care, to be mindful of one another's wellbeing. Choosing to trust, to be mindful, requires then that we think carefully about what we say and how we say it, considering as well the impact of our words on fellow listeners" (hooks, 2010:87).

hooks' description of the relationship between trust, accountability and voice is echoed in the paradigm of 'transformative justice'. Transformative justice practitioners such as Mariame Kaba and Mia Mingus have an understanding that, in order to uphold collective accountability, all members of a community need to consent to being part of the underpinning processes of dealing with conflict and harm. This is based on the idea that, ultimately, I can only hold *myself* accountable; calling out another member of the community for harm caused is not enough. We need to know they will listen, that they will commit to doing the work needed to transform the situation. Thus, while freedom of speech comes with a duty to consider others, it is also predicated on the assumption that others are doing the same and considering *us*. In other words, true community is dependent on, as one participant put it, the "values we share" (Rebecca); otherwise we are just individuals on a university course who happen to be in the room together for the sake of getting a degree. Such a space isn't safe for anyone, because consideration of one another's needs is absent. Without a collective commitment to the values underpinning our behaviour, it's little use having careful procedures for helping people to learn from their words and from how they might make others feel.

The distinction between 'calling in' and 'calling out' helps to highlight these processes of collective accountability. While these are primarily tools for dealing with harm rather than simply 'difference', it helps to illustrate the significance of shared values in all instances of disagreement. 'Calling out' is a way of clearly and swiftly drawing those 'lines in the sand' (discussed earlier) about what perspectives are simply incompatible with justice. 'Calling in' is a way of helping members of our community engage in a process of furthering knowledge and understanding. Rather than simply seeking to put an immediate stop to clear instances of harm, 'calling in' is about engaging in critical discussion and reflection about *how and why harm has been caused*, and what can be done to transform the situation to prevent it in future. In other words, 'calling in' places a greater emphasis on trying to help people to understand when and why lines are being drawn, and – crucially – to engage in dialogue.

Evidently there are always some things that fall into the former category of non-negotiable – as identified earlier in this chapter. For instance, the reproduction of video footage of violence against Muhlaysia Booker should be seen as a clear instance of violating baseline ethics. However, as Neve suggested earlier, the CCM could have provided an important opportunity for collective learning around *why* it's problematic to platform violent content in general. By raising the concern in the CCM, Neve was arguably attempting to 'call out' the showing of the video, but to 'call *in*' the issue of platforming violence in general. Unfortunately, however – as discussed earlier – many felt the conversation became a polarised debate rather than a process of collective reflection and listening. This is because 'calling in' is only appropriate if there is already collective consent to these 'transformative' approaches. In other words, 'calling in' should not be used as a means of justifying creating a space in which people never feel directly challenged. It is not about treading on eggshells around people simply for the sake of avoiding offence – it's about trusting that fellow members of the community are willing to engage in 'transforming' the situation. As activist Loan Trần puts it, "calling in [is for] people who we want to be in community with, people who we have reason to trust or with whom we have common ground. It's not a [...] free-for-all for those with privilege to demand we put their hurt feelings first regardless of the harm they cause" (Loan Trần, 2013).

The role of staff in supporting collective trust and accountability

We think it is worth highlighting that staff have an important role to play in upholding the ethos of collective trust and accountability described above. An education space founded on trust and comfort with opposition and with challenge includes, of course, normalising and challenging teachers: engaged pedagogy is surely about helping students to realise precisely that teachers' words are *not* "God's words" (Erica) – but part and parcel of collective dialogue. Nonetheless, treating students as partners does not mean accepting their opinions uncritically. As Dan and Joe identify below, there is a danger that if staff simply take a step back on the grounds of egalitarianism, they allow marginalisation to go unchallenged:

> Joe: [T]his is something I don't actually often get right, [in] stepping back and letting [students] take ownership of the space. [B]ecause actually we have responsibility for that space, both emotionally and intellectually [...] [and] sometimes if I let conversations just go free, sometimes they actually stray into areas in ways that I find quite problematic. And then things go unchallenged, and I think that means I'm being complicit in, like, the perpetuation of narratives that actually this space is meant to be challenging.

> Dan: [There have been times in seminars] when students have literally unburdened themselves about struggles that they've faced in their lives – really real struggles, material struggles, personal stuff... and the response has been [insensitive or judgemental]. That kind of a response, like absolute, like, unpleasantness. [...] [S]o initially I said that I wasn't gonna talk- 'Don't look at me, I'm gonna talk as little as I can'. After that particular episode, I said 'I'm sorry, but I'm gonna be intervening quite a lot from now on'. [...] [A]nd I'm sorry about that but I just felt that [not intervening] was so risky. And a lot of students were upset. [...] Yeah, I just don't know that I feel comfortable letting them loose on each other.

Educators are always vested with some degree of authority and influence in the classroom. Much of this is to do institutional hierarchy which vests staff with power (whether they like it or not) and which clearly needs resisting and deconstructing. But in any given space, some people taking on the role of facilitators may be justifiable and even desirable. For instance, on our programme, some people have knowledge and consciousness which is not shared by everyone in the room. One would hope that staff would be among them as 'experienced learners'. But what *also* marks staff apart in the institutional context in which the programme operates is that they are uniquely positioned to act as facilitators: it is part of their positionality as an educator to help others acquire that knowledge and consciousness. They can thus often do so with fewer social costs (such as upsetting personal friends) and greater sway than students. In other words, while as a community we seek to work towards a more egalitarian way of educating – in which the role of facilitator could be played by anyone with the right skills – we can't ignore the existing institutional dynamics, which mean staff are – in effect – already positioned to play a facilitator role. Given this, it seems reasonable that staff are the ones who uphold baseline principles around how the space is conducted. This might include making certain training compulsory or initiating foundational conversations around topics such as anti-racism or structural oppression, as some participants suggested:

> Rebecca: Yeah [we need to] not replicate oppressive structures in the classroom. [...] The fact [is] that we've just been given these really heavy topics, with no discussion about how we deal with these topics.

Staff providing students with a framework for engaging with social issues in a non-harmful way need not be an act of authoritarianism which undermines the capacity for partnership. Rather, it is about setting the scene in which partnership takes place. This may mean, as May and Rebecca identify in their exchange below, that a tension sometimes emerges between the desire to support "student-led" approaches in the community while also upholding a commitment to an "ethos" of recognition in other respects:

> May: I mean, I know I understand they want to make this like a [...] student-led course, whatever. But like when it comes to stuff like [the Muhlaysia Booker video], they need to stand their ground and say, 'Hey, like we shouldn't be showing videos like that', not like, 'Oh, let the students decide'.

Rebecca: [It's] like where is the line between letting the course be student-led and also enforcing the ethos?

In other words, the programme's commitment to recognition as equality and partnership should not be at the expense of recognition of the harms of marginalisation! Navigating the "line" between these competing versions of recognition is not necessarily straightforward. But acknowledging the challenge is part of the process of constant critical reflection integral to any community committed to social justice. This process of critical reflection must inevitably be a shared one, which includes both students and staff; nonetheless, for all the reasons identified above, staff have a unique responsibility to act as its facilitators. If anything, this is what distinguishes their role from the rest of the community.

Some final thoughts

As hooks writes, "no true supporter of free speech endorses censorship, hence it is all the more important to be aware as teachers and students that our speech can be verbally abusive, that it can perpetuate domination and breed hate" (2010:87). Thus, our right to freedom of speech comes with an attendant responsibility: to consider others. You cannot 'say what you want' without consideration of the consequences; freedom of speech must go hand in hand with collective values around challenging the reproduction of harm.

What counts as 'harm' or as 'domination' and 'hate' is often contested. Sometimes the lines are very blurred. But sometimes they are very clear. We have tried to delineate a baseline for who should be 'heard' in the classroom, grounded in the philosophical premise that your views do not deserve equal recognition if they are predicated on the non-recognition of others. This has significant consequences for education: it means that views upholding the rights and lived experiences of marginalised groups will often need to be at the heart of deliberative exploration of social and political issues. We can name this political bias on the grounds that it violates a particular vision of neutrality; or we can call it ethical practice on the grounds that it recognises – and seeks to redress – deep, historical, entrenched inequalities.

The role of staff is of course integral to upholding this pedagogical vision, as explored above. But ultimately, it needs to be a collective endeavour. The hope is that we can, collectively, develop precisely the forms of community accountability which minimise situations which require staff to step in for the sake of harm-prevention, and instead help us to be okay with both challenging and being challenged, safe in the knowledge that we trust and care for one another. This, ultimately, is the best terrain for the most interesting, thought-provoking and life-affirming forms of difference and personal expression to flourish.

One final, closing thought: earlier this year, in the wake of the BLM protests, the long-standing student campaign at Oxford University, 'Rhodes Must Fall' (inspired by the campaign of the same name at the University of Cape Town), gained an unexpected victory (Mohdin, 2020). Rhodes has finally fallen. But that campaign was always about so much more than statues of colonialists: it's about critically debating what people, ideas, and histories should be given the spotlight in educational discourse and institutions. It's about questioning the idea that taking certain, deeply destructive narratives *off* privileged platforms (whether literally or figuratively) is 'erasing history', rather than recognising the deep silences in our collective memories. It is, in short, about putting a politics of difference front and centre in how we think about the priorities of Higher Education: seeing acknowledgement of people's lived experiences of structural marginalisation and inequality as a core commitment of recognitional justice. As educators, we should be unapologetic about this commitment. As Fanon wrote, somewhat provocatively, in their famous text *Black Skin, White Masks:*

> "I put the white man [sic] back into his place; growing bolder, I jostled him and told him point-blank, "Get used to me, I am not getting used to anyone." I shouted my laughter to the stars." (1952:100)

Storms of Change

by Eleni Koutsouri

In the storms of change, all water drops are one.
All equally powerful,
All equally important.
In the challenges of learning,
the "I" becomes "we",
Serenity is disturbed,
And lost questions look for temporary shelter in temporary answers.
In the eyes of the world,
Neither time nor any crime could prevent change from happening.
The ultimate form of kindness,
For one's soul,
For one's mind,
Its impact can be priceless,
Its power divine.
From spring to summer,
From sunshine to rain,
No natural or taught laws could ever fail change.
Raised from the ashes or born on fertile land,
Change will always be the most loving form of art.

Epilogue

Throughout this book we have attempted to explore how participants' experiences of the BA Social Sciences programme can be understood through the lens of recognition. We have explored recognition in various forms: through love, care and kindness, through partnership and equality, and through practices associated with tackling marginalisation. Our data offer much positivity and affirmation of the programme's practice in these respects, but also a lot of scope for critical reflection about how things could be better.

For instance, in chapter 2 we explored the need for clearer procedures on handling interpersonal conflict, for stronger lines of communication, for building greater shared understanding of institutional constraints, and for finding more time to spend together as a community. In chapter 3, we explored the need to build skills and awareness in inclusive, critically reflexive decision-making as well as to improve levels of engagement with the CCMs. We raised similar issues around engagement in relation to learning and teaching and covered various specific concerns about pedagogical approach. In chapter 5 we highlighted the need to improve diversity in HE access, and to develop greater critical consciousness about the fact that people's positionalities *do* have a powerful impact on their experiences of the programme, and mean that not everybody feels as included in the community as some would claim. Chapter 5 also raised a number of critical questions around clarifying the meaning of openness and free speech in education. We explored how to create learning spaces based on openness – where people feel they can be 'heard' even where their views differ from the majority, how to build greater collective accountability through shared values around harm-prevention and conflict resolution, and how recognition might require us to foreground experiences and histories of marginalisation.

The capacity of the programme to respond to these crucial critiques cannot, of course, be detached from its context; many participants, alongside highlighting important work for the community to reflect on, also pointed to the limitations of wider structures. Some of these structures related to the context of contemporary HE, such as its increasing marketisation: the reduction of HE to the function of preparing students to become 'successful' economic agents (Hess, 2009), in a competitive market of 'providers', has clearly generated workload pressures, consumer mindsets and resource constraints which place real strain on attempts to embed recognition in our practice. Other (connected) challenges were to do with the hierarchical and elitist structures of mainstream universities, which mean admissions practices, for instance – as well as a host of other factors – are out of the programme's hands (and patently clash with its attempts to promote forms of democratic self-governance). Almost all of these challenges were framed by entrenched, systemic inequalities, such as the historical and contemporary marginalisation of particular groups of people within both HE and wider society.

The impact of these broader structures should not be underestimated. Indeed, a powerful theme in our data – among staff in particular – was concern about the limits of what the programme can achieve, given both the institutional and wider social context in which it operates:

> Luke: [I]t's difficult 'cos I think on the one hand, we sort of have to have these aspirations for the programme knowing that the institutional context will mean it's very difficult... to enact.

> Joe: [I]t's happened so many times this year [laughs] where I've come home and I've just gone 'We're trying to do something *really* big at a very *late* point in people's educational journeys' – and that goes for [both] staff and students. And there is a lot of damage to undo, and a lot of preconceptions to challenge, and sometimes I get exhausted by the enormity of that task, to be completely honest.

> Rosa: [S]ometimes I think what we're doing is like... it's the minimum, you know? [laughs] It's the minimum. And I don't mean by that to put it down in any way, 'cos I also think it's amazing [...] but in another way I just think [...] you know, if this was the norm [...] then it would be really exciting. We could think 'Right, how do we make it really [work], you know, [...] [and] push it further'.

Evidently, the programme's attempts to realise recognition are not without their many dilemmas and shortcomings. And evidently, many of these *are* shaped by powerful limitations associated with both the immediate and broader context. None of this can be eradicated just by a single individual, team, or community "trying to do things differently" (Simon). But we'd like to field the question: what is the alternative to trying? Accepting the enduring power of structures is not about resigning ourselves to determinism; just because we cannot completely transform the broader picture does not deny the significance of resistance. We might be shaped by structures, but we are *also always shaping them*. And when enough people do things differently, persistently, structures can change.

Blaming the constraints of context does little to transform Higher Education into the kind of space we all allegedly want and call for. Perhaps everyone is just too "exhausted" (Joe) to do anything else – and arguably the self-care from which such a position stems is, in so many ways, inseparable from recognition itself. But we have to accept that going with the tide may contribute to perpetuating – rather than simply 'leaving be' – the status quo in HE. And given the entrenched inequalities and prejudice of the Academy highlighted throughout this book, that's a concerning prospect. Indeed, if theories of recognition tell us anything, it's that *how we see and treat others* can generate identities with extraordinary permanence and power. That means our relationships, in our everyday lives, matter. We get to decide what characterises those relationships. We can opt to refuse hierarchical micropolitics which erode people's self-esteem and professional dignity. To refuse to contribute to the reproduction of marginalisation and non-recognition. To refuse to treat students as customers, strangers, or people whose voices don't matter (perhaps all the easier to do if we feel valued and recognised within our own professional teams).

We can strive for these things and still keep in mind the limitations of context. In other words, maybe there is a way to, as Gewirtz and Cribb put it, "steer a careful course between the twin dangers of naive optimism and pessimistic determinism" (2020:228). But that does mean expecting the journey to be difficult. Rebecca Solnit's book on the history of activism, *Hope in the Dark* (2016), points out how common it is, especially among activists, to cling to misplaced notions of 'victory' as some kind of idealised end point against which every step of the journey is measured. With such a high bar it's no wonder, Solnit says, that people get frustrated with the two-steps-forward-one-step-back reality of change. Because there is only ever a learning curve, only ever little breakthroughs within a landscape made up of lots of mistakes and lots of 'good enoughs'.

So we can spend all our time reminiscing about some "golden age" of Higher Education's past (Holden, 2014:24) or talking about how we wish we were in a different, more perfect future. But, as the French philosopher Blaise Pascal (1670) once famously pointed out: all we can really do is decide what kind of contribution we want to make to *the present* – to the world we are actually in. And in fact, one of the most consistent themes in our data – alongside a lot of honesty about challenges and shortcomings – was one of optimism about what the programme is trying to build:

> Rachel: [W]e're trying to be [...] a community. And we're actually trying to, in a way, as students, [...] help create the programme, as we're going through it, with the staff members. So we can [...] help the next few cohorts to have an even better programme. [...] [A]nd, like, especially during the strikes I think, our course did, like, the most teach-outs? Yeah so I thought that was really interesting to know that, like, people who are studying social sciences – they're not only trying to like, get a degree and get a job but they're actually trying to change the world. And I feel like the majority of our course feels the same way? [...] [A]re trying to change the world in some way or another.

> Luke: [T]his programme [...], it *is* going to be delivered at this institution so, you know, it- you can't really get away [laughs] from that [...]. We need to be realistic about that side of things. But that's not to say that we can't [...] push for a version of the programme that we think is meaningful. And that we can't seek to carve out, you know, a vision [...] which is distinct [...] [from] the culture and practice of the rest of the institution.

Joe: I admit that cold professionalism might be a hell of a lot easier to pull off – a bit like authoritarianism is a much easier thing to enact than democracy. But, well, life is way too short to not build meaningful relationships.

It doesn't matter that we don't always succeed in this "vision" – that we get things wrong, that we stumble. What matters is that, as bell hooks writes, we do not "act as though it is somehow a naive moral position to believe that our lives [can] be a living example" of our educational values (1994:48). The fall out would be to accept that nothing can change and – surely – "life is too short" for that.

Executive summary

Below we have attempted to highlight the key points – and some key data – from each chapter of the book. We also have tried to summarise theoretical concepts, where relevant. However, this is not a comprehensive account of all issues addressed, nor should it be seen as representative of the text as a whole. Attempting to crystallise takeaway messages is a tricky task: it means some things – not least the messy 'human' bits (which are often the most interesting) – are necessarily lost. Nonetheless, we hope that this executive summary provides a useful accompanying document to the main text, as well as an indication of its core components.

Chapter 1: Relationships and Recognition

Chapter 1 provided an overview of the core thematic focus of the book and our theoretical lens. Our data seemed to tell a story of a programme trying to emphasise meaningful educational relationships in spite of many contextual constraints. In attempting to make sense of this, we applied the concept of 'recognition' – a core tenet of social justice theory through which writers have tried to articulate what it means to affirm, value and esteem other people. This theoretical approach felt particularly appropriate because the BASS programme defines itself as seeking to facilitate social

> "Higher Education has become individualised and [...], you know, the marketisation of education has kind of promoted a sense in which individual customers are receiving services from an institution and the service providers that work at that institution. And if there is any way in which we are going to escape and transcend that model [...] it's through establishing a *community of learners.*" (Luke, staff member)

justice and social change; it therefore seemed to make sense to use a core part of social justice theorising – the concept of recognition – to analyse the programme itself. We analysed our data in relation to various well-established articulations of recognition – exploring both the ways in which the programme can be seen to realise recognition as well as the challenges it faces in doing so.

Chapter 2: Recognition as Love, Care and Kindness

In chapter 2 we explored one of the most prevalent themes in our data, which related to participant descriptions of the programme as a space which emphasises love, care and kindness. Axel Honneth defines this form of recognition as "emotional concern for [people's] wellbeing and needs" (van Leeuwen, 2007:182). This manifested in several specific ways in the data, through references to:

The informal, non-hierarchical nature of student-staff relationships, which participants suggested enables students to feel comfortable approaching staff with their needs and concerns, whether academic or personal.

The programme's emphasis on valuing and talking about mental health in the community. The sense that such discussions are normalised seems to have made it easier for students to open up to staff, and to see staff concern for their wellbeing as authentic rather than tokenistic.

> "The staff, like, actually care about you as well. So it's not just the students but the community feel comes from the staff as well, like being able to kind of say how you feel, or if something's wrong, you feel comfortable doing that. [...] It's like a constant message that 'You can speak to us', sort of thing? [...] [T]he message is reiterated all the time." (Maya, student)

The importance of knowing one another. The opportunity to learn things about one another's lives – not just people's names, but their interests and needs and struggles – was seen as core to building emotionally meaningful relationships on the programme.

Dealing constructively with interpersonal conflict – in particular, building a 'working agreement' outlining principles governing community interactions.

Several challenges were identified in terms of building relationships based on love, care and kindness:

Consumerist framings of HE and student identity. Some participants felt that mutually caring relationships can be obscured by student demands around 'value for money' (demands which became particularly apparent during the 2020 strike action). It was suggested that these demands can undermine consideration for staff and do not tally with phenomena like love and kindness – which are about upholding inherent ethical values rather than pursuing commodified outcomes. Nonetheless, it is notable that a significant number of participants indicated strong forms of resistance to consumerist framings of their learner identity.

Lines of communication. It was suggested that when strong lines of communication are absent (which was, again, especially apparent during the strike), it can generate anxiety on the part of students, and erode their confidence in approaching staff about concerns. It was also suggested that a lack of face-to-face contact can lead to a reliance on electronic media, which are less conducive to compassionate communication. Finally, it was suggested that lack of communication erodes the possibility for building understanding across the staff-student divide – e.g. for helping students understand the realities of the institutional constraints faced by staff.

Institutional culture/set-up. Many participants suggested that the bureaucracy and anonymity of the College is not set up to care for them as students. Staff pointed to the way they sometimes feel complicit in 'symbolically violent' institutional practices such as standardised marking procedures.

Interpersonal conflict was highlighted as something which does not always have a clear procedure or 'place' within the programme community – particularly when students have concerns about specific members of staff. The Course Community Meeting (CCM) remit does not extend to conflict between individuals, but a small number of students felt that raising things informally through other routes – e.g. their personal tutor – had not led to necessary action/change.

Time was one of the most consistently mentioned challenges throughout the dataset. Time (or lack thereof) was considered to have a particularly significant impact on the possibility of building emotionally meaningful relationships. The need for more time to 'be together' was consistently highlighted by both students and staff. It was also suggested that quality of time is more important than quantity when it comes to relationship building, perhaps best exemplified by participants' emphasis on the small-group seminars as a space in which they feel able to express themselves and get to know others in depth (in comparison to lectures, which were considered more 'anonymous'). The importance of both physical contact and space was also highlighted as key. Among staff, concerns about time often manifested in concerns around workload (which in turn was linked to the impact and pressures of the marketisation of the sector). Some staff also pointed out that the programme's ethos and philosophy is *particularly* time-consuming; in light of this, some raised questions around its sustainability, and others raised concerns about the extent to which the philosophy could be truly realised given the context.

"I think one of the biggest challenges is… […] the pressures on people's time. […]. I know if I spent more time on […] planning my sessions, on the […] Course Community Meetings, on the democratic elements, […] on having more time to read – so choosing better readings – on having more time to just engage with the students outside of formal class time, on having more time, crucially, to engage with my colleagues and to really reflect on what we're doing, to meet together, informally/formally, you know […]. If we had more time, there's a huge amount more that could be done." (Rosa, staff member)

Chapter 3: Recognition as Equality and Partnership

In chapter 3 we explored another core recognition theme in our data, which related to perceptions that the programme actively pursues equality and partnership between students and staff. This articulation of recognition is deeply rooted in the work of Hegel, who (rather ironically, given his own racism and sexism) suggested that recognition is impossible when predicated on inequality, because inequality is rooted in denigrating the humanity of 'the other'. Paulo Freire is among the most well-known thinkers to apply this principle to education contexts, and the connotations are significant: as one participant put it, treating each other as "human beings" (Rosa) who are part of a community of equals means challenging fundamentally hierarchical categories of institutional 'difference' – categories, indeed, such as 'students' and 'staff'. We argued that this commitment to recognition as equality and partnership must manifest not only in our day to day attitudes towards one another, but in our *institutional structures*. We suggested the programme pursues equality/partnership through two such institutional structures: a) quasi-democratic shared decision-making spaces (the Course Community Meetings) and b) learning oriented around 'engaged pedagogy'.

3a – Participatory democracy: Course Community Meetings

The CCM is a quasi-democratic discussion and decision-making space for raising and negotiating issues relating to the programme. They are led by a team of student facilitators, supported by staff, and happen at least twice per semester. Most decisions are made by majority vote. All decisions (except for those relating to CCM procedure) are considered recommendations until ratified by the staff team.

Many participants described *the CCMs as contributing to a feeling that their voices genuinely matter on the programme.* Often, this was contrasted with perceptions or experiences of other educational spaces where student perspectives are either not taken seriously or not elicited. Some participants also expressed a feeling that *the CCMs contribute to the deconstruction of traditional educational power structures,* helping to build more equal working relationships between students and staff.

> "[The CCMs are] where the students can actually have a voice, and how if we want to change something we can actually do that and discuss it with other people [...]. [W]e actually can co-create the course." (Selena, student)

Some participants – particularly staff – pointed to *the importance of the CCMs occurring in a structurally recognised space.* Not least given the severe time and resource constraints of HE, it was felt that having a delineated space for decision-making makes it easier to embed democratic values in the programme.

The importance of staff support for and investment in the CCMs was also noted as significant for their functioning and credibility.

A number of challenges were identified in relation to the CCMs:

A consumerist framing of HE and student identity was once again highlighted by participants. It was suggested that this can encourage a one-sided, demands-oriented form of engagement with the CCMs. It was argued that the CCMs should, instead, be grounded in people taking collective responsibility for deliberation and decision-making.

Instrumental attitudes were raised as a separate challenge (though related to consumerism). Concerns were raised that some members of the community see the programme as simply about instrumental ends – such as getting a degree or 'good grades' – and thus less readily engage with non-credentialised aspects of the programme such as the CCMs. There was some suggestion that this problem can be traced to instrumental norms within the wider education system – which some argued the College in turn perpetuates with its strong focus on outcomes and academic competitiveness. There was some concern that students are forced into this mindset by wider socioeconomic pressures – such as a highly competitive job market and expectations around 'success'. Again,

> "I just feel like sometimes people see this course as… like just a course? But we're so much more than that, we're trying to actually like do things, to make it like better, like we're just not- like some people see it as [...] somewhere they wanna get their BA and kind just like wave goodbye to everyone else after that. But I feel like we're so much more than [that]."
> (Leanne, student)

however, there were themes of resistance in the data, with several student participants articulating their belief in the inherent value of both learning and community-building.

Wider educational attitudes. Though connected to the issues of consumerism and instrumentalism, this issue also goes beyond these two phenomena. For instance, some felt that the student passivity encouraged by much mainstream education makes it difficult for community members to feel like empowered agents who are able or willing to engage in collective deliberation and decision-making. It was also suggested that staff reproduce residual attitudes derived from wider norms – for instance, around 'authority' or 'normal practice' – which sometimes limit the extent to which they feel able to prioritise student-staff partnership, or take risks with 'unusual' approaches.

"So King's is very ambitious but in a sort of- I would say in quite a conventional sense. So it sees itself as, like, an institution guided by ambitions for 'academic excellence' for example [...]. That kind of approach doesn't lend itself to experimentation or kind of devolving decisions, you know, beyond a certain point [...] [because of] a concern with image, a concern with reputation." (Luke, staff member)

Institutional culture/set-up was again raised as a core concern, with participants pointing to how the wider institution of the College is not especially democratic, and also has a broad remit to make decisions affecting the programme; this led to some frustration with the limited capacity of the CCMs to enact change, as well as concerns that the broader institutional culture was affecting the extent to which students can feel like empowered agents within HE.

Scope and conflict. Some participants suggested that the scope of the CCMs can be too narrowly practical and that there should be greater engagement with social and political issues – relating to both the programme and wider world. However, concerns were also raised about the extent to which the CCMs are equipped to deal with more challenging or sensitive discussions – perhaps because of a lack of familiarity with collective decision-making practices and attendant skills around non-harmful conflict resolution and community accountability. It was suggested that more training and consciousness-raising was needed to generate a better context in which CCM discussions can take place. There was also some suggestion – linking back to the issues raised in chapter 2 – that the quality of underlying relationships is

> "I think when you're not sort of used to having accountability processes- [...] cos, like, in the communities that I'm in, if I do something wrong I expect to be called out like straight away, and, like, we'll have a conversation about it and then we move on. [But] I think for a lot of people, you know, these processes are very new [...], so people become very defensive when they're criticised on something, and then that sort of tension is what carries through." (Neve, student)

integral to the success of collective decision-making spaces, and that strengthening our relationships on the programme would thus strengthen our democratic processes.

Time was once again considered a key factor, both for working through the complexities of democracy (especially conflict), and for engaging with the challenging social and political issues covered in the classroom.

3b – Learning and teaching: engaged pedagogy

The term 'engaged pedagogy' comes from bell hooks (e.g. 1994, 2010). It refers to classroom practice rooted in student-teacher partnership, in students' active, critical involvement in learning, and in emphasising the significance of the 'personal' in relation to the academic. Our data suggests that learning and teaching on the programme echoes this approach in several ways:

> "I guess previously we were just kind of fed information? [...] Like we would sit in the classroom and then there would just be like a teacher talking to us and preparing us for an exam. But [...] [here we're] given the material, [and] then we're given, like, an opportunity to kind of navigate it and figure out what it means and kind of come up with our own ideas from it." (Rachel, student)

Participants strongly foregrounded *the programme's commitment to students' active engagement with their learning*, often comparing this to what Freire might call the "banking" model of education (1993:75) – in which students are seen simply as passive recipients of teacher-led content. Though large-group lectures and workshops do form part of the programme timetable, most of these are structured to invite student contributions and smaller-group activities or discussions. In addition, small-group seminars form a large proportion of the week's contact time.

An emphasis on student engagement was also mentioned in relation to assessment practices specifically; participants positively highlighted the level of choice and autonomy afforded to students in relation to their assignments.

A number of challenges were identified in relation to engaged pedagogy:

The core concern was about a *lack of student engagement* – both in terms of attendance and work preparation. It was suggested that these factors generate serious challenges for creating a classroom environment based on participation. For instance, when some people don't do prep, it means there's an imbalance in people's capacity to contribute meaningfully to the discussion (partly because seminar tutors end up leading the space by re-explaining content, rather than facilitating dialogue). Connectedly, it was suggested that student non-engagement limits the extent to which staff are able to see students as equal partners who are invested in a collaborative learning journey.

> "I've noticed some people being… too relaxed, about the course [...]. Yeah, it's easy to misunderstand that individuality and that freedom that we have in the course and take it for granted and be like, 'Oh yeah I don't have to do anything'." (Tia, student)

Several participants pointed to *wider educational attitudes* – particularly, again, the normalisation of passivity, hierarchy and instrumentalism – as an explanation for some students' non-engagement in the classroom. In response to this problem, some participants suggested people need more incentive to engage and recommended informal testing or greater oversight. Others, however, pointed out that the

> "I still feel weird and good with this kind of freedom. At the same time [...] I feel like if I didn't have this kind of freedom I would miss it [...]. I think it's necessary and I think this is something that both students and teachers have to get used to, in a way?" (Susan, student)

programme's ethos is oriented around self-direction and supporting an inherent love of learning. A number of students referred to going through a process of *un*learning aspects of their approach to education and discovering greater comfort with self-direction and agency.

Other, more **specific and practical concerns around pedagogy** were also raised by participants. A small number of student participants said they felt that there was too much emphasis on student opinions and personal experience, at the expense of engagement with literature. Some expressed a desire for slower, simpler language by teachers and for more structured input on breaking down difficult texts. Some referred to struggling with consolidating their learning on the programme – not least because of constraints on contact time. Although some participants, as discussed above, suggested more frequent assessment exercises as a solution, others suggested creative pedagogical approaches, such as using storytelling techniques, or tying critical discussion more specifically to reading material. It was also proposed that conversations about how to help people consolidate material could take place collectively. A final concern was centred around a perceived need to better connect academic content to 'real-world issues'. Although a number of participants felt the programme does a good job of building that bridge, some felt it could be given greater emphasis.

It was suggested that **the above concerns underline the importance of equality and partnership in learning and teaching**; by building an environment in which people feel able to speak out about problems (and not just in the context of research projects!), the hope is that challenges can be identified and addressed. And, indeed, there was some encouraging evidence of this in the data.

Chapter 4: The Context of Recognition on the Programme

Chapter 4 explored two further core themes in the data, which related to aspects of the programme which appear to *facilitate* the various forms of recognition explored so far. These were: 1) the ethos of the staff team and of the wider departmental culture in which the programme exists and 2) the size of the programme community.

4a – Recognition on the staff team

The programme team ethos was described by staff participants in ways which strongly echoed the recognition themes explored in relation to the programme as a whole. Staff spoke about what they perceived as a clear effort within the team to break down professional hierarchies and normalise equality in decision-making and also how meaningful relationships and emotional support are a core part of the programme team ethos.

"So this team is kind of special for me, because although we have differences in our opinions, there are a certain set of first principles that are kind of like, 'No actually we're not debating those, 'cos they're kind of at the heart of what we do'. Around, like, treating people as people, around emotional wellbeing, around people's rights to actually not be subject to constant paternalistic surveillance or oversight, around the idea that intellectual rigor need not be traded off against personal experience and emotional engagement." (Joe, staff member)

We suggested it should not be seen as a coincidence that the staff team culture so strongly echoes that of the programme, but rather as a prerequisite. We suggested that staff can much more easily reproduce a resistant culture in their teaching practice and in their relationships with students if they feel accepted, valued, and cared for in their own workplace. This

269

notion of positive reproduction was echoed in the staff data – with many explicitly noting the significance of the staff team ethos for generating a culture on the programme as a whole – including students' enactment of it.

Some staff participants went beyond discussions of the programme team ethos and invoked the importance of both the wider culture of the School (ECS) and one of its research groups – the Centre for Public Policy Research – which was heavily involved in developing the BASS programme. This included particular reference to the role of senior staff, whose values and behaviour were considered crucial for enabling the programme ethos.

4b – Sheer numbers: why community size matters for recognition

Participants consistently highlighted the crucial importance of the small size of the programme community, in ways that have relevance for both recognition themes explored in the preceding chapters. For instance, it was suggested that having a small community makes it much easier to build depth of knowledge about one another's lives and, connectedly, to develop empathy. In relation to classroom practice and pedagogy, participants suggested that small-group learning was a crucial part of them feeling safe expressing themselves – evidently a core part of engaged pedagogy.

> "I think a thing that would be important [for the programme] is to keep a relatively small number of students? [...] [T]hat would be [...] essential [...] for the kind of identity of the programme. [...] [It's] not just that, you know, staff are [...] caring and kind and available but also, like, the [...] small size of the programme, right, makes this kind of interaction possible. And in a sense more- more human, right?" (Belle, staff member)

It was noted that participants' emphasis on the importance of small-group learning for participation raises questions around how comfortable students feel expressing themselves in the larger-group context of CCMs. While concerns about this were not raised explicitly in the data, some participants did point to people feeling "shy" in CCMs, as well as to people feeling less comfortable speaking when a large number of *staff* are present. There was a call for greater experimentation with "creative techniques" (Rosa) to help people share their opinions and ideas in CCMs, including breaking into groups that are smaller in size.

Chapter 5: Enacting Recognition Through the Politics of Difference

Chapter 5 had a different theoretical focus – and to some extent a different format – to the rest of the text. The themes of recognition explored in the preceding chapters all focus on ideas about how we should treat *everyone*, regardless of their positionality or identity. We related this to Charles Taylor's notion of 'the politics of universalism'. Yet Taylor and other theorists have challenged the idea that 'universalist' principles go far enough in realising recognition, particularly for those who start out in a position of marginalisation. Taylor lays out an alternative vision of recognition, grounded in what he calls the 'politics of difference'. This approach asks us to attend to the lived experiences of marginalised groups, and recognise that specific forms of affirmative action may be required to ensure equitable recognition. Chapter 5 focused on the critical questions raised by the politics of difference in terms of our programme and HE practice more broadly, drawing on themes around marginalisation in our dataset. Thus, while the first four chapters are, by and large, about adopting a particular articulation of recognition and describing – albeit critically – the ways in which the programme may or may not manage to realise it in practical terms, this chapter sought to more explicitly problematise how we *define* recognition.

5a – Class, 'race' and critical consciousness

In 5a Samira Salam explored how our data appeared to indicate limited critical consciousness within the community about the way that students' race and class positionality affect their lived experiences of the programme.

A large number of participants focused on nationality and gender as core demographic features of the programme; comparatively few extended their analysis to race and class. Some participants acknowledged that the demographic of the programme community is predominantly middle-class, and an even smaller number referred to the predominance of 'whiteness'.

However, it was argued that this differs from evidence of critical consciousness. Firstly, very few participants, in discussing these demographic factors, acknowledged how minority groups on the programme might be impacted, nor how their own positionality might affect their perceptions. Secondly, those who did directly acknowledge the significance of race and class positionality were, almost exclusively, students identifying as working-class and/or Black, Brown or an ethnic minority. These participants described forms of race and class-based exclusion along the following lines:

> "Sometimes [with where I come from] – like, people don't understand like the struggles? [...] Like, I don't really think about class a lot, like, 'Oh I'm working-class' but [...] when you see like people with Macbooks for example [laughs] and, like, just other stuff and they're just talking about it like it's normal. It's not normal for me." (Ali, student)

Feeling that they didn't 'fit in', including references to 'imposter syndrome' or the feeling that others did not share the same life experiences and background.

Feeling excluded from social events, for instance due to their prohibitive cost, or because they take place in spaces in which people did not feel comfortable.

Feeling excluded in the classroom, for instance due to comments from peers which invalidate lived experience of marginalisation, or due to the dominance of certain voices (e.g. those from Western middle-class backgrounds).

272

Several possible actions were identified, namely:

a. Ensuring that social and community events do not exclude people on the basis of their positionality, by considering factors such as cost, caring responsibilities, and cultural/religious factors.

b. Fighting for better access to HE for students from working-class and/or ethnic minority backgrounds (though it was noted that 'Widening Participation' schemes should not be a tick-box exercise but attend to the complexities of intersectionality).

c. Generating greater critical consciousness through our pedagogy. It was argued that at the same time as recognising the uniquely valuable contributions of people with lived experience, we need to avoid relying on those who are already facing intersectional marginalisation to educate people. We need to develop critical consciousness amongst everybody, regardless of who is actually in the room.

5b – The effects of institutional and societal structures on access to HE

In 5b Eleni Koutsouri argued that pursuing meaningful recognition requires 'making space' for voices which are usually sidelined. It was suggested that this means we need to think about not only who gets a voice in the room and how, but who gets into the room in the first place. Otherwise, the relative homogeneity in the demographic of the cohort risks the reproduction of silencing certain narratives, which could have a detrimental effect on our efforts to centre critically reflexive approaches to learning. The nature of the cohort demographic was related to wider inequalities in HE access, and a number of reasons for these inequalities were explored, drawing primarily on secondary literature. For instance, it was highlighted that:

> "The makeup of our course reflects, wider, higher, problems within higher [education] institutions, [...] in that, you know, you're more likely to go to university if you're white middle-class, and that's reflected on our course in terms of the demographic in the room."
> (Rebecca, student)

Many students feel alienated by the elitism, demographic imbalances, and often discriminatory practices of HE institutions; this exacerbates the lack of representation of BAME and working-class students and practitioners. This was also linked to sector marketisation and the way that competition – especially among 'elite' institutions – means attempts to widen participation are not always in universities' financial or reputational interest.

Wider educational inequalities affect who can even apply to university, and educational attainment is strongly affected by the intersecting forces of socioeconomic inequality and systemic discrimination.

5c – The politics of difference in the classroom

Finally, in 5c we grappled with the role of learning and teaching in relation to the politics of difference. Drawing on participant data around safety, freedom of speech, and harm in the classroom, we explored the question of which voices should be foregrounded and/or challenged in the classroom in the name of recognition. Various authors provided their own responses in the form of opinion pieces:

Minkyung Kim called for *a general commitment to 'openness' in the classroom* to enable all students to feel recognised and valued as well as to learn to become democratic citizens. They argued, based on participant data, that the programme's commitment to kindness is sometimes misconceived as conflict averseness, and that openness in the classroom can help to overcome this. To facilitate openness, they suggested teachers adopt an approach called 'procedural neutrality', whereby they present their own viewpoints alongside justifications for *contrasting* positions. Some limitations and weaknesses of the idea of openness were explored, though it was suggested that these could be overcome through teachers' interventions. For instance, it was suggested that traditionally marginalised voices can be presented with equally strong conviction by staff, that inappropriate ethical conduct could be prevented through the co-creation of a 'working agreement' with students, and that teachers should seek to promote reflexivity.

SooYeon Suh argued that while diversity in the classroom can enrich learning, it does not necessarily lead to the deconstruction of social divisions and marginalisation. They argued that the roots of marginalisation are deep-rooted – stemming from collective histories to the present day – which have led to the reproduction of powerful forms of exclusion in society, including in HE. Suh called for *greater levels of dialogue in the classroom to allow marginalised voices to be foregrounded* and suggested this would help facilitate greater empathy with and understanding of difference. They emphasised that this must be pursued hand in hand with kindness and reflexivity; it was suggested this would enable people to critically reflect on how the threads of colonial histories, in particular, have come to define HE. They also suggested it would also enable the community to foster shared values around how to handle conflict without silencing or diminishing anyone's validity in the space.

Tope Mayomi and Freya Aquarone suggested that the right to freedom of speech comes with an attendant responsibility: to consider others. They argued that suggestions (from participant data) that staff should strive for 'neutrality' or 'manufacture debate' in order to generate greater diversity of discussion in the classroom too often lead to the reproduction of marginalisation. Instead, they delineated a baseline for who should be 'heard' in the classroom, grounded in the philosophical premise that your views do not deserve equal recognition if they are predicated on the non-recognition of others. Drawing on principles of transformative justice, they suggested that *we must develop forms of collective accountability and trust* – for instance, around how to take others into consideration when we express our perspectives, and how to challenge the reproduction of harm.

Some recommendations

Much of what is raised in this book (not least in chapter 5) takes the form of difficult-to-answer or open questions. Nonetheless, we think there are some takeaway messages which are worth highlighting. These are certainly not reflective of all the possible interpretations of the analysis but are instead based on what we felt were particularly clear implications for people seeking to build relationships based on 'recognition' in HE practice. These include:

That normalising talking about mental health matters for building emotionally meaningful relationships, as does breaking down hierarchy and formality.

That strong lines of communication are key for navigating challenges and building shared understanding.

That it is important to establish clarity about how to resolve interpersonal conflict.

That people need time to be together and to get to know one another – and community space may be key to this also.

That having time to reflect upon and support new, experimental practices (like the CCMs) is integral to their development.

That the sustainability of staff workload (and, connectedly, their wellbeing) needs to be borne in mind.

That staff (as well as student) attendance at CCMs is crucial to their legitimacy.

That 'engagement' is crucial for all aspects of the programme: whether for relationship building, community organising/decision-making, or learning and teaching.

That training and input on realising inclusive decision-making practices may be key to managing conflict and engaging with challenging issues in a constructive way, both in CCMs and in day to day life on the programme.

That programmes would benefit from much greater independence from institutional constraints (e.g. around assessment, decision-making, employment practice, resource allocation, and admissions).

That the ethos of the staff team and broader local working culture are foundational to the programme itself.

That class size and the overall size of the programme community are fundamental considerations which underpin what it is possible to achieve in terms of the development of relationships on the programme, and subsequent cultures of recognition and engagement.

That the diversity of students and staff needs attention (and not just surface internationalism).

That we need to work to develop greater critical consciousness about intersectional positionalities and how these affect people's lived experiences of the programme.

That there should be ongoing, open debates about pedagogy – particularly about how to strike a balance between openness and tackling marginalisation, and about what is 'good practice' in enacting a 'politics of difference' as part of a culture of recognition.

Afterword

As we write this, major changes are taking place in HE in response to the impact of COVID-19. Among these, drastic staffing cuts across multiple HE institutions, threats of unilateral pay freezes, and larger cohort sizes on certain programmes, to make up for admissions shortfalls elsewhere. For this academic year, the BASS programme's student intake almost doubled and staff have struggled to keep up with the workload – not least because of the extra labour involved in incorporating both face-to-face and online learning. We are also even more reliant on casualised labour. And if human contact in HE was already fragmented or time-constrained, the necessity of online learning has generated even greater challenges for relationship- and community-building. So only one year into the programme, we are starting to see the erosion of some of the things that we felt were really working (e.g. relationships, community size), and the exacerbation of difficulties we were already grappling with (e.g. staff working conditions). In short, the pandemic has brought more dramatically into the spotlight many of the existing challenges within the sector; these risk undermining possibilities for generating and sustaining meaningful educational relationships based on mutual recognition.

It is vital that senior management at the College take into account the experiences of people who have helped establish the programme to protect the valuable progress that has been made in its first year. We accept that the programme needs to fit into the institution and needs to be responsive and constructive in relation to contextual challenges and institutional priorities. But we would take it for granted that the institution should also be responsive to the programme community, both students and staff. *We have cultivated this garden. We have got up early in the morning every day to do so. We are lucky to have inherited it and been given some stock but we have also put more labour into it than some people think is sensible. It is far from perfect but it is full of care and promise and many of us take pride in it as well as appreciating it as a special space in an often hostile physical and human environment. Not everything in it is either useful or beautiful but there is a lot of beauty in the imaginations and effort it represents. Obviously we would be upset if it was decided that the bulldozers should come and flatten it to make a car park. But it is just as devastating when the bulldozers push through with no deliberate intent to do damage but simply because no one has even noticed there is a garden here or thought to ask who has been working the land and what matters to them.*

Acknowledgements

This project would not have been possible without the support and expertise of John Owens – the BASS programme director – and Alan Cribb – a professor in our School and one of the original co-creators of the programme. The team is immensely grateful to them not only for their input but also for trusting us to research and write about a programme which both of them were involved in many years before any of us were on the scene. We'd like to thank LISS-DTP for the opportunity afforded by their funding, as well as the Centre for Public Policy Research for hosting the project and publishing the resulting book. Finally, we would like to thank all our participants for giving up their time and for sharing their stories and experiences, as well as the wider BASS programme community for their interest in and support of the project. There are many more people to whom this project is indebted, including Sharon Gewirtz, Tania de St Croix, Antonia Dawes, Evie-May Ellis, Neil Brogan, and Emile Burgoyne. In addition, each author has listed their personal acknowledgements below.

SooYeon: Given our current situation with the pandemic I would like to thank all the project team members who have shown so much resilience throughout this journey. Especially all the hard work and efforts the collective has put in to make this project possible. I appreciate how the writing team has persevered despite being spread out all across the globe and relying on the screens of our laptops to stay connected. I would also like to thank Freya for reading through my drafts, providing me with immense guidance and encouragement throughout the writing process and helping me find the words needed to write this section. I would also like to thank the professors in our course for supporting us throughout this journey. And finally, I would like to thank my parents and my brother who have helped me find balance and the confidence to finish this writing.

Eleni: I dedicate my work to my sweet mother whose acts of kindness and love inspired my ambition to make the world a more loving place.

And to Freya – thank you for your continuous support, motivation and enthusiasm. I am forever grateful for your patience and guidance.

Minkyung: I wish to express my sincere gratitude to the team members for their efforts and contributions to the final outcome of this project while undergoing the pandemic. I would like to specially thank Freya Aquarone for the opportunities to be involved in this project and providing me with invaluable guidance, suggestions and recommendations in regard to my work. The completion of this project could not have been possible without her assistance. Besides that, I sincerely thank all the staff who provided additional support and guidance in carrying out this project. Last but not least, I would like to thank my parents and sisters, whose love and support are always with me in whatever I pursue.

Tope: to my partner, Leonie and my people: Loy, Meg and Rowan, for their endless love and support.

Propa: I'd like to firstly immensely thank the pillar of my life: my mother Dr Zaki Rezwana Anwar FRSA who I'm immeasurably indebted to. I remember my late father Dr Udoy Syeed Anwar too, for also having instilled within me a love for research. I'm grateful as well for my school teacher Charlotte Humphreys, who continues to serve as a mentor / huge supportive force in my academic journey. As well as to Dr John Owens and Professor Alan Cribb for their guidance, thanks to the whole research team for being a pleasure to work with – but especially Laura Nehéz-Posony for the strength she gave me during the pandemic. Of course thanks Freya Aquarone – as well as for further piquing my interests in the field of education – for being the best colleague, supervisor, big sister, friend and role model any researcher could wish for. Annika Brigitte Heike Hansen must be commended for her tireless efforts in enhancing our course community from the outset. I would like to end by thanking Allah for everything: all the growth opportunities, good memories and strengthened relationships that came about as a result of this project – leaving me feeling very fulfilled and hopeful about the future of the Social Sciences BA.

Laura: I am forever indebted to Freya for motivating me and cheering me on throughout these months. She was a teacher, a big sister and a confidant all in one person, who kept believing in me when everything in the world seemed hopeless. Without her I would not have been able to keep going – I am eternally grateful.

Samira: First, I would like to thank my parents and my two younger siblings for allowing me to understand the world from different perspectives and encouraging me to seek new opportunities to grow, particularly my mother who has always taught me the importance of speaking out on injustice and taking action to do right. I would also like to thank one of my closest friends Faiza for just being there for me and being the sounding board for advice, knowing how indecisive I can get at times! I have to also express my gratitude to my team members on the research team, considering some of the challenges we have faced due to the situation of the pandemic – your collective endeavours to achieve this final outcome of the project are greatly appreciated. To Freya especially, I must say that I am deeply grateful for the support and passion you have put into making this project come to life – your guidance is truly invaluable. Lastly, I would like to appreciate the wider organisations and mentors that have worked with me both towards my journey into university and within it, including the staff team on our course. I am indebted for all of the help.

Freya: Thanks to John Owens, Sharon Gewirtz and Tania de St Croix for their enduring friendship and academic solidarity – which kept me sane during the uphill moments – and to Jamie Rose, for his humanity, creative insight and frankly saintly levels of patience. I am indebted to the rest of the research team, who have demonstrated such integrity and commitment (and tolerance for my persistently terrible time-keeping!) throughout this project: working with you all has been a truly humbling experience. Neil Brogan deserves enormous recognition Finally, I want to extend my thanks to Alan Cribb: Alan, knowing and working with you has taught me so much about what genuine educational partnership can look like – as well as the crucial role of trust and emotional openness in academic work. Thanks for putting up with me throughout not only the intensity of these past few months, but also the past few years! It has all meant more to me than I can say.

References

Adam, B. (2003) 'Reflexive Modernization Temporalized'. *Theory, Culture & Society*, 20(2), 59–78

Anderson, S. C. (2011) *Hegel's Theory of Recognition: From Oppression to Ethical Liberal Modernity*. London: Bloomsbury Publishing Plc

Andersson, J., Sadgrove, J., and Valentine, G. (2012) 'Consuming campus: geographies of encounter at a British university'. *Social & Cultural Geography*, 13(5), 501-515

Annamma, S. A., Ferri, B. A., and Connor, D. J. (2018) 'Disability Critical Race· Theory: Exploring the Intersectional Lineage, Emergence, and Potential Futures of DisCrit in Education'. *Review of Research in Education*, 42, 46–71

Archer, L. and Leathwood, C. (2003) 'Identities, Inequalities and Higher Education' in *Higher Education: Issues of Inclusion and Exclusion*, Archer, L. et al. (ed.). London: RoutledgeFalmer

Arday, J. (2018) 'Understanding Racism within the Academy: The Persistence of Racism within Higher Education' in *In The Fire Now: Anti-Racist Scholarship in Times of Explicit Racial Violence*, Johnson, A., Joseph-Salisbury, R., and Kamunge, B. (eds.). London: Zed Books

Ashencaen Crabtree, S. and Shiel, C. (2019) '"Playing Mother": Channeled Careers and the Construction of Gender in Academia'. *SAGE Open*, [Online] Available at: https://doi.org/10.1177/2158244019876285

Back, L. (2010) 'The Listeners'. *New Humanist*, [Online] Available at: https://newhumanist.org.uk/articles/2346/the-listeners

Back, L. and Puwar, N. (2012) *Live Methods*. Oxford: Blackwell Publishing.

Bailey, M. P. (2011) *The Role of Consensus in the Neutrality/Advocacy Debate*. PhD thesis. University of North Florida, [Online] Available at: https://digitalcommons.unf.edu/cgi/viewcontent.cgi?article=1140&context=etd

Ball, S. (2003) 'The teacher's soul and the terrors of performativity'. *Journal of Education Policy*, 18(2), 215-228

Bates, A. (2019) 'Character education and the 'priority of recognition''. *Cambridge Journal of Education*, 49(6), 695-710

BBC (2018) 'Stormzy launches Cambridge scholarship for black students'. *BBC*, [Online] Available at: https://www.bbc.co.uk/news/newsbeat-45206266

Bereiter, C. and Engelman, S. (1966) *Teaching Disadvantaged Children in the Pre-school*. New York: Prentice Hall

Berliner, D. C. (2002) 'Comment: Educational Research: The Hardest Science of All'. *Educational Researcher*, 31(8), 18–20

Bhambra, G., Gebrial, D., and Nişancıoğlu, K. (2018) *Decolonising the University*. London: Pluto Press

Bhopal, K. (2010) *Asian Women in Higher Education: Shared Communities*. Stoke-on-Trent: Trentham Books.

Bhopal, K. (2017) 'Addressing racial inequalities in higher education: equity, inclusion and social justice'. *Ethnic and Racial Studies*, 40(13), 2293-2299

Bhopal, K., Brown, H., and Jackson, J. (2018) 'Should I Stay or Should I Go? BME Academics and the Decision to Leave UK Higher Education' in *Dismantling Race in Higher Education*, Arday, J. and Mirza, H. S. (eds.). London: Palgrave Macmillan

Black, L. N. (2014) 'Why Isn't My Professor Black? On Reflection'. *Runnymede Trust*, [Online] Available at: http://www.runnymede trust.org/blog/why-isnt-my-professor-black

Boliver, V., Gorard, S., and Siddiqui, N. (2015) 'Will the Use of Contextual Indicators Make UK Higher Education Admissions Fairer?'. *Education Sciences*, 5(4):306-322

Boliver, V. (2015) 'Are there distinctive clusters of higher and lower status universities in the UK?'. *Oxford Review of Education*, 41(5), 608-627

Boliver, V. (2017) 'Misplaced optimism: how higher education reproduces rather than reduces social inequality'. *British Journal of Sociology of Education*, 38(3), 423-432

Boliver, V. (2018) 'Ethnic Inequalities in Admission to Highly Selective Universities' in *Dismantling Race in Higher Education*, Arday, J. and Mirza, H. S. (eds.). London: Palgrave Macmillan

Bomstad, L. (1995) 'Advocating Procedural Neutrality'. *Teaching Philosophy*, 18(3), 197-210

Bourdieu, P. (1984) *Distinction: A Social Critique of the Judgement of Taste.* Translated by Nice, R. Cambridge, MA: Harvard University Press

Bourdieu, P. (1993) *Sociology in question.* London: Sage.

Bovill, C., Cook-Sather A., and Felten, P. (2011) 'Students as co-creators of teaching approaches, course design, and curricula: implications for academic developers'. *International Journal for Academic Development,* 16(2), 133-145

Bowl, M. (2003) *Non-traditional entrants to higher education: 'They talk about people like me'.* Stoke on Trent: Trentham Books

Brait, E. (2015) 'Princeton Students Demand Removal of Woodrow Wilson's Name from Buildings'. *The Guardian,* [Online] Available at: https://www.theguardian.com/education/2015/nov/23/princeton-woodrow-wilson-racism-students-remove-name

Bunce, L., Baird, A., and Jones, S. E. (2017) 'The student-as-consumer approach in higher education and its effects on academic performance'. *Studies in Higher Education,* 42(11), 1958-1978

Byrom, T. and Lightfoot, N. (2012) 'Transformation or Transgression? Institutional Habitus and Working Class Student Identity'. *Journal of Social Sciences,* 8(2), 126-134

Byron, K. (2008) 'Carrying too heavy a load? The communication and miscommunication of emotion by e-mail'. *The Academy of Management Review,* 33, 309–327

Clegg, S. and Rowland, S. (2010) 'Kindness in pedagogical practice and academic life'. *British Journal of Sociology of Education,* 31(6), 719-735

Cohen-Almagor, R. (1991) *The Boundaries of Liberty and Tolerance: Liberal Theory and the Struggle Against Kahanism in Israel.* PhD Thesis. University of Oxford, [Online] Available at: https://ora.ox.ac.uk/objects/uuid:e02067a0-ba42-428c-967a-1f3ba11c64bf/download_file?safe_filename=602327189.pdf&file_format=application%2Fpdf&type_of_work=Thesis

Constanti, P. and Gibbs, P. (2004) 'Higher education teachers and emotional labour'. *International Journal of Educational Management,* 18(4), 243-249

Cook-Sather, A., Bovill, C., and Felten, P. (2014) *Engaging Students As Partners in Learning and Teaching: A Guide for Faculty*. Hoboken, NJ: John Wiley & Sons

Cribb, A. and Gewirtz, S. (2013) 'The hollowed-out university? A critical analysis of changing institutional and academic norms in UK higher education'. *Discourse: Studies in the Cultural Politics of Education*, 34(3), 338-350

Cribb, A. and Gewirtz, S. (2005) 'Navigating justice in practice: An exercise in grounding ethical theory'. *Theory and Research in Education*, 3(3), 327-342

Crozier, G., Burke, P. J., and Archer, L. (2016) 'Peer relations in higher education: raced, classed and gendered constructions and Othering'. *Whiteness and Education*, 1(1), 39-53

Crozier, G., Reay, D. and Clayton, J. (2010) 'The sociocultural and learning experiences of working-class students in higher education' in *Widening Participation through Improving Learning*, David, M. (ed.). London: Routledge

Cullen, D. (2016) 'Leopold Must Fall.' *Imperial and Global Forum*, [Online] Available at: https://imperialglobalexeter.com/2016/06/28/leopold-must-fall/

Curran, R. (2017) 'Students as Partners—Good for Students, Good for Staff: A Study on the Impact of Partnership Working and How This Translates to Improved Student-Staff Engagement'. *International Journal for Students as Partners*, 1(2), 1-16

De Benedictis, S. (2012) 'Feral Parents: austerity parenting under neoliberalism'. *Studies in the Maternal*, 4(2), 1–21

Deem, R. and Brehony, K. J. (2005) 'Management as ideology: the case of 'new managerialism' in higher education'. *Oxford Review of Education*, 31(2), 217-235

Denzin, N. K. and Lincoln, Y. S. (2011) *The SAGE Handbook of Qualitative Research*. Thousand Oaks, CA: SAGE

Derounian, J. (2011) 'Shall we dance? The importance of staff–student relationships to undergraduate dissertation preparation'. *Active Learning in Higher Education*, 12(2), 91-100

Dewey, J. (1916) *Democracy and Education*. Reprint, University Park, State College: Pennsylvania State University Press, 2001, [Online] Available at: https://www.academia.edu/24704521/Democracy_and_Education_A_Penn_State_Electronic_Classics_Series_Publication

Dewey, J. (1939) 'Creative Democracy – The Task before Us' in *Teachers, Leaders, and Schools: Essays by John Dewey,* Stack, S. F. (ed.). Reprint, Carbondale, IL: Southern Illinois University Press, 2010

Dorling, D. (2016) 'Mind the opportunity gap: it's time to take the lie of the higher education landscape'. *Times Higher Education,* [Online] Available at: https://www.timeshighereducation.com/comment/danny-dorling-on-university-admissions-and-inequality

Dunbar, R. I. M. and Sosis, R. (2018) 'Optimising human community sizes'. *Evolution and Human Behavior,* 39(1), 106-111

Ecclestone, K. and Hayes, D. (2009) *The Dangerous Rise of Therapeutic Education.* London: Routledge

Egerton, M. (2001) 'Mature Graduates I: Occupational attainment and the effects of labour market duration'. *Oxford Review of Education,* 27(1), 135-150

Engle, J. and Tinto, V. (2008) *Moving beyond access: College for low-income, first-generation students.* Washington, DC: The Pell Institute

Fanon, F. (1952) *Black Skin White Masks.* Translated by Markmann, C. L. Reprint, London: Pluto Press, 2008

Felten, P., Bagg, J., Bumbry, M., Hill, J., Hornsby, K., Pratt, M., and Weller, S. (2013) 'A Call for Expanding Inclusive Student Engagement in SoTL'. *Teaching & Learning Inquiry,* 1(2), 63–74

Feucht, F. C., Lunn Brownlee, J., and Schraw, G. (2017) 'Moving Beyond Reflection: Reflexivity and Epistemic Cognition in Teaching and Teacher Education'. *Educational Psychologist,* 52(4), 234-241

Fielding, M. (2004) 'Transformative Approaches to Student Voice: Theoretical Underpinnings, Recalcitrant Realities.' *British Educational Research Journal,* 30(2), 295-311

Foucault, M. (1977) *Discipline and Punish: The Birth of the Prison.* Translated by Sheridan, A. Reprint, London: Penguin, 1991

Fraser, N. (2008) 'Heterosexism, misrecognition, and capitalism: A response to Judith Butler' in *Adding Insult to Injury: Nancy Fraser Debates Her Critics*, Olson, K. (ed.). London: Verso

Freire, P. (1970) *Pedagogy of the Oppressed.* Translated by Ramos, M. B. Reprint, London: Penguin Books, 1996

Freire, P. (1998) 'Cultural action for freedom'. *Harvard Education Review,* 68(4), 71-521

Freire, P. and Macedo, D. P. (1995) 'A dialogue: Culture, language and race'. *Harvard Educational Review,* 65(3), 377-402

Friedman, R. A., and Currall, S. C. (2003) 'Conflict escalation: Dispute exacerbating elements of e-mail communication'. *Human Relations,* 56(11), 1325–1347

Galletta, A. and Torre, M. E. (2019) 'Participatory Action Research in Education' in *Oxford Research Encyclopedia of Education,* [Online] Available at: https://oxfordre.com/education/view/10.1093/acrefore /9780190264093.001.0001/acrefore-9780190264093-e-557

Gannon, M. (2016) 'Race Is a Social Construct, Scientists Argue'. *Scientific American,* [Online] Available at: https://www.scientific american.com/article/race-is-a-social-construct-scientists-argue/

Gebrial, D. (2018) 'Rhodes Must Fall: Oxford and Movements for Change' in *Decolonising the University,* Bhambra, G., Gebrial, D., and Nişancıoğlu, K. (eds.). London: Pluto Press

Gewirtz, S. and Cribb, A. (2020) 'Can Teachers Still Be Teachers? The Near Impossibility of Humanity in the Transactional Workplace' in *Knowledge, Policy and Practice in Education and the Struggle for Social Justice: Essays Inspired by the Work of Geoff Whitty,* Brown, A. and Wisby, E. (eds.). London: UCL Press

Giannakis, M. and Bullivant, N. (2016) 'The massification of higher education in the UK: Aspects of service quality'. *Journal of Further and Higher Education,* 40(5), 630-648

Gibbons, M. M., Woodside, M. Hannon, C., Sweeney, J. R. and Davison, J. (2011) 'The lived experience of work and career: Women whose parents lack postsecondary education'. *Career Development Quarterly,* 59, 315-29

Green, P. (1998) 'Conclusion: egalitarian solidarity' in *The Last Best Hope: A Democracy Reader,* Goodland, S. J. (ed.). San Francisco, CA: Jossey-Bass.

Grenier, F. (2016) 'How Can Reflexivity Inform Critical Pedagogies? Insights from the Theory versus Practice Debate'. *International Studies Perspectives,* 17(2), 154-172

Gunn, A. (2018) 'Metrics and methodologies for measuring teaching quality in higher education: developing the Teaching Excellence Framework (TEF)'. *Educational Review,* 70(2), 129-148

Harlow, R. (2003). "Race Doesn't Matter, but…': The Effect of Race on Professors' Experiences and Emotion Management in the Undergraduate College Classroom'. *Social Psychology Quarterly,* 66(4), 348-363

Harris, J. C. (2017) 'Multiracial College Students' Experiences with Multiracial Microaggressions.' *Race, Ethnicity and Education,* 20(4), 429-445

Hegel, G. W. F. (1807) *The Phenomenology of Spirit.* Reprint, Notre Dame: University of Notre Dame Press, 2019

Hess, D. (2009) *Controversy in the Classroom: The Democractic Power of Discussion.* New York: Routledge

McAvoy, P. and Hess, D. (2013) 'Classroom Deliberation in an Era of Political Polarization'. *Curriculum Inquiry.* 43(1), 14-47

Hess, D. and McAvoy, P. (2014) *The Political Classroom: Evidence and Ethics in Democratic Education.* New York: Routledge

Hill Collins, P. and Solomos, J. (2010) *The SAGE Handbook of Race and Ethnic Studies.* London: SAGE

Hirsch, D. (2007) 'Chicken and Egg: Child Poverty and Educational Inequalities'. *Child Poverty Action Group briefing, September 2007,* [Online] Available at: https://www.researchgate.net/publication/26 5630069 Chicken and Egg Child Poverty and Educational Inequalities

Holden, K. (2015) 'Lamenting the Golden Age: Love, Labour and Loss in the Collective Memory of Scientists'. *Science as Culture,* 24(1), 24-45

Honneth, A. (2005) *Reification: A New Look at an Old Idea.* New York: Oxford University Press 2008

Honneth, A. (2013) 'Love, society and agape: An interview with Axel Honneth. Interviewed by Iorio, G. and Campello, F., *European Journal of Social Theory,* 16(2), 246-258

Honneth, A. (2014) *Freedom's Right. The Social Foundations of Democratic Life.* New York: Columbia University Press

Honneth, A. and Margalit, A. (2001) 'Recognition'. *Proceedings of the Aristotelian Society, Supplementary Volumes,* 75, 111-139

hooks, b. (1994) *Teaching to Transgress: Education as the Practice of Freedom.* New York: Routledge

hooks, b. (2010) *Teaching Critical Thinking: Practical Wisdom.* New York: Routledge

Hopper, K. (1999) 'John Berger and Erick Holtzman'. *Social Policy,* 30(2), 13–21

Johnson, A. and Joseph-Salisbury, R. (2018) "Are You Supposed to Be in Here?' Racial Microaggressions and Knowledge Production in Higher Education' in *Dismantling Race in Higher Education,* Arday, J. and Heidi, H. S. (eds.). Basingstoke: Palgrave Macmillan

Joseph-Salisbury, R. (2020) 'Race and Racism in English Secondary Schools'. *Runnymede Trust,* [Online] Available at: https://www.runnymedetrust.org/uploads/publications/pdfs/Runnymede%20Secondary%20Schools%20report%20FINAL.pdf

Kazantzakis, N. (1961) *Report to Greco.* Reprint, New York: Simon & Schuster, 2001

Kellner, D. (2010) 'Toward a Critical Theory of Education'. *Democracy & Nature,* 9(1), 51-64

Kincheloe, J. (2005) 'On to the Next Level: Continuing the Conceptualization of the Bricolage'. *Qualitative Inquiry,* 11(3), 323-350

King's College London (KCL) website (2020) *Social Sciences BA,* [Online] Available at: https://www.kcl.ac.uk/study/undergraduate/courses/social-sciences-ba

Kose, B. W. (2009) 'The principal's role in professional development for social justice: An empirically-based transformative framework'. *Urban Education,* 44(6), 628-700

Ladson-Billings, G. (2006) 'Once upon a Time When Patriotism was What You Did'. *Phi Delta Kappan,* 87(8), 585-588

Lammy, D. (2010). 'The Oxbridge Whitewash'. *The Guardian,* [Online] Available at: https://www.theguardian.com/commentisfree/2010/dec/06/the-oxbridge-whitewash-black-students

Lammy, D. (2017) 'Seven Years Have Changed Nothing at Oxbridge. In Fact, Diversity Is Even Worse'. *The Guardian,* [Online] Available at: https://www.theguardian.com/commentisfree/2017/oct/20/oxford-cambridge-not-changed-diversity-even-worse-admissions

Lareau, A. (2003) *Unequal Childhoods.* Berkeley, CA: University of California Press

Leach, D. (2013) 'Prefigurative Politics' in *The Blackwell Encyclopedia of Social and Political Movements,* Snow, D. A., Della Porta, D., Klandermans, B., and McAdam, D. (eds.). Oxford: Blackwell Publishing

Leathwood, C., Maylor, U., and Moreau, M. (2009) 'The experience of black and minority ethnic staff working in higher education'. *Equality Challenge Unit,* [Online] Available at: https://www.ecu.ac.uk/wp-content/uploads/external/experience-of-bme-staff-in-he.pdf

Leathwood, C. and Read, B. (2020) 'Short-term, short-changed? A temporal perspective on the implications of academic casualisation for teaching in higher education'. *Teaching in Higher Education,* [Online] Available at: https://www.tandfonline.com/doi/full/10.1080/13562 517.2020.172681?needAccess=true

Leonardo, Z. and Porter, R. K. (2010) 'Pedagogy of fear: toward a Fanonian theory of 'safety' in race dialogue'. *Race Ethnicity and Education,* 13(2), 139-157

Less, T. and Coutts, C. (2020) 'How King's College London has become Cancel College'. *The Critic,* [Online] Available at: https://thecritic.co.uk/how-kings-college-london-has-become-cancel-college/

Levy, P., Little, S., and Whelan, N. (2010) 'Perspectives on Staff-Student Partnership in Learning, Research and Educational Enhancement' in *Staff-Student Partnerships in Higher Education,* Little, S. (ed.). London: Continuum International Publishing Group

Lincoln, Y. (2000) 'When Research Is Not Enough: Community, Care, and Love'. *The Review of Higher Education,* 23(3), 241-256

Lingard, B. and Thompson, G. (2017) 'Doing time in the sociology of education'. *British Journal of Sociology of Education,* 38(1), 1-12

Loan Trần, N. (2013) 'Calling IN: A Less Disposable Way of Holding Each Other Accountable'. *BGD,* [Online] Available at: https://www.bgdblog.org/2013/12/calling-less-disposable-way-holding-accountable/

Loke, G. (2018) 'So What Next? A Policy Response' in *Dismantling Race in Higher Education,* Arday, J. and Mirza, H. S. (eds.). London: Palgrave Macmillan

Maguire, M. (2012) 'Identity Work in a London Primary School: A Head Teacher's Perspective' in *Schools for Marginalized Youth – An International Perspective,* Pink, W. (ed.). New York: Hampton Press

Malešević, S. (2004) *The Sociology of Ethnicity.* London: Sage Publications

Mansbridge, J., Bohman, J., Chambers, S., Estlund, D., Føllesdal, A., Fung, A., Lafont, C., Manin, B., and Martí, J. (2010) 'The Place of Self-Interest and the Role of Power in Deliberative Democracy'. *Journal of Political Philosophy,* 18(1), 64-100

Marquis, E., Puri, V., Wan, S., Ahmad, A., Goff, L., Knorr, K., Vassileva, I., and Woo, J. (2016) 'Navigating the threshold of student–staff partnerships: a case study from an Ontario teaching and learning institute'. *International Journal for Academic Development,* 21(1), 4-15

Martinez, G. and Law, T. (2019) 'Two Recent Murders of Black Trans Women in Texas Reveal a Nationwide Crisis, Advocates Say'. *Time,* [Online] Available at: https://time.com/5601227/two-black-trans-women-murders-in-dallas-anti-trans-violence/

McAllister, M., Wynaden, D., Happell, B., Flynn, T., Walters, V., Duggan, R., Byrne, L., Heslop, K., and Gaskin, C. (2014) 'Staff experiences of providing support to students who are managing mental health challenges: A qualitative study from two Australian universities'. *Advances in Mental Health,* 12(3), 192-201

McArdle, K. and Mansfield, S. (2007) 'Voice, Discourse and Transformation: Enabling learning for the achieving of social change'. *Discourse: Studies in the Cultural Politics of Education,* 28(4), 485-498

Mcavoy, P. and Hess, D. (2013) 'Classroom Deliberation in an Era of Political Polarization'. *Curriculum Inquiry,* 43(1), 14-47

McBurney, S. (2016) *The Encounter*. London: Nick Hern Books

McLeod, J. (2011) 'Student voice and the politics of listening in higher education'. *Critical Studies in Education*, 52(2), 179-189

Megoran, N. and Mason, O. (2020) *Second class academic citizens: The dehumanising effects of casualisation in higher education*. University and College Union, [Online] Available at: https://www.ucu. org.uk/article/10527/Casualised-staff-are-second-class-citizens-warns-report

Mills, M. and McGregor, G. (2014) *Re-engaging young people in education: learning from alternative schools*. Abingdon: Routledge

Mohdin, A. (2020) 'Campaign doesn't end with Rhodes statue, says Oxford group'. *The Guardian*, [Online] Available at: https://www. theguardian.com/education/2020/jun/18/campaign-doesnt-end-with-rhodes-statue-says-oxford-group

Moreau, M. and Leathwood, C. (2006) 'Balancing paid work and studies: working (-class) students in higher education'. *Studies in Higher Education*, 31(1), 23-42

Morrison, T. (1975) 'A Humanist View'. Speech from Portland State University's Oregon Public Speakers Collection. *Black Studies Center public dialogue Pt. 2*. [Online] Available at: https://www.mackenzian.com/wp-content/uploads/2014/07/Trans cript_PortlandState_TMorrison.pdf

Muddiman, E. (2015) *The instrumental self: student attitudes towards learning, work and success in Britain and Singapore*. PhD Thesis, Cardiff University, [Online] Available at: http://orca.cf.ac.uk/70902/

Neary, M. (2016) 'Teaching Excellence Framework: a critical response and an alternative future'. *Journal of Contemporary European Research*, 12, 690-695

Netting, F. E. and Rodwell, M. K. (1998) 'Integrating Gender into Human Service Organization, Administration and Planning Curricula' in *The Role of Gender in Practice Knowledge: Claiming Half the Human Experience*, McDonough, J. F., Netting, F. E., and Casebolt, A. N. (eds.). New York: Routledge

Nylander, F. 2017. 'Why Did Oxford Circulate a Criminalised Image of Me – Because I'm a Black Man?' *The Guardian*, [Online] Available at: https://www.theguardian.com/commentisfree/2017/feb/10/oxford-university-circulate-criminalised-image-black-man

Office for National Statistics (2018) *Socioeconomic Status*, [Online] Available at: https://www.ethnicity-facts-figures.service.gov.uk/uk-population-by-ethnicity/demographics/socioeconomic-status/latest

O'Donnell, P., Lloyd, J., and Dreher, T. (2009). 'Listening, pathbuilding and continuations: A research agenda for the analysis of listening'. *Continuum: Journal of Media and Cultural Studies*, 23(4), 423–439

Pascal, B. (1670) *Pensées*. Translated by Krailsheimer, A. J. Reprint, London: Penguin, 1995

Pateman, C. (1970) *Participation and Democratic Theory*. Cambridge: Cambridge University Press

Pearl, A. (1997) 'Democratic education as an alternative to deficit thinking' in *The evolution of deficit thinking: Educational thought and practice*, Valencia, R. R. (ed.). New York: RoutledgeFalmer

Peters, M. A. (2018) 'Why Is My Curriculum White? A Brief Genealogy of Resistance' in *Dismantling Race in Higher Education* by Arday, J. and Mirza, H. S. (eds.). London: Palgrave Macmillan

Pitt, R. and Mewburn, I. (2016) 'Academic superheroes? A critical analysis of academic job descriptions'. *Journal of Higher Education Policy and Management*, 38, 1-14

Platt, L. (2007) 'Poverty and Ethnicity in the UK'. *Joseph Rowntree Foundation*, [Online] Available at: https://www.jrf.org.uk/report/poverty-and-ethnicity-uk

Popper, K. (1945) *The Open Society and Its Enemies*. Reprint, Abingdon: Routledge, 2011

Putwain, D. W. (2009) 'Assessment and examination stress in Key Stage 4'. *British Educational Research Journal*, 35(3), 391-411

Puwar, N. (2004) *Space Invaders: Race, Gender and Bodies Out of Place*. Oxford: Berg Publishers

Rainford, J. (2017) 'Targeting of widening participation measures by elite institutions: widening access or simply aiding recruitment?'. *Perspectives: Policy and Practice in Higher Education*, 21(2-3), 45-50

Read, B., Archer, L. and Leathwood, C. (2003) 'Challenging Cultures? Students Conceptions of 'Belonging' and 'Isolation' at a Post-1992 University'. *Studies in Higher Education,* 28(3), 261–277

Reay, D., Crozier, G., and Clayton, J. (2009). "Strangers in Paradise'? Working-class students in elite universities'. *Sociology,* 43, 1103–1121

Reay, D., Crozier, G., and Clayton, J. (2010) "Fitting in' or 'standing out': working class students in UK higher education'. *British Educational Research Journal,* 36(1), 107-124

Reay, D. (2018) 'Race and Elite Universities in the UK' in *Dismantling Race in Higher Education* by Arday, J. and Mirza, H. S. (eds.). London: Palgrave Macmillan

Roberts, R. (2017) 'Demands of 'snowflake' students pose threat to freedom of speech, universities warned'. *The Independent,* [Online] Available at: https://www.independent.co.uk/news/education/education-news/university-rankings-top-threat-snowflake-students-demands-a7516316.html

Rollock, N. (2011) 'Unspoken Rules of Engagement: Navigating Racial Microaggressions in the Academic Terrain'. *International Journal of Qualitative Studies in Education,* 25(2), 517–532

Roome, T. and Soan, C. A. (2019) 'GCSE exam stress: student perceptions of the effects on wellbeing and performance'. *Pastoral Care in Education,* 37(4), 297-315

Ross, A., Archer, L., Hutchings, M., Gilchrist, R., Thompson, D. Charine, J., and Akantziliou, K. (2002) 'Potential Mature Students Recruitment to HE'. *Institute for Policy Studies in education, Department for Educational and Skills Research Report 385,* [Online] Available at: https://dera.ioe.ac.uk//4706/

Rowland, S. (2003) 'Teaching for Democracy in Higher Education'. *Teaching in Higher Education,* 8(1), 89-101

Russon, J. (2011) 'The Project of Hegel's Phenomenology of Spirit' in *A Companion to Hegel,* Houlgate, S. and Baur, M. (eds.). Oxford: Blackwell Publishing Ltd.

Said, E. (1978) *Orientalism.* Reprint, London: Penguin Books, 2003

Savage, M., Devine, F., Cunningham, N., Taylor, M., Li, Y., Hjellbrekke, J., Le Roux, B., Friedman, S., and Miles, A. (2013) 'A New Model of Social Class? Findings from the BBC's Great British Class Survey Experiment'. *Sociology*, 47(2), 219-250

Shields, C. (2003) *Good intentions are not enough: Transformative leadership for communities of difference.* Lanham, MD: Scarecrow

Simone, J. (2012) *Addressing the marginalized student: the secondary principal's role in eliminating deficit thinking.* PhD Thesis. University of Illinois, [Online] Available at: https://core.ac.uk/download/pdf/4838923.pdf

Slaughter, S. and Leslie, L. (2001) 'Expanding and Elaborating the Concept of Academic Capitalism'. *Organization*, 8(2), 154–161

Solnit, R. (2016) *Hope in the Dark: Untold Histories, Wild Possibilities.* Edinburgh: Canongate Books

Solomos, K. and Solomos, J. (2005) *Racialization: Studies in Theory and Practice.* Oxford: Oxford University Press

Spiegler, T. and Bednarek, A. (2013) 'First-generation students: what we ask, what we know and what it means: an international review of the state of research'. *International Studies in Sociology of Education*, 23(4), 318-337

Stephen, D. E., O'Connell, P., and Hall, M. (2008) "Going the extra mile', 'fire-fighting', or laissez-faire? Re-evaluating personal tutoring relationships within mass higher education'. *Teaching in Higher Education*, 13(4), 449-460

Strand, S. (2012) 'The White British-Black Caribbean achievement gap: Tests, tiers and teacher expectations'. *British Educational Research Journal,* 38(1), 75-101

Streeting, W. and Wise, G. (2009) Rethinking the values of higher education - consumption, partnership, community? *Quality Assurance Agency for Higher Education,* [Online] Available at: https://www.sparqs.ac.uk/ch/F2%20Rethinking%20the%20Values%20of%20Higher%20Education.pdf

Taylor, C. (1994) 'The politics of recognition' in *Multiculturalism and the politics of recognition,* Gutmann, A. (ed.). Princeton, NJ: Princeton University Press

Terenzini, P. T., Springer, L., Yaeger, P. M., Pascarella, E. T., and Amaury, N. (1996) 'First-generation college students: Characteristics, experiences, and cognitive development'. *Research in Higher Education,* 37(1), 1–22

Throsby, D. (1999) 'Cultural Capital'. *Journal of Cultural Economics,* 23, 3-12

Times Higher Education (2016) *THE University Workplace Survey 2016: results and analysis,* [Online] Available at: https://www. timeshighereducation.com/features/university-workplace-survey-2016-results-and-analysis

Tomlinson, M. (2017) 'Student perceptions of themselves as 'consumers' of higher education'. *British Journal of Sociology of Education,* 38(4), 450-467

Turner, C. (2018) ''Snowflake' generation of students' hostility to free speech revealed'. *The Telegraph,* [Online] Available at: https://www.telegraph.co.uk/education/2018/06/28/snowflake-generation-students-hostility-free-speech-revealed/

Tutu, D. (1984) in *Unexpected News: Reading the Bible with Third World Eyes,* McAfee Brown, R. Louisville, KY: Westminster John Knox Press

University and College Union (UCU) (2016) 'Workload is an education issue'. *UCU Workload Survey Report 2016,* [Online] Available at: https://www.ucu.org.uk/media/8195/Workload-is-an-education-issue-UCU-workload-survey-report-2016/pdf/ucu_workloadsurvey_fullreport_jun16.pdf

University and College Union (UCU) (2019) *Counting the costs of casualisation in higher education,* [Online] Available at: https://www.ucu.org.uk/media/10336/Counting-the-costs-of-casualisation-in-higher-education-Jun-19/pdf/ucu_casualisation_in_HE_survey_report_Jun19.pdf

University and College Union (UCU) (2020) 'UCU members to defend most vulnerable staff as universities refuse to come clean on job cut plans', [Online] Available at: https://www.ucu.org.uk/article/10911/UCU-members-to-defend-most-vulnerable-staff-as-universities-refuse-to-come-clean-on-job-cut-plans van Leeuwen, B. (2007) 'A Formal Recognition of Social Attachments: Expanding Axel Honneth's Theory of Recognition'. *Inquiry*, 50(2), 180-205

Warikoo, N. (2016) *The Diversity Bargain: and Other Dilemmas of Race, Admissions and Meritocracy at Elite Universities.* Chicago, IL: University of Chicago Press.

Weale, S. (2020) 'BAME students make up one-fifth of new Oxford undergraduates', *The Guardian.* [Online] Available at: https://www.theguardian.com/education/2020/jun/23/bame-students-make-up-one-fifth-of-new-oxford-undergraduates

Wiesel, E. (1986) 'Nobel Prize Speech'. *The Elie Wiesel Foundation for Humanity,* [Online] Available at: https://eliewieselfoundation.org/elie-wiesel/nobelprizespeech/

Young, I. (1990) *Justice and the politics of difference.* Woodstock, NY: Princeton University Press

Index